Newspapers in Transition

ALSO BY JIM COX

*Radio After the Golden Age: The Evolution
of American Broadcasting Since 1960* (2013)

*Radio Journalism in America: Telling the News
in the Golden Age and Beyond* (2013)

*Musicmakers of Network Radio: 24 Entertainers,
1926–1962* (2012)

*Rails Across Dixie: A History of Passenger Trains
in the American South* (2011)

American Radio Networks: A History (2009)

*Sold on Radio: Advertisers in the Golden Age
of Broadcasting* (2008; paperback 2013)

*This Day in Network Radio: A Daily Calendar of Births,
Deaths, Debuts, Cancellations and Other Events
in Broadcasting History* (2008)

The Great Radio Sitcoms (2007; paperback 2012)

*Radio Speakers: Narrators, News Junkies, Sports Jockeys,
Tattletales, Tipsters, Toastmasters and Coffee Klatch Couples
Who Verbalized the Jargon of the Aural Ether from the 1920s
to the 1980s—A Biographical Dictionary* (2007; paperback 2011)

The Daytime Serials of Television, 1946–1960
(2006; paperback 2010)

*Music Radio: The Great Performers and Programs
of the 1920s through Early 1960s* (2005; paperback 2011)

*Mr. Keen, Tracer of Lost Persons: A Complete History and Episode
Log of Radio's Most Durable Detective* (2004; paperback 2011)

*Frank and Anne Hummert's Radio Factory: The Programs and
Personalities of Broadcasting's Most Prolific Producers* (2003)

*Radio Crime Fighters: More Than 300 Programs
from the Golden Age* (2002; paperback 2010)

Say Goodnight, Gracie: The Last Years of Network Radio (2002)

*The Great Radio Audience Participation Shows: Seventeen
Programs from the 1940s and 1950s* (2001; paperback 2009)

The Great Radio Soap Operas (1999; paperback 2008)

Newspapers in Transition

American Dailies Confront the Digital Age

JIM COX

McFarland & Company, Inc., Publishers
Jefferson, North Carolina

LIBRARY OF CONGRESS CATALOGUING-IN-PUBLICATION DATA

Cox, Jim, 1939–
 Newspapers in transition : American dailies confront the digital age / Jim Cox.
  p. cm.
 Includes bibliographical references and index.

 ISBN 978-0-7864-7829-3 (softcover : acid free paper) ∞
 ISBN 978-1-4766-1649-0 (ebook)

 1. Newspaper publishing—United States—History—21st century. 2. Newspaper publishing—Technological innovations—United States. 3. Journalism—Technological innovations—United States. 4. Electronic newspapers—United States—History—21st century. I. Title.
 PN4867.2.C69 2014
 071'.309051—dc23   2014013728

BRITISH LIBRARY CATALOGUING DATA ARE AVAILABLE

© 2014 Jim Cox. All rights reserved

No part of this book may be reproduced or transmitted in any form or by any means, electronic or mechanical, including photocopying or recording, or by any information storage and retrieval system, without permission in writing from the publisher.

Cover images © iStock/Thinkstock

Printed in the United States of America

McFarland & Company, Inc., Publishers
 Box 611, Jefferson, North Carolina 28640
  www.mcfarlandpub.com

*To the memory of the late
Ralph McGill and Eugene Patterson,
journalists of impeccable integrity—
with fertile pens they initiated
sweeping perceptions in judgment*

Table of Contents

Acknowledgments   ix
Prologue: Blazing a Paperless Trail   1

1. The *Times* of Our Lives   5
2. A Nation of News Readers   15
3. The Last Word   26
4. The Only Thing Constant   34
5. Supply and Demand   50
6. The Bad News Is   55
7. Out of the Hybrid an Oxymoron   63
8. You Get What You Pay For   83
9. Paywalls: Like Hitting Pay Dirt?   90
10. An Endangered Species   98
11. Cutting to the Paper Chase   107
12. Are We Missing Anything?   113
13. An Alternating Landscape   122
14. Families in Distress   127
15. Falling from Grace to Disgrace   143
16. Connecting in a Multimedia Epoch   150
17. Digital Mags: Feel the Magic?   158
18. The Future of the Form   173

Table of Contents

Epilogue: Gimme Five   180
Appendix: Highlights of American Newspaper History   185
Chapter Notes   193
Bibliography   209
Index   215

Acknowledgments

Many disparate members of the Fourth Estate have provided inspiration and shaped my long-standing interest in journalism. From instructors to editors and publishers to authors, colleagues, freelance writers, and still others, these skilled craftsmen profoundly affected my consciousness. I am not only grateful but also inordinately blessed by their contributions and influence.

One of the earliest in that enduring line was my uncle, Ernest Camp, owner-publisher-editor of *The Walton Tribune,* the county-seat semi-weekly at Monroe, Georgia. His whole career was devoted to news journals. For more than a half century Uncle Ernest edited that one. My visits to his little enterprise were among the highlights of my boyhood and may have started the ink flowing in my veins. Dr. Sidney Kobre, a professor in the School of Journalism at Florida State University, was another early influencer. I think he initially saw possibilities in me that few others of his status recognized. With his ringing endorsement, for the first time I felt I could actually make it in a vocational communications capacity.

A handful of professionals of similar persuasion kept the flame alive. I was genuinely fortunate to win a summer internship at *The Atlanta Constitution* in the Ralph McGill–Eugene Patterson epoch and was humbled and grateful for that break. To walk the very corridors with two iconic heroes of that day created within me a jubilance never lost. During a subsequent summer, I was offered a similar spot at *The Tampa Times.* Ultimately I declined it to fill a summer public relations appointment, thereby expanding my scope into another journalistic sphere. Some other equally valuable opportunities in training followed.

I'd like to thank a few added contributors whose oversight substantially influenced my progress in sundry journalistic endeavors: David

Acknowledgments

K. Alexander, Bob Bell, Jr., Muriel E. Blackwell, Lucien E. Coleman, Jr., E. Odell Crowe, Chauncey R. Daley, Wilmer C. Fields, Agnes G. Ford, Robert G. Fulbright, Herbert C. Gabhart, Oscar Hoffmeyer, Jr., Gomer R. Lesch, James B. Lewis, W. Mark Moore, James R. Newton, Robert O'Brien, Susan B. Riley, Quentin E. Scholtz, Hubert B. Smothers, Neta B. Stewart, Keith C. Von Hagen, Willard K. Weeks, and Ruth Williams.

In addition, my research assistant of long standing, Irene Heinstein, contributed significantly to the finished product. I am deeply indebted to her for many efforts that make my task easier and result in a far more comprehensive work. She labors relentlessly and is a perpetual inspiration in every assignment.

Finally, to my devoted companion of many years, Sharon Cox, I pay absolute homage. Were it not for her willingness to share me with these interests, you wouldn't be reading about them. I am intensely grateful for her abiding encouragement in my quests.

May the efforts of all of the contributors to this volume help you to have a greater appreciation for newspapers and a fuller comprehension of the plight that newsprint journalism is up against. These are crunch times for U.S. dailies and weeklies. Not all are expected to survive. Not all will do so in their current form. The story that follows is a composite of many individuals' perspectives. I trust it has been told with the same sense of fervor, detail, precision, and impartiality that so many of those named here have shared with me.

Prologue:
Blazing a Paperless Trail

Early in 2013, the Associated Press reported that, of all things, cash registers in retail emporiums were beginning to be transferred to the recycling bins and landfills. In an increasingly cashless society, one of modern technology's latest implementations is suddenly allowing merchants to chuck the machines that their salespeople have depended upon since the first one was introduced shortly after the Civil War. Now smartphones and tablet computers are performing their tasks, supplying cheaper devices that claim little space and afford ease of operation while allowing clerks to interact with the patrons.

The new gadgets are also eliminating those pesky inflexible spots at the head of lines where cashiers have been tethered behind counters since time immemorial. In some scenarios the customers are even scanning their own merchandise without staff intervention.[1] It's a new day in technology's revolution as more and more possibilities emerge to improve the functions that the public habitually encounters.

Are you familiar with pixels?

Pixels are the smallest controllable components of images produced on screens. A picture (or image) is constituted when a cluster of pixels combine forces. As a vital element in contemporary communication, pixels are an application of Internet technology that creates meaning on the display surfaces of myriad electronic devices now in use. Pixels are emblematic of the innovative methods of conveying data, illustrations, and information that many could not have fathomed prior to the latter years of the 20th century or even the early years of the 21st.

While we may have been getting used to the new proficiencies in the interim, the potential for much larger expansion had hardly crossed the minds of most Americans prior to the last few years. (You can count cash register–less vendors among the bright ideas.) Things are changing rapidly as pixels start to leapfrog, for example, over rolls of omnipresent newsprint that Americans have taken for granted for as long as print media have existed.[2] In what seems like an ostensibly appropriate symbol, paper is quickly being trashed by pixels. Either fully or partially so, the conversion is already in effect, expanding with each passing month.

Although the transition from paper to pixels hasn't occurred everywhere, it's happened in enough places to constitute a mounting trend. And as ancillary journalistic enterprises introduce online alternatives to the standard ink-and-paper delivery process, the shift may envelop the trade. The reasons for its escalation will be examined in much greater detail in the following pages.

In the meantime the current period may be viewed as one of transition. As previously noted, an extensive segment within print media (including those responsible for producing magazines, newsletters, and other periodicals in addition to newspapers) has bought into the model of dispatching their wares online. Others that have not done so—as yet, anyway—may be holding back for any of a number of reasons that will be examined herein.

Before the pendulum swings any further in the direction of electronic transmission and the potential displacement of newsprint altogether, nevertheless, many organizations are tentatively dipping their toes into the water prior to wholly diving in. In a hybrid interval in which the two extremes (paper and pixels, our emblems for the dual structures) are exhibited, we're experiencing a fusion of distribution systems that could actually impart the best of both worlds. It's a smorgasbord of options that may suit the tastes of more than one type of newshound.

At the outset this author wishes to make clear that he has no particular dog in this fight, no personal cause in the contest between paper and pixels. I attempt to acknowledge realities in which a preponderance of evidence dictates an overwhelming preference for an idea among many. Accepting that sometimes takes readers where they may not wish to go.

This author is an inveterate wordsmith who's devoted a career to various journalistic pursuits. They include advertising, editing, inter-

Prologue: Blazing a Paperless Trail

viewing, freelancing, marketing, photography, public relations, teaching, and writing—disciplines that encompass both vocational as well as avocational absorptions. Yet my immersion in all things journalistic isn't to lead you to any stance that paper or pixel is superior to the other. I can and will defend both models and will criticize them when I deem them vulnerable. But any thought you may draw about which is a cut above the other should be your choice.

My intent will be to explore the possibilities of a mixed bag of keyboard-originated communications and its prospective impact on the conventional newspaper in America. As technology continues to fabricate newer methods of conveying what people want to know in the Information Age, with each passing month it seems there are more indications that we are reaching a few lofty summits from which it will be difficult to descend. The current screen versions of the traditional daily or weekly newsprint edition have opened a fascinating panorama that will be with us for a while. Where it could lead is only a part of the story of an industry fully immersed in reinvention at a dizzying pace.

In the meantime there is mounting evidence that we could be getting our daily dose of headlines solely online in the not-too-distant future. (In some U.S. cities it is already happening.) This may be true of more and more communities soon. Those subscribers who own computers or any of a variety of mobile devices and future wireless offshoots may be the winners in the tug-of-war between paper and pixel.[3] And the paperless trail they blaze will rewrite journalism's history just as surely as Johannes Gutenberg did almost six centuries ago: He overturned 1500 years of scribal practice to cultivate a method of mass producing the hard copy, you may remember.

When Lady Macbeth washes her bloodstained hands in Shakespeare's *Macbeth* in an effort to rid her conscience of a murder for which she is guilty, she exclaims: "Here's a spot. Out, damned spot! Out, I say! ... All the perfumes of Arabia will not sweeten this little hand." It's a splendid metaphor that conjures up images of yesterday's newspaper readers. America's news junkies may no longer be rushing to their washbasins to eradicate themselves of ink-stained hands after perusing the daily headlines. Lady Macbeth finally admonishes to herself: "Come, give me your hand. What's done cannot be undone."[4]

The psalmist upholds the virtues that are evidenced in possessing "clean hands and a pure heart."[5] The readers of tomorrow's editions might not unremittingly offer up pure hearts. But if they're getting their news online, surely they can flaunt some spotless hands. And this could be another small satisfaction derived from undoing what we have perpetually thought could never be undone.

1

The *Times* of Our Lives

The very idea that a newspaper could be printed on anything other than newsprint and read in the traditional columned broadsheet or tabloid would hardly have been given a passing thought only a few years ago. Almost too impossible to fathom would have been any notion that might have challenged the deeply rooted status quo that made a newspaper a news*paper,* giving it certain characteristics that were inviolable. After all, it had been around for half a millennium in something approximating its conventional form.

Don't mess with success, right?

Nobody did for several centuries.[1] The newspaper served its function, primarily one of providing the details of events occurring in past or future tenses, and was circulated to an audience of copious readers who sometimes were scattered across widely disconnected geographical territory. The newspaper—published daily, semiweekly, weekly, semimonthly, monthly, or on some other recurring schedule of release—has given us the news on a consistent basis in a mode that we have easily held in our hands and read at our leisure for all of our lives.

One of the newspaper's defining characteristics has been construed as "a periodicity entirely dependent upon the habit of the customer."[2] But nothing lasts forever. The business model of the stable traditional newspaper is changing: unmistakably, swiftly, and profusely. "We do need a new model. Those of us who worked for newspapers in better times often wish we could go back to the golden age of newspapers. But it's over," enduring practitioner Philip Meyer solemnly proclaimed, and seemingly a little wistfully. "The world moved on while we were thinking about other things."[3]

A few years ago fertile penman Eric Alterman, an English and journalism scholar whose recent assessments appear to brand the newspaper trade with "a palpable sense of doom," expounded on the shifting environment faced by the modern American paradigm. "Few believe that newspapers in their current printed form will survive," said he. "Newspaper companies are losing advertisers, readers, market value, and, in some cases, their sense of mission." Alterman quotes Bill Keller, a *New York Times* editor, who lamented on the dais in a speaking role before one assemblage: "At places where editors and publishers gather, the mood these days is funereal. Editors ask one another, 'How are you?' in that sober tone one employs with friends who have just emerged from rehab or a messy divorce."[4]

According to Alterman, the time-honored news daily that Keller portrays as "that lovable old-fashioned bundle of ink and cellulose" is beginning to resemble "an artifact ready for display under glass." He confirms, "Newspapers are dying; the evidence of diminishment in economic vitality, editorial quality, depth, personnel, and the over-all number of papers is everywhere."[5]

While the newspaper still does "most of the original reporting in America," it is nevertheless "the most endangered of the journalism species," another long-term observer, Stephen B. Shepard—concerned about whether "quality journalism is to survive"—admonished in 2013.[6] An electronic messaging system has been adopted by a growing sector of the newspaper industry already, at least by many, if not wholly so by the time this discourse is circulated. And getting used to the changes are millions of American newspaper subscribers.

The introduction of the computer, the Internet, and the World Wide Web (one of the protocols embraced by the Internet) has jointly anointed a formula for dispensing the news that has revolutionized this undertaking.[7] The result is a far faster and cheaper method of production requiring fewer bodies to physically derive and distribute the end product.

At the same time it proffers the added benefit of realizing a far more environmentally friendly outcome than that derived through the time-honored approach. The most obvious difference to the end user of the newer style is that the finished work is read on some type of electronic screen (PC, laptop, iPhone, tablet, e-reader, or thingamabob by another designation) instead of on newsprint.[8] And it's usually updated several times a day rather than by the normal once-a-day dispatching method that most newspaper readers have been accustomed to all their lives.

Persuaded by the possibilities of electronic extensions, by the turn of the 21st century three out of five of America's dailies had inaugurated those editions, the Newspaper Association of America reported.[9] That figure almost doubled the percentage of journals with Web-based spin-offs just two years before. Meanwhile every one of the 100 largest circulating U.S. newspapers was providing online versions prior to 2000's arrival. Such reflections underscore the industry's common acceptance and even adoption of the enhancements proffered by the Internet.

In the meantime a contemporary insider insists that some of our routine jargon also has been affected by significantly increased reliance upon cyberspace. The label *print* has encountered a fate similar to that of the buggy whip, says media analyst Ken Doctor.[10] *Print* is now popularly replaced with the alternative *tag text* in depicting the widespread communication publishing pursuits that are being currently conducted.

Welcome to the new *Times* of our lives.

The daily newspaper hit its stride during the 1960s, rising to the peak of its popularity with readers, marketers, and owners. In the same epoch it was valued at a high level of intrinsic significance among commercial enterprises. In addition, possibly influenced by some of the same reasons just mentioned, it gained a high degree of adulation from within and outside the milieu of mass communications as a noble profession for those privileged to pursue it as their source of livelihood. That venerated assessment of newspapers was gathered not solely in the United States but in some other highly industrialized societies as well.[11] For a fleeting instant at that intersection the newspapers occupied the proverbial catbird seat among the traditional information providers, doing so briefly all by themselves. But that moment of glory was to vanish in little more than the blink of an eye. There were a number of factors that contributed to the downhill slide starting at the very zenith of the newspapers' heyday in the sun:

> It was already beginning to suffer from the problem of having fallen slightly out of step with its readers. Social and demographic structures had shifted.... It was no longer possible or necessary for an individual to take interest in all the areas his newspaper covered. Large sections ... came to seem irrelevant to many of the readers and therefore to many of the advertisers, who

could see that the other media ... could reach audiences more easily and more cheaply. The newspaper's readers now seemed to be living in the wrong places, traveling to work at the wrong times to pick up their papers, or destined for workplaces outside the downtown areas, the traditional site for the newspaper kiosk. The paper's manufacturing plant, now vast and ancient, was often situated on valuable pieces of city real estate many miles from the zones in which the newspaper had to be distributed. These zones were now expensive to reach because of traffic blocks and high-priced oil. In the seventies, even newsprint became expensive. Most important ... the newspaper is a labor-intensive medium in an era when labor has become highly organized and very expensive.[12]

Publishers attempting to deliver their papers to homes in excess of 100 miles from the printing plant have encountered an especially tough challenge. "Just to get them all to the local delivery points consumes 450,000 gallons of gasoline," noted media veteran Anthony Smith. "In the outlying areas the cost of delivering the paper is equal to the total revenue collected from the reader." His assessment, incidentally, is based on late 1970s economics. "Were the cost of gasoline to rise above a dollar fifty per gallon, the whole operating profit of the newspaper would disappear," Smith professed.[13] Based on that data, the stark realities of today's energy-focused environment would seem to insinuate that making a profit from readers living in distant geographical territories could be virtually considered an absurd myth.

Citing the aforementioned period that he identifies as the "old analog world," media industry analyst Ken Doctor estimates that newspaper publishers may have seen a quarter of their out-of-pocket expenses channeled into production and distribution. With the Internet in place, however, he figures a budgetary appropriation of no more than five to ten percent covers that territory—"negligible," he says, by sheer contrast.[14]

Before becoming a recognized authority on media culture and politics, penning diverse volumes on those topics, Anthony Smith—quoted earlier—invested much of his career in broadcasting in his native England and in America. Despite the dynamics that he cites that contribute to the newspaper's declining momentum, Smith never misses a cue, proposing a ready alternative for rescuing the troubled enterprise.

Be fully aware that his submission was derived at least a third of a century ago (1980), at a time when few people had even heard of the Internet. Most, in fact, wouldn't be conscious of its existence until the middle of the next decade or afterward. Just 11 percent of U.S. domiciles were equipped with Internet connections by April 1996 (including home computer, modem, and online service with Internet access). According to one study, the Internet didn't reach half of America's residences until June 2000.[15] What extraordinary perception Smith demonstrated in regard to technology's future!:

> Electronics and the computer were clearly the instruments to extricate the … industry from the problems that had grown up around it.... The computer will do more than help newspapers smear a fifth of an ounce of ink across a kilo of newsprint. It has the capacity to store and disseminate information, … to give a person only what he wants and relieve him of the necessity of paying for what he does not....
>
> In some ways the newspaper has become like a telephone directory. Both involve the printing and transportation of a large amount of paper to a large number of homes where only a small proportion of the material will even be consulted.... A computer-based information system could provide each directory subscriber with the numbers he needs, up-to-date, because the computer offers a more malleable form of storage … as well as a variety of nonphysical methods for distributing it (via an operator, a TV screen, a printout, etc.). The impact of the computer on the newspaper and other print media is thus potentially very profound … to offer … new ways of collecting, storing, and disseminating information to readers.[16]

Was this man dreaming dreams and seeing visions? He appeared to be living well ahead of the preponderance of Earth's population. Smith proposed: "The next technological stages in newspaper history and in the history of communication devices in general must lead to the stripping away of some forms of information from the newspaper and to their transmission to readers in other ways."[17] In 1980, he was a telepathic clairvoyant indeed!

More recently, Stephen Shephard—whose lifelong rendezvous with journalism extends from print media to preparing protégés for it in the halls of learning—penned a few lines about what readers of a mythical newspaper might anticipate in the not-too-distant future. Writing from the viewpoint of the paper's CEO, he attests:

> I'm pretty sure we can charge readers for our digital content. Our research shows that a well-designed pay system does not reduce traffic in any meaningful way. Yes, page views [visitors to a site] may drop a bit, but they often do not carry any advertising, or they are sold at remnant rates that have little financial value to us. A metering system [rates applied to one or more digital

platforms] may well offer us the best of both worlds: we can allow our casual readers to access up to 10 articles a month in the *Daily Bugle,* thus maintaining the bulk of our traffic. But readers who want the convenience of mobile devices, bless them, will pay for digital delivery on a variety of platforms, including tablets and smartphones, via a web browser or a mobile app. And we're starting to develop some premium products for our real fans. We even ... believe ... our most-engaged readers, ... paying for the privilege, may command higher rates from advertisers.[18]

Shepard's fabricated CEO goes on to allow that "the Internet is an engine of efficiency that can drive down our analog-world costs." He elaborates further: "Ultimately, we won't have to pay for printing, paper, or distribution in the emerging digital world.... We can outsource other tasks.... Our company will probably be smaller with lower revenue, but we will be profitable and sustainable." To which an interviewer poses the inquiry: "So you're saying you will one day stop printing the *Daily Bugle?*"[19] And the newspaper CEO replies:

For the next few years, we'll be a hybrid—print plus digital. But going all digital is probably inevitable if print advertising continues to decline. We'd start by ending print editions on the days with the least advertising—typically Monday, Tuesday, and Saturday. Or give up every day except Sunday, if that makes sense.[20]

The questioner hastily asks the CEO: "Doesn't that make you sad?"

"It breaks my heart," the CEO responds, "but I try not to be sentimental about these things."

"It sure is a new world, for better or worse," the journalist wraps up.

"For better *and* worse. Get used to it," cautions the CEO.[21]

Given the veracity of what's been happening within a growing segment of the newspaper-publishing world in a handful of recent years, this may not be the first time you have imagined a scenario like this with the supposition that it could actually come to pass. Now we know that such a case not only *could* but already *has* transpired. And it's done so more than once. Indeed, since about 2012 mounting evidence has been exhibited in diverse branches of the print media that appear to reverse a familiar maxim—"the more things stay the same, the more they change."

As subscribers and advertisers fall away and the costs linked with labor and production sharply escalate, print publishers find themselves in hastily worsening financial chaos. Some are deeply in debt, some are just meeting their essential obligations, and not very many (if any) are experiencing the fantastically gargantuan profits that they were hauling in a few decades ago when they seemingly had a license to print money.

Paradoxically, you might be surprised to learn that there are longtime practitioners of the trade, including a few wags who are acclaimed as *visionaries*, who are painting still more ominous circumstances for news journals down the road. Two of them are Robert W. McChesney and John Nichols. While the duo already doesn't extend much hope for print editions, concurring that "newspapers will be predominantly digital in the foreseeable future," they presume still worse for the enterprise in time: "There is no particularly meaningful or long-term future for the corporate system of daily newspaper publishing, even in digital form. Some businesses may survive in communities as profit-making entities; but if they do, the evidence suggests they will not be doing much journalism, or they will be producing *niche* journalism, pitched at a sliver of the community."[22]

While this opinion may not be broadly shared, it's out there nevertheless, and probably one that traditionalists hope never becomes true. Even the purists who are addicted to the newsprint model likely could wish for a surviving online ancillary if that becomes the sole alternative to a panorama without newspapers. In reality, for many, 'tis not a pretty thought to contemplate.

Yet there's yet another bright spot in all of this online activity, one particularly advantageous to the newspaper owners, investors, and publishers. Shortly after the turn of the current century Harvard Business School researcher Clark Gilbert scrutinized prevailing conditions within the newspaper sector. This canvasser was able to draw a few early conclusions shortly before the electronic manifestation became so widely entrenched. With their inception on the Internet, he reported, newspapers are primarily reaching new clientele. Furthermore, Gilbert found that a somewhat surprising social response existed wherever the online edition was introduced. He discovered, for instance:

> Four out of 10 newspaper Web site readers read the traditional print product, two out of 10 actually subscribe. The overwhelming growth is Web readership. More importantly, even where it overlaps, people use the online product much differently than they use print.

> They use the online product as a utility, as a way to get quick access to information that's useful to their lives. The overwhelming net use of all these sites, even the most local, small market ones, is that they create net readership.[23]

Although we will see these findings subsequently borne out elsewhere, Gilbert rendered a good day's work in underscoring the tendencies he encountered. Where this will lead may be anybody's guess at the moment, but it's an encouraging sign that the industry is drawing added pairs of eyes to focus on what newspapers have to offer. Ultimately this may turn into something exceedingly promising as the trade flails in a sea of murky waters, facing the uncertainties that have plagued it, which it can't seem to shake in the contemporary age. While there is more journalism being performed today by more people on more platforms than ever before, the profession itself has encountered a "best-of-times, worst-of-times" state of affairs that is "in fundamental transition."[24]

There are other well-grounded sources warning of proliferating dangers to the industry as a result of the availability of the World Wide Web's accessibility and myriad types of capitalists. Respected journalism academic Philip Meyer is among them, cautioning that electronic innovation brings its own ills as easily as it irons out problems:

> The chief threat to newspapers in the twenty-first century will come from entrepreneurs who figure out how to use the more favorable cost structure of Internet-based media to provide better services to the same kinds of communities that newspapers have served so well.... If newspapers harvest [abandon] their goodwill to maintain their historic profitability, they will create opportunities for entrepreneurs who are willing to try new things and be satisfied with smaller returns.[25]

Before imparting the indisputable notion that the wholesale departure of the ink-on-paper newspaper model is an inescapable supposition, you may rest assured that there are some outspoken informants who believe such will never be the case. And the likelihood of the electronic newspaper becoming the dominant form is pretty slim, too, a contingent of clairvoyants predicts. Even the revered TV news anchorman Walter Cronkite perturbed one crowd by cautioning that the Internet could turn out to be a "frightful danger to all of us."[26] Plenty more skeptics abound.

In more recent times a couple of seasoned print journalists—Leonard Downie, Jr. and Robert G. Kaiser—purported that newspapers

1. The Times of Our Lives

"may prove to be the last real mass medium in America" in an age in which the Internet is flourishing. The pair alludes to a mushrooming glut of TV channels that are divvying up the viewership, while at the same time maintaining that the Internet is "taking audience away from television, not newspapers."[27] A strong case can be made for this hypothesis and will be considered in a later chapter. While on the one hand, this twosome isn't alone in their assumptions, on the other hand there is unmistakably an active craze that is open to some other interpretations.

Parenthetically, before rushing to final judgment on the matter keep in mind, too, that there are still tens of millions of Americans who remain on the sidelines of the digital revolution.[28] In late summer of 2013, *The New York Times* reported that one out of five adults in the United States does not tap into the Internet at home, at work, or at school, nor with any mobile device. Government officials and policy experts say that 60 million denizens are presently disenfranchised due to an inability to afford Internet service or because of a lack of interest or computer literacy. Not only does this create disparities in economic opportunities; it also generates lagging implications for health care, education, government services, social, cultural, racial, and other dimensions. And it knocks that deprived segment out of the possibility of receiving a newspaper electronically as well. In this case, if newsprint is someday totally banished one size simply does *not* fit all.

Whatever the outcome to all the debate, there can be little doubt that the publishing industry is in serious jeopardy and—in the meantime—it's looking everywhere for solutions. Technology is offering the prospect of a way out without unconditional surrender. Although predicting the demise of newsprint probably would be unrealistic at the current time, there may come a day in the near future when the actual paper on which certain documents are printed is no longer there. For real. This includes but definitely is not limited to such published materials as today's newspapers, tabloids, magazines, newsletters, advertising circulars, brochures, and a whole lot more that as yet we can hold in our hands and peruse at our leisure.

Presumably you are familiar with the axiom "not worth the paper it's printed on"? That expression may no longer be apropos (or even make sense) to some future generations: They may be utterly unaccustomed to holding copies of some mass-produced printed works in their own hands in a very literal sense.

In the 20th century Americans initially gathered around their radios, and subsequently around their televisions, to learn the details of up-to-the-minute major events as they happened—news that affected their world. Not anymore. "That's the way it was," noted ex-TV, magazine, and wire journalist Christopher Harper. "Today and tomorrow, digital journalism is the way it will be."[29]

Many readers may not be happy about the conversion as it arrives (we're assuming that its near-universal certainty is an inescapable outcome, although probably not one transpiring overnight). Neither were some people very enthusiastic when the automatic answering machine surfaced in the 1970s and began replacing live human beings, taking telephone calls and recording their messages in homes and workplaces across the land. That is, until people got used to it and found it not only convenient but also significantly beneficial to them. Today most Americans might wonder how we ever got along without such a device. More recently, adherents of GPS technology would be "lost" without it. Future cultures may be in a fix if theirs should ever fail. The same may exist for tomorrow's electronic editions. Yet in the transitional period between, some *readers* may find it an extremely bitter pill to swallow.

Never think that something can't go away. It can, and it very well may. While there's nothing as old as yesterday's newspaper, you might want to devour it while you have it. Given a little more time, your newspaper delivery person may not be stopping by your house with tomorrow's edition.

2

A Nation of News Readers

The foremost testaments to our collective attempts to connect with other individuals beyond face-to-face communication are manifest in some crude carvings that were found traced on cave walls. These remnants of a bygone era were sketched by inhabitants who populated the earth much, much earlier and are indicative of the narrow culture to which they were exposed. Those figures were discovered at Lascaux, France, and at Altamira, Spain. It is believed they may have originated as far back as 15,000 BC—or some 17,000 years ago.[1] A restricted scribal or priestly social order is thought to have produced the drawings that modern anthropologists have tagged *pictograms*.[2]

In the intervening time the spoken word has come into play in recording and communicating people's thoughts, activities, and conduct. As best as experts researching ancient *Homo sapiens* can conclude, that first occurred around 6000 BC. Those investigators deduced that another millennium faded before any written words were enduringly exhibited (around 5000 BC).[3] Numerical signs comprised the earliest writing (rather than drawings), followed by codifying spoken words into scribbled symbols.

A function of the written word was that ideas could be preserved. In oral communication, the intended meaning could be mistakenly ignored or distorted when repeating something. But writing proffered the advantage of permanence, being reliable and precise. It was also characterized by its mobile trait: It was easily transportable between venues. As a result individuals experienced the reflections of unseen and sometimes unknown scribes. This was nevertheless light-years ahead of communicating in a darkened past as did previous generations.

With art being such exchanges' first distinguished advancement, then language the second, and writing the third, the fourth revolution was touched off in the 15th century when blacksmith/goldsmith Johannes Gutenberg (ca. 1398–1468) of Mainz, Germany, perfected a mechanism for setting movable type. Mass quantities of books and pamphlets were readily produced on Gutenberg's printing press, which he completed about 1450. Prior to that breakthrough's inception it took an average monk a full year to copy a lone Bible by hand. In the initial year of this primitive (to us) hand-cranked contraption, nonetheless, 180 Bibles were reproduced.[4] This epochal event clearly signaled the wave of the future.

"Great oaks from little acorns grow," as a 14th-century proverb put it.[5] Educational institutions apart from religious orders surfaced and the reading public gradually increased. The printed word proliferated and became available to virtually all of Earth's populace. Reading was an informational and edifying source of knowledge as well as a pastime of contentment pursued by almost everybody who had been taught the skill. And one of the advantages of printing, which would be obvious for all time, was just this: "It shifted control of the text away from the keeper of the original and over to the author."[6]

As we look back from our vantage point it seems almost inevitable that someone would ultimately discover a need for conveying the events and occurrences of a contemporary age that people could find useful in printed form. It would keep them abreast of what was going on around them and possibly even provide what was happening at distant sites. And of course, somebody did come to that conclusion and as a result the monthly, weekly, and daily news journal was conceived. There were hand-lettered manifestations of a "daily gazette" in Rome that dated as far back as 59 BC. Yet not until 1621 were there any rudimentary expressions of what we might roughly christen a newspaper that were available to the citizens of London.[7]

Parenthetically, just four decades afterward (1661) one of the early harbingers of the newspaper's initial rival in mass communications (in the form of radio) was forecast. At the time it was nearly three centuries before "the wireless" was to become a popular and reliable disseminator of newsworthy topics. On that occasion English clergyman Joseph Glanvill prophesied: "The time will come, and that presently, when by making use of the magnetic waves that permeate the ether which surrounds our world, we shall communicate with the Antipodes."[8]

2. A Nation of News Readers

Although the clergyman's timing was a few centuries off, his knowledge of physics was astonishingly adept. In the 1920s and 1930s, before television began a long, slow expansion to overtake it, radio was to become a major competitor to newspapers for the affections of the American news junkies:

> Nothing before had knit America together as closely as network radio. The railroads, the automobile, and aircraft all shrank distance and time, and thus gave the country a physical unity. But radio gave America unprecedented cultural unity. Books, the theater, newspapers, and magazines had not been able to achieve such swift, all-encompassing homogenization.... Before this phenomenon, communities were still somewhat culturally atomized. No such swift highway had ever linked them before. With network radio, the era of mass culture, of universal if passive experience, for good or ill ... had arrived.[9]

So powerful was radio's contribution to become in informing the nation's inhabitants in their quests for information that during the Second World War the medium's instantaneous reportage of eyewitness accounts on the battlefield superseded that of newspapers and other print forms. While the news journals often provided greater depth, they couldn't do it virtually as consequential events occurred. The four days of national mourning that surrounded the assassination of President John F. Kennedy in 1963 elevated television to a similar unassailable level during national and international crises as well. It's a role that television ever since—now aided and abetted by the World Wide Web—continues to govern when the colossal newsbreaking actions transpire.

Returning to the focus of early newspapers, there really wasn't any reliability in those productions' release, a commonly held tenet of newspapers today. Widely accepted criteria for modern journals include this trio of key irrefutable points: (1) availability on a regular schedule, predominantly daily or weekly at least; (2) appeal to readers with broad interests rather than narrowly defined tastes and relevance; and (3) up-to-date reporting.[10]

America didn't get into newspapering until 1704, or about 84 years following the founding of the first permanent English settlement by the Pilgrims in New England in 1620. Concerned for the edification of their offspring, Massachusetts Bay colonists established Harvard College by 1636. They intended to replicate the advantages their own well-educated generation had been afforded in the Mother Country. Those early settlers installed the English colonies' inaugural press at Cambridge two years hence (in 1638). Their attention to education and culture resulted in making Boston the "intellectual capital" of their newly acquired land: "Here were all the ingredients for the development of a newspaper—high literacy, interest in community matters, self-government, prosperity, and cultural leadership."[11]

Copying the traditions witnessed in British newspapers that were delivered to the American Colonies, in 1690 Boston's Benjamin Harris (fl. 1673–1716) launched what was considered to be the first locally produced newspaper in the New World. *Publick Occurrences, Both Forreign and Domestick* was a solo 7-by-11-inch double-columned sheet issued on September 25, 1690. But Harris' English superiors suspended it forever after that issue fell into their hands.[12] Another 14 years would roll by before anybody was brave, stupid, or determined enough to try it again. That time was successful, however (perhaps they had learned from Harris's mistakes, by then omitting anything of a controversial nature, at least initially so). The second attempt carved out a pattern for subsequent and proliferating aspirants to duplicate.

On April 24, 1704, local postmaster John Campbell published his initial weekly *Boston News-Letter,* a single dual-columned sheet containing advertising on both sides.[13] Acquiring British sanction with his effort, Campbell and his heirs persisted in that quest for 72 years, to 1776, the year U.S.–British ties were irretrievably ruptured: The former was finally separated from the Mother Country and established as an independent nation. By then many other entrepreneurs had taken up newspapers as their vocational quests.

When electricity was eventually harnessed, printed materials—including newspapers, books, and pamphlets—earned still more capacity and velocity than had been possible previously. Mechanical power increased the capacity of communicators to supply greater substance and to do it much faster. Moreover, electricity paved the way for still added wonders. In the decades preceding, during, and following the second Industrial Revolution (the latter years of the 19th century and earliest years of the 20th), the capabilities for narrowing gaps in accessing Earth's inhabitants were considerably abridged.[14] All of this laid the groundwork for still greater applications in the 20th and 21st centuries.

2. A Nation of News Readers

In the meantime a pioneering nation that had won its right for independence—starting out pretty much with a strong dependence upon its own resources and resolve—acquired not only an intense work ethic but one that was augmented by high ethical standards, a love of country, and a dedication to cultural and educational advancement. Among the latter passions was a growing awareness of current events. Americans wanted to remain abreast of what was transpiring in the lives of others on the planet, including residents living nearby as well as those stationed in remote domestic and foreign territories.

In 1844, Samuel F. B. Morse (1791-1872) successfully demonstrated an application using electric signals of dots and dashes to transmit language electronically over wires.[15] For the very first time Morse's appliance, labeled the *telegraph,* made it possible to acquire fresh details virtually at once across vast distances. This capability provided something that hadn't previously been possible: news as an accurate reflection that was totally removed from the eyewitness who recorded it on paper. By 1846, existing newspapers jointly launched a nonprofit enterprise under the still-familiar name of the Associated Press. With it news could be fed to distant papers by way of the telegraph, a service available for publication to any member paper.

As the United States developed its own educational systems, often patterned after those of the European civilizations its citizens had left behind, the ability to read and comprehend world affairs increased. At the same time an abiding interest in knowing still more was fostered. In the formative decades of the new nation, newspapers—with precious little competition in mass communications—readily gained a monopoly as the reliable structure for keeping citizens aware of whatever may have been of interest to them widespread. In many households reading a news journal daily or weekly became a perpetual ritual. Eventually, in fact, it was to become a part of the normal routine of a majority of the new country's growing numbers of residents. Great stress was placed on reading daily newspapers. This really didn't come about from any romantic attachment to ink and newsprint but was due to the fact that news journals were responsible for so much of original journalism—in an earlier age and now as well.[16]

In the 1960s in the United States, daily newspaper circulation achieved its highest watermark in history. That pinnacle wasn't to last forever or even for long, however. Attitudes shifted from newspapers as many people turned to embrace television in particular but to specialized periodicals as well. The latter category attempted to gratify certain narrowly defined audiences as targets. Social and demographic structures had altered by then while competition proliferated and distinctive lifestyles emerged. Large portions of the newspaper were becoming immaterial to many readers and extraneous to many advertisers as well.[17]

Ah, but in the age of online activity, technology tells a different tale!

> For the computer, there is no advantage in wastage. If the information is collected, and the machinery for distribution and reception available, it can be stored and transmitted to those who want it. Economies of scale achieved by mass replication are balanced by the computer's innate capacity to offer material to the individual.
>
> In some ways the newspaper has become like a telephone directory. Both involve the printing and transportation of a large amount of paper to a large number of homes where only a small proportion of the material will even be consulted.... A computer-based information system could provide each directory subscriber with the numbers he needs, up-to-date, because the computer offers a more malleable form of storage for the material as well as a variety of nonphysical methods for distributing it.... It is in the nature of the computer ... to offer society a variety of new ways of collecting, storing, and disseminating information to readers.[18]

One of the grandest benefits of all of these options is that readily offering one's specific favorite pursuits coupled with speed and ease may cause even the so-called lesser-inclined bookworms to feel a coercion (and maybe even a compelling exigency) to read, read, read, and to do so zealously—a passion that librarians and teachers have always encouraged. Researchers have discovered that as typical households have diminished in size and leisure time has multiplied, a teeming "growth in the use of information media" is keenly observable.[19] It reinforces the notion that America is a reading nation and now is even more so as individuals can pick and choose easily from a great range of reading material.

Parenthetically, "By the year 2000 or 2010," wrote Anthony Smith (1938–) in the year 1980, "systems of information will be far more interactive and abundant, based more upon electronic transfer than physical carriage, upon individual selection than generalized transmission." At the time of this writing, Smith is still around and is surely justified if he's saying to himself, "See! I told you so!" In 1980, incidentally, he further maintained: "The first stage of the journey of computer-based information into our culture ... is taking place more publicly in the newspaper industry than in any other area of society."[20] Certainly there is substantial evidence to support that theory now.

The growth in technology applies to an online newspaper as well as an abundance of quests for added data, answers, knowledge, and specifically tailored pursuits. Never have the planet's inhabitants had so much detail so readily available to them. It's literally at their fingertips! It's an endless bequest to reading enthusiasts who could never absorb it all in a lifetime but who are nevertheless continually dazzled by the provisions of the Internet and all it brings. One might ask, is this nirvana or what?

As swiftly as we experience adjustments to the technological platforms and to so much else that is included in Computerology 101, it hasn't yet been lost on the adults of every living generation in the United States that the marvels of the World Wide Web have been with us only a minuscule proportion of time. Especially is this true when one considers that brief moment within the total time frame of human existence. Writing in the mid–1990s, W. Russell Neuman brought into focus just how speedily technology is evolving in the modern era:

> News and information, let alone computers, are actually quite new. If you consider the time frame of human life on earth and imagine it as a twenty-four hour day, the information age is a fraction of that day. The invention of speech, which occurred about 100,000 years BC, would not take place until 9:30 p.m. Writing occurred about eight minutes before midnight. The ability to store and transmit speech and writing electronically through the telegraph, telephone, radio and television happened about eleven seconds before midnight. The digital computer just made it under the wire two seconds before midnight in our communication day.[21]

Under these hasty "time flies" conditions of Neuman's 24-hour day, if we'd been given a book to read when Gutenberg invented the printing press (ca. 1450) we'd be hard-pressed to reach the dedication page by the end of the day! And reading a newspaper? Maybe we'd get the front page scanned. Talk about the speed of light!

In the meantime, just before the turn of the 21st century communications Prof. Christopher Harper delineated an abridged overview of the brief history of the Internet. According to him it began in 1969 when the U.S. Defense Department commissioned the creation of a computer network, laying a foundation for the Internet. A few more highlights from Harper's compendium are adapted here:

1982 The *Fort Worth Star-Telegram*'s StarText opens the first online entity of a newspaper, a dial-in bulletin board service. The BBS moves to the Web in 1995.

1983 The Internet begins operating based on the underpinning efforts begun in 1969.

1991 America Online goes public offering news and information services for a fee.

1994 In January approximately 20 newspapers with online services are available globally, mostly of the bulletin board variety. The Raleigh (N.C.) *News & Observer* initiates its online adjunct (NandO) the same month. Also, Time Inc. then commences Pathfinder, a Web site comprised of a periodicals mix. By 1997, Pathfinder is losing $10 million annually. In December, prestigious papers such as *The Atlanta Journal-Constitution* and the *Los Angeles Times* are among 100 with or anticipating online editions/services. America Online reaches a million subscribers.

1995 In April *USA Today* inaugurates an online version. There is a fee for the service via CompuServe initially, but it quickly lapses into a freebie. That verdict is overturned later to secure paid subscribers for plans encompassing a range of electronic platforms (e-edition, e-reader, various mobile devices). By December 700 newspapers worldwide maintain online versions, a boost of 600 in a year.

1996 *The New York Times* crafts an e-edition in January. It will take several years for the company to settle on a viable plan for recouping what it's giving away at first. America Online claims 5 million subscribers at the *Times* start-up. At the same time Japan's third-largest newspaper, *Mainichi Shimbun*, is the first to issue daily papers received on a portable electronic display (a handheld Zaurus). By April *The Wall Street Journal Interactive Edition* is offered free online; five months hence it's by paid subscription. Others will implement pay plans down the road. Before the year ends 700 global newspapers with online editions in 1995 have mushroomed to more than 1,600. Almost every major paper in Europe and North America is among them. The wave of the future is clearly evidenced.[22]

Despite America's long-standing love affair with the printed press, Moody's Investors Service (MIS) announced in June 2009 that paper-and-ink dailies were no longer commercially feasible. A study by MIS investigators disclosed that 70 percent of the newspaper industry's revenue was then being channeled into printing and "maintaining old-media infrastructure and corporate expenses." At the same time 16 percent of the papers' budgets were being funneled into advertising sales while just a mere 14 percent was designated for content generation. The latter was the function (and product) for which a newspaper theoretically exists, at least in the collective public's mind.

A well-regarded Moody's recommended that the combined trade rid itself of as much of the expenditures linked to the 70 percent as possible in order to amplify the 14 percent available for substance development. To create a sustained future, according to Moody's, newspapers would do well to turn onto the cyberspace information superhighway and to do so quickly. Even with that, said Moody's, there could be still more downhill stresses on the industry's credit ratings.[23]

Actually, for some time certain segments of the media already had been looking in the direction of Moody's 2009 recommendation. The British Broadcasting Corporation tested videotext, an interactive communications model, as early as 1969. Videotext displayed an ability to combine telephone, a tailored TV set, and keyboard for dispatching words and images. In the meantime U.S. newspapers initially began experimenting online in the summer of 1980. Not long afterward San Francisco's KRON-TV informed its viewers of something that is now commonplace but must have been astonishing to many of its patrons then: "Imagine, if you will, sitting down to your morning coffee—turning on your computer to read the day's newspaper. Well, it's not as far-fetched as it may seem."[24]

The author begs the reader's indulgence for a moment of personal reflection. It was a genuine privilege for this wordsmith to labor in the 1960s in an advertising post that was guided by a farsighted superior, E.

Odell Crowe. His premonitions at times were little short of startling. More than once he demonstrated an ability to forecast the future accurately. On one occasion during the summer of 1965, Crowe confidently remarked to a handful of protégés: "There will come a day when we will be reading the daily newspaper on screens in our living rooms." While he wasn't precisely sure of the size and scope of those screens or whether they would be physically affixed to walls or applied in some other way ("perhaps television," he added), he was nevertheless boldly assertive that it would become a reality within our lifetimes.

Crowe's words were, of course, prophetic. Following a heart attack the insightful telepath passed away a few decades ago, failing to witness the outcome of this shrewd declaration. Yet he probably wouldn't be surprised by the myriad desktop, freestanding, wall-mounted, and handheld devices we now employ in catching up with the news whenever and wherever it transpires. And although his prediction was uttered nearly a half century back, yours truly is just as amazed now by what has occurred in recent years as when Crowe's calculation was projected. Being on target was for him as much a natural phenomenon as witnessing those predictions coming true is for us now.

For a century or longer it has been commonplace in communal spots in this country (at public transportation gate areas, in physicians' waiting rooms and hotel lobbies, at coffee shop/tearoom/café/restaurant booths and tables and sports venues, on subways and buses, and wherever else crowds accumulate to pass the time for many reasons) to find Americans catching up with what's happening in their world. Only now it's routine to view them gaining their insights from e-readers, laptops, smartphones, and a proliferation of gizmos that habitually debut onto the communications stage. While those in preceding generations customarily harvested their knowledge from newsprint, many younger Americans have reversed that trend by taking their cues from pixels on a multiplicity of platforms (the "Crowe theory" in actual practice):

> Today, as bytes of information move through cyberspace in nanoseconds and as citizens in remote corners of the world are awash in the latest news, it can be difficult to contemplate how slowly information moved four hundred years ago. But there are clear echoes in the history recalled here. The written word or printing press was in every way as profound a change as the Internet. The emerging newspapers of the seventeenth and eighteenth cen-

tury were analogous to the embryonic blogs, social networking sites, video sharing platforms, and other online forums for citizen conversation of the twenty-first century.... In the simplest terms, newspapers made information that was once held by a few more transparent to many. The readership of the press in the 1730s was certainly not widespread, but nonetheless, information that was once essentially confined at court traveled in dramatic and profound ways. A century later the rise of a commercial press in the United States increased the spread of information and helped previously marginalized citizens become involved in public affairs.[25]

Today's contrasting camps reaffirm the commitment of the masses to keeping informed, drawing their information from myriad sources. It's a demonstrated trait that has persisted for as long as there has been a nation, and that quest doesn't appear to be ending anytime soon.

3

The Last Word

The venerated columnist Walter Lippmann once affirmed the newspaper as "the bible of democracy, the book out of which a people determines its conduct."[1] Today, however, its role is questioned, as in the following response:

> The passage captures the idea of the press as "gatekeeper" on behalf of the public. Journalists select and order the medley of fact, propaganda, rumor, and suspicion and transform them into news that is true and reliable. This gatekeeper notion governed newsrooms for most of the twentieth century and instilled the sense of civic responsibility in the journalist. After all, who else could stand sentinel at the gate of public knowledge? The newsroom was the sole intermediary between the citizen and newsmaker. Anyone who wanted to reach the public with information needed to go through the "working press...."
>
> Now, however, the metaphor of the solitary gatekeeper mediating facts on behalf of the public is increasingly problematic—or even obsolete. There are many conduits between newsmakers and the public. The press is merely one.... A third of Americans now get news recommended to them from non-journalists they follow on social networks. Almost half of all Americans have watched or read news that was sent to them by friends in e-mails. Six in ten of those online get news assembled for them by aggregators. A third of those online read blogs, and six in ten watch videos on sites like YouTube. And the same technology that makes it easier for citizens to produce their own content also makes it easier for government or corporations or any other entity to communicate directly. With all this, journalists stand sentinel at a gate with no fence surrounding it.[2]

Technology has complicated the plight of the journalist. Its impact is almost certain to be much greater than we have already experienced, however.

"It is now possible to contemplate a time in the near future when major towns will no longer have a newspaper and when magazines and network news operations will employ no more than a handful of reporters,"

Time's ex–managing editor Walter Isaacson wrote in 2009.³ After being "central to the American experience through the country's entire history," media's predicament has "reached meltdown proportions," Isaacson warned. And journalism scholars Robert McChesney and John Nichols echoed that sentiment in regard to once almost revered print dailies and weeklies: "They are in crisis, and may soon become extinct."⁴

> We believe ... there is no particularly meaningful or long-term future for the corporate system of daily newspaper publishing, even in digital form....
> ...Newspapers will be predominantly digital in the foreseeable future. And that means the rhythm will change to the Web's clock of constant publishing. This will erase many of the traditional distinctions between daily and weekly newspapers.... Likewise, the newspaper will increasingly be audio-visual....
> What will remain constant is that newspapers—the term of art we continue to employ, although we are really talking about newsrooms—will be institutions responsible for covering communities with a sense of duty that is unmatched by other media ventures. Newspapers are the place where the buck stops in a community; where people can logically expect to see coverage of what is important in their locale.... A collection of niche Web sites covering different aspects of a community are well and good, but in combination they cannot recreate the coherence and unity a well-edited and resourced newspaper can deliver.⁵

To the *very idea* of the tangible expressions of newspapers that we have *always* known and loved and depended upon for their status reports about the current events that are transpiring in our contemporary world—to those oracles of journalistic expression—must we now add the possibility (or even maybe the probability) that print newspapers might literally vanish from everyday life? Say it isn't so! But indeed, the likelihood is looming before us as time advances. And it may be sooner than you think! If you're wed to the status quo, this may be the interval when you may want to start thinking about making a peace pact with the devil.

In 1998, advertisers pumped a record $44 billion into the coffers of American newspapers. Of that aggregate, $18 billion was in classifieds all by itself.⁶ Yet those gross figures reveal only one measure of the media's coup as papers posted profit margins of 20 percent or more annually. The U.S. dailies and weeklies were fundamentally cash machines in effect that the Wall Street crowd of investors zealously courted. But keep in mind that nothing is forever. It's a theme you'll see, by the way, reiterated over and over as this volume unfolds.

Newspaper revenues plunged a whopping 29 percent from the previous year in 2009, the greatest single thrashing in a single year that the trade had experienced since the Great Depression three-quarters of a century earlier![7] By then newspapers' revenues had plummeted in every consecutive quarter for a trio of years. Is that indicative of a trend? And if that news isn't utterly dreadful enough, as if in tandem at the very same juncture (2009) American dailies' print display advertising had slumped by a historically unprecedented 29.7 percent.[8] All of this painted a bleak outlook for the newsprint crowd and a potential sign of the times alluding to further calamity as the years moved along.

Noting in 2009 that 395 major U.S. dailies reported that they had collectively experienced 7.1 percent losses in circulation in a six-month interlude, McChesney and Nichols sounded the alarm, stating that if newspapers persist in dropping readers at the rate of seven percent every six months, "they've got less than eight years to go before no one is reading them." By my calculated timetable that would be 2017 at the very latest. But, those observers added, if acceleration in circulation decline continues to prevail "it's probably closer to six years" (2015). "In view of the ongoing cutbacks that make daily newspapers less and less attractive," the writers envisage, it isn't an "unreasonable" projection.[9]

Lo, if their forecast is even close to accurate then we may want to start stockpiling our newspapers today for their value to some collector on eBay for some time in the future. What is increasingly clear is that something has to give to prevent the eventual eradication of the nation's leading news journals. We've lost too many of them already.

In the matter of diminishing newspaper staffs during the current millennium the news has been anything but optimistic. In 2008 alone, the American Society of Newspaper Editors (ASNE) acknowledged a reduction of 5,900 reporters, columnists, and editors. That's an 11.3 percent tumble in newsroom employment in a single year.[10] At that point it was the largest one-year newsroom decline that ASNE had witnessed over its 87-year history, more than doubling the losses that had occurred in the previous year. That revelation notwithstanding, the total for the industry gets still worse—much worse, in fact.

The ASNE figure was compiled from the responses of 931 of the 1,405 daily American newspapers at the time. This meant that nearly a third of those journals were never heard from. Nor were more than 6,500 weekly, biweekly, and triweekly papers included in the ASNE accounting despite the fact that they, too, were shedding jobs at seismic levels. No source could produce a reasonably responsible rough calculation of the total number. Waves of closures, buyouts, and layoffs made a proper estimate impractical. All we may be certain of is that the figure is likely phenomenally high.

There are many contributing factors to this development. A national economic slump is frequently cited as a leading cause of the crisis, a favorite whipping boy of sorts. Advancements in communications technology have encouraged most classified advertising to shift from newsprint to the Internet, depriving newspapers of a major traditional source of revenue.

Readers, too, in very large numbers not only have discovered the Internet but also liked what they found there, particularly from the news sources that—for quite a while—remained accessible to them without charge. (Many now assess a fee for those efforts, to be examined in detail in chapter 9.) Competing against the conventional paper-and-ink publications, electronic news purveyors are in most instances saving their backers a bundle (and a substantial bundle at that) in both costly production and delivery system disbursements.

Nor are some conglomerate owners of major U.S. dailies and weeklies still committed to newspapers' traditional role in society. They don't particularly view their responsibilities as delivering the candor expected by a readership relying upon them for news of the cities, states, and regions where the bulk of their readers reside. The capitalists no longer exercise the fervor and dedication that their predecessors displayed before they were bought out. The paramount premise of some media superchains today appears to be concerned with generating as much return on investment as possible regardless of the product that "the business" is generating.

One wag, James O'Shea, a product of the industry himself, with impressive editorial stints at the *Chicago Tribune* and *Los Angeles Times* to his credit, contends that neither the Internet nor declining circulations are responsible for the deaths of newspapers any more than long stories, skimpy attention spans, or haughty journalists with axes to grind. Instead he gives the plight a different spin: "What is killing a system that brings reliably edited news and information to readers' doorsteps every morning for less than the cost of a cup of coffee is the way that the people who run the industry have reacted to those forces. The lack of investment, the greed, incompetence, corruption, hypocrisy, and downright arrogance of people who put their interests ahead of the public's, are responsible for the state of the newspaper industry today," purports O'Shea.[11]

As a result of the myriad factors that funnel into this frenzy, "Newspapers are going to die. We are undergoing a millennial transformation from the industrial, mass economy to what comes next. Disruption and destruction are inevitable," prophesied Jeff Jarvis of *Buzz Machine* in 2009.[12]

No less sagacious mystics than McChesney and Nichols echo these sentiments. Sparing few words as they assess the chances of newsprint's survival, they sound like voices of gloom and doom: "Eventually the Internet and digital revolution are going to bring ink-and-paper newspapers and all traditional commercial news media to their knees. It is in the process of doing so to all major media industries, from book publishing and recorded music to radio and television."[13] For some who are reading these words, it must be an overwhelming thought. It could even leave some with the feeling that they've had the breath knocked out of them.

During the final decade of the 20th century—a time marked by substantial abundance in this country, and this includes the media enterprises that saw newspapers and broadcast networks swimming in prosperity—managers of those organizations began to be driven by their investors' ultimatums for escalating returns. Those overseers did so primarily on two fronts: through wholesale deletions of news staffs and by presiding over a significant number of news bureau closures. In the ten-year interval from 1992 to 2002 for instance, a total of 6,000 broadcast and newspaper posts disappeared from the editorial side of those ventures.[14] And we know this to have been but the instigation of the banishments. Tens of thousands of moderately paid career news junkies were dismissed during the decade succeeding the year 2002. (You'll encounter still more inquisitions into this circumstance in chapter 15.)

The development that followed has been recounted by various media historians in much the same manner that McChesney and Nichols perceived it: "Stock prices built up expectations for continually massive earnings so there could be no letup, or a CEO might walk the plank."[15] A vicious cycle had been unleashed that was to be repeated over and over—with precious little hope of abandoning its gale-force winds. It led to the destruction of the professional livelihoods of legions of lifelong journalists. By then the smell of blood (money) netted a voracious appetite among still more investors.

To keep them happy CEOs directed the observable dismantling of many great American media enterprises. There is evidence in many places that all that really mattered was the corporate bottom line by that time. The scenario resembled that of scavenging crows picking over the corpses of fallen comrades that had given their all. The crows were the investors, of course, demonstrating an insatiable quest to gain more and more profits for themselves.

With their careers in abject disarray, the perspective of contemporary journalism became a "nightmare" to the besieged laborers of newsroom staffs. At the turn of the century Howard Gardner of Harvard University guided a crew of researchers inquiring into the current state of the journalist's profession. In findings published in 2001, those investigators revealed that the demoralized survivors of the trade were operating in collective despair. No longer could they "pursue the mission that inspired them to enter the field," for that mission as such didn't exist anymore.[16]

Not long afterward the *Columbia Journalism Review* released its own study of yet another branch of the communicators' tree, having polled TV news directors. The venerable periodical concluded that cynicism and negativity were running rampant in TV newsrooms.[17] Needless to say, those results indicated that that era wasn't a particularly propitious time to invest formal training and livelihood in the pursuit of news reportage. Due to continuing draining of U.S. newsrooms, some of the intrinsic expectations are still missing in many situations. The job satisfactions have hardly intensified for most of those wordsmiths in the years since.

Commensurate with the depression filling America's newsrooms, and at least partially because of it, "the general quality of journalism in the United States today is dreadful," McChesney and Nichols insist. "It is likely to get worse, as dire economic circumstances push commercial media firms to lessen remaining professional standards if they stand in the way of a cash infusion."[18] Does this sound like the newspapers we want to read and the stations we want to watch? For most it hardly sounds comforting or promising.

Even with all this carnage, including the deletion of thousands of jobs and the subtraction of long-standing news journals bearing brandished names with sterling histories, what remains in many communities could be fittingly described as genuine embarrassments to the forebears they timidly emulate. It was just a few years ago that Harvard's Alex S. Jones was affirming that 85 percent of what was then currently generated as professionally reported news was originating with daily newspapers. That includes news Web sites and all the other forms of general news, including that dispatched by varied methods of electronic communications. Jones disclosed additionally that his figure might be on the low side—that something closer to 95 percent origination with newspapers was quite likely more realistic.[19]

"What is really frightening is that newspapers appear to be dying so quickly that they may disappear, or at least disappear as a serious part of our lives, before we have a replacement for them. That's a grave danger to democracy," professes David Maraniss, Pulitzer Prize–winning journalist of *The Washington Post*. "As flawed as journalism as practiced in newspapers is, we don't have another vehicle for journalism that picks up where newspapers leave off."[20]

Could cyberspace be a plausible hope? Is there a way we can corral its increasing prospects into performing the diversified services required by a well-informed nation that we have typically relied upon print journalism to supply? And isn't that electronic wizardry doing precisely that already, expanding increasingly with each passing year? Can we figure out a way to harness all this information and refocus the nation's attention if and when newspapers vanish off our radar screens? Surely some of our best thinkers are on to the immense possibilities for that already.

Before we write them off entirely, however, there are still some seers out there who maintain an intense belief that the newsprint edition—to which many of us have long held absolute allegiance—may be with us for yet some time to come:

3. The Last Word

After years of steady, ominous decline in the face of digital disruption, the long-derided dinosaurs are showing signs that they may not be leaving the building anytime soon.

The business will be smaller. The sky-high profits of years past are as over as the Spice Girls. But oblivion is not necessarily part of the equation.

The core question for newspapers in recent years has been, where is the money going to come from? The Internet blew up their lucrative advertising monopolies. Craigslist took their classifieds. And while newspaper websites significantly increased the size of their audiences, digital advertising, once seen as the holy grail, has been profoundly disappointing.[21]

But, maintains *USA Today* media columnist Rem Rieder, there are a few sources of revenue that are already contributing substantially to some newspapers' bottom lines. In demonstrating their adaptability for replacing evaporated advertising, these sources are helping their applicants to survive. By charging readers for digital content—something most journals were loath to do for several years—these newspapers have added appreciably to their cash flow. They've done it not merely with digital-only prepayment plans but also by supplying bundled subscriptions, thereby letting readers receive content via a cornucopia of digital platforms.

Beyond these, news journals are making money with measures unrelated to their core businesses such as advising local retailers, organizations, and entrepreneurs about marketing while furnishing allied services. They are concurrently earning revenues centered around e-commerce pursuits and hosting local events. In 2012, new ventures added nearly $6 billion to the coffers of the U.S. newspaper trade.

All of this seems to suggest that newspapers in America—including those that are still appearing in newsprint editions, which continue to be thrown on the front porches of America—may have some life in them yet. At least some of them will be hanging on for a while. The last word has yet to be written on the subject. According to media analyst and *American Journalism Review* columnist John Morton, the digital juggernaut isn't going to kill the newspaper industry. "But," Morton adds summarily, "it's certainly going to change it."

"What past is prologue," wrote William Shakespeare. And the changes that have already transpired there would seem to be keeping the old girl alive.

For the moment, at least.

4

The Only Thing Constant

It may strike us as just a little bit funny now. Not so long ago (a few decades at the most distant point) there were farsighted media gurus who shared their superior comprehension of just what the public at large would and wouldn't stand for in the way of technological expansion. This came about as more and more new discoveries, innovations, and revelations appeared on the horizon, well before the current proliferation of gadgets and gizmos that seemingly has been driven mostly by escalating online activity. So thoroughly did many of us accept the disclosures submitted by the sages of old that we, too, probably grew communally skeptical about some of the futuristic concepts, regarding them more as novelties than as literal realities. Those images that seemed so far out probably couldn't be adopted by any rational beings, we may have assumed.

The print media was among the conventional systems influenced by some of that rumination. We were reasonably confident, persuaded by multiple insiders, that our deeply rooted traditions would scarcely be affected by any new communications marvels that might arise. The enduring purveyors of knowledge—some of which we virtually deemed as sacrosanct—were unconditionally secure. At least, they were so then. The intellects we put our trust into seemed convinced that we would never encounter a jolt akin to the drama that often accompanies pitching out the baby with the bathwater. Hastily discarding a dependable lifelong source simply wasn't in the cards.

Alas, that was then, and this is now.

With the passing of time such a possibility has come across as nearly inescapable in the modern world. Back in 1980, however, it never seemed to cross anyone's mind:

4. The Only Thing Constant

At the brink of a new era of communication devices, one inevitably has cause to stop and ask, Who wants them? How will the demand for them be generated? The public will have to buy their way into these new media, as they have already done in the case of radio and television, but which they have not had to do in the case of film, newspapers, magazines, and other printed forms. The balance of investment has already swung from center to periphery, from publishers to receiver, from producer to audience, in the electronic era, and the pendulum will swing farther yet in the same direction if printed information is to reach a sizable section of the readership by way of the new devices.... Nor is it going to be as easy ... for a series of new devices to be marketed en masse and simultaneously to societies already brimful of entertainment and information gadgetry.

Of one thing we may be certain, these new devices will not take off with the rapidity of the radio in the 1920's, for they supplement and replace, rather than provide a fundamentally new experience.... There are, to be sure, certain historic trends that make the new media inevitable but not in so dramatically short a period.[1]

On the contrary, apparatus and ancillary instruments of countless persuasions have firmly established their places in capturing and conveying communications in the 21st century. (Shortly after the turn of the century some burgeoning electronic doohickeys were dubbed "information appliances" by cutting-edge futurists then on a tear to be among the early adopters who put that pioneering gear to use.)[2] The revolutionary appliances have thwarted a few established powerhouses from the previous century that had long satisfied our hunger for current events. Now humbled and derided by the doodads of legions of news seekers in the Information Age, the conventional methods have been threatened by the competition with their very survival. Chief among the forces encountering the possibility of ruin and even potential extinction is the paper-and-ink business model—the daily newspaper categorically elevated to Exhibit A.

The first two decades of the 21st century have already witnessed unprecedented upheaval in the historic principles and traditions normally accorded to communications media. Sterling improvements in the modern era have become commonplace, attaining a high level of approval. Those innovations may be rivaled by just a couple of signal delivery systems introduced earlier: the fashioning of the hand-cranked printing press in the mid–1400s and—in the early 1920s—the inception of aural broadcasting.[3]

Even those stimulating upstarts—as widely heralded as they were—

could pale in the current climate that is witnessing a shift away from long-established distribution systems to newer strategies. Contemporary advancements almost appear to be discontent with merely competing alongside established systems long in place. This can be not only disconcerting but also petrifying to the operatives who maintain conventional structures. Demoralizing and diminishing long-standing news dissemination methods like print and broadcasting media may not be completely satisfying to enterprising revolutionaries.

Boosted by increased momentum and incentive, they may not only occupy the prized turf of the historic conveyances but also effectively eliminate the thinning clout that those long forms still possess in a race to get the news to the customers. The bottom line in a worst-case scenario would see the existence of enduring models eliminated altogether. While that won't happen overnight, if it does at all, the fact that we are talking about the possibility seems foreboding in itself. Whatever happens, it's clear that the conduits of yesteryear cannot escape unscathed as Americans become more and more invested in and reliant on Internet delivery of information we used to receive in other ways.

In the meantime, as a nation of news junkies, not many rely on a single news source any longer. In 2010, a joint Project for Excellence in Journalism and Pew Internet and American Life Project indicated that 93 percent of Americans spread their daily quests for reporting on local, regional, national, and international activities to several suppliers.[4] Dubbing the modern generation seeking to know what's going on "news grazers," longtime newspapermen Bill Kovach and Tom Rosenstiel candidly observed how things have changed from the time when we did pursue single sources for most of our searches for current events. Even the conditions surrounding the timing of those quests have been radically altered for many people:

> We get our news now throughout the day, in bits and pieces, not all at once at prescribed times, the way we did a generation ago. These two changes, the reliance on multiple sources and continuous news consumption, represent an enormous shift with profound implications about public learning. Instead of getting the news all at once in an ordered way, scanning the newspaper or watching the whole newscast, we increasingly acquire our news one story at a time, subject by subject, at different times and in fragments. News consumption online, for instance, spikes after lunch, after people hear about something during their lunch break and then go back to their office

to read about it and other subjects. What this means is that the news has become unbundled from the news organization. We don't turn to our favorite morning newspaper or evening newscast to have them tell us what's happening. Instead, increasingly we check the news to find out more about the stories we are curious about. We seek the news today, in effect, by a story rather than by news organization.[5]

The evolutionary variations have been ushered in by a handful of effects that banded together after the turn of the century. Their roots are embedded in technology, culture, economics, control, and entrepreneurial ambitions. Together those diverse phenomena have fused some extraordinary courses for conveying information in ways that most current observers could hardly have imagined as recently as the waning years of the 20th century.

As wide-ranging deviations began to appear on the landscape, it became evident to some visionaries that a few habitual means of doing things weren't going to be useful any longer. In April 2005, one member of an elite circle, media mogul Rupert Murdoch, revealed to the American Society of Newspaper Editors, "Many of us have been remarkably, unaccountably complacent ... quietly hoping that this thing called the digital revolution would just limp along."[6] But, so he realized in time, it wasn't to be.

For a segment of communications practitioners the prospect was extended that some deeply embedded, virtually consecrated incarnations that had traditionally distinguished how their profession was conducted might go away in time—not just partially but altogether, and possibly sooner rather than later. Grasping that reality has been difficult for many in the business.

James O'Shea, one of a handful of editors in fairly rapid succession at the *Los Angeles Times* after that paper was acquired by Chicago's Tribune Company, was especially proud of his affirmation of the Web's potential to the storied *Times* in the years ahead. During his brief tenure (O'Shea was at the helm of the *Times* for 14 months, 2006–2008) he departed from predecessors John Carroll (1995–2005) and Dean Baquet (2005–2006) to include increased recognition of electronic journalism. O'Shea's machinations may have been typical of what was occurring at about the same time in many more newsrooms across the country:

The biggest change I made at the *Times* involved the relations between the printed newspaper and www.latimes.com. Both Baquet and Carroll agreed that they, like a lot of editors around the country, had failed to pay enough attention to the Internet as a medium for news. When I took over, relations between the paper and its online effort were awful. Many Internet journalists viewed print reporters at the *Times* as stodgy old coots who didn't get that the world had evolved to a new diet of news with more liberal standards. Journalists could no longer wait for the daily deadline to post a story; they had to do it now and be judged by how many people clicked on the story, not by how important it was deemed by some ivory-towered editor. Print journalists viewed their online brethren as a bunch of naïve kids unschooled in the basics of journalism.... Both sides ignored one another, and almost all stories had to run in the newspaper before they got posted online....

...I decided to launch an initiative to change the staff's thinking about www.latimes.com.... I said the *Times* would break news on the Internet twenty-four hours a day and explain or analyze it in the newspaper, a complete change in thinking.[7]

On the surface at least an almost irresistible tendency currently exists for isolating the Internet as the principal—if not only—driving force behind the restructuring of the communications media. "The Internet is the most important medium since the printing press," professes widely read syndicated columnist Dan Gillmor. "It subsumes all that has come before."[8] Well, now, not quite. Although the Internet may be transformative as Gillmor envisages, anyone could gamely make an argument that the arrival of the telegraph, the telephone, movies, radio, transistor, television, fax, satellite, and cable may have been equally impressive to Earth's inhabitants in *their* day as the Internet is to us now.

While the rise of the World Wide Web (a derivative of the Internet) is awe-inspiring, especially as its tentacles perceptibly invade more and more of our daily lives, its commanding influence—admittedly powerful and pervasive—hasn't brought about any derailment of established practices all by itself. To hint that the proud family from which mainstream media descends is being singularly endangered by the root of all evil (ah, well, those pesky modifications) would be an oversimplification of the facts. Quite plainly, it would also be a misnomer of sorts. Alongside all that online activity there are some additional factors at work here. Perhaps of seemingly lesser consequence, they are nevertheless incredibly influential. All of this has coalesced into a few enveloping reforms that we are presently witnessing in the renovations that are taking place during the Information Age.[9]

Social change, for instance, has been affected by a fusion of cultural dynamics that regularly impinge on civilization: They include, but are not limited to, society's values, attitudes, and ideologies. The instability of such variants is dictating constant alterations that permeate the environment shared by the political, educational and communications realms, and other leading forces. This ongoing volatility is a consequential determinant in shaping how old-school systems are being revolutionized currently.

Another source that is heavily manipulating the outcome of media's makeover relates to financial practices. In the modern age provincial economies have united to form a massive international fiscal channel that, as time goes on, is directed more and more by powerful commercial transnational enterprises. This phenomenon has impacted the fiscal core of not only journalism but the processes that encompass a broader range of media as well.

Meanwhile, the Telecommunications Act of 1996 enacted by the U.S. Federal Communications Commission initiated a few important modifications of some of the traditional methods of conducting mass media. Lifting long-standing boundaries that had restricted competition as one example, the landmark legislation markedly altered the landscape that surrounded media ownership. As a result ever more daunting rivalries in journalism and communications were given green lights, yielding a handful of gigantic commercial ownership enterprises. In an era of nearly unlimited restrictions they have been permitted to thrive, powerfully dominating the nation's broadcast operations. Consequently, in many places the era of the smaller family-run media venture unmistakably appeared to be passing from the landscape that it had dominated through some of the 20th century.

Then there were the unwavering aspirations of the capitalists who arrived on the scene to spearhead a movement that was to ultimately transform a sequence of complex issues into something quite likely unanticipated. Maneuvering themselves into pivotal roles of leadership within existing media empires, the progressives were well-placed to be on the cutting edge of innovation. Ultimately they would shoulder much of the weight in overhauling some of the prevailing standards of practice—some virtually regarded as untouchable by wordsmiths whose lifelong careers had been devoted to their trade. The final decision makers, in their sovereignty, weren't only to be responsible for renovating the finished products but also—perhaps even more menacingly—to be responsible for disturbing the very lives and livelihoods of a workforce who had dedicated their careers to laboring in the vineyards of their periodicals. For many of the veterans the outcome was to be a consequential life-changing experience.

The late James W. Carey, a revered communications theorist, media critic, and college professor of journalism, whose scholarly authorship defined his profession for a generation, pinpointed what may have been the original medium of universal interactive exchanges. Thus far at least it's the one with the most promising impetus. In a leading trade periodical late in the 20th century Carey observed:

> The Internet should be understood as the first instance of a global communication system. That system ... is displacing a national system of communications which came into existence at the end of the nineteenth century as a result of the railroad and telegraph, and was "perfected" in subsequent innovations through television in the network era.[10]

Carey's assertions notwithstanding, a fellow traveler, John V. Pavlik, is convinced that the Internet is "merely a product, or symptom, of a more fundamental technological change" that has been progressing for more than a half century. "Only now," Pavlik insists, it "is beginning to crystallize: the convergence of telecommunications, computing, and traditional media." With professorial stints at Penn State, San Diego State, Columbia, and Rutgers universities on his résumé, Pavlik expounds: "This new media system embraces all forms of human communication in a digital format where the rules and constraints of the analog world no longer apply."

He contends further, for any who would possibly think differently, that the unification of diverse forms of communicative schematics (e.g., satellite TV systems, digital video, telephone, and the Internet, as some examples) has made linkages a reality between the computer and telecommunications. At the same time, Pavlik proposes that such alliances are "neither inevitable nor necessarily good." He holds the belief that, in this century, such fusion simply presupposes a "better, more efficient, more democratic medium for journalism and the public."[11]

4. The Only Thing Constant

Today more than 5,000 news sites published by newspapers and other print-generated media, radio and TV broadcasters, and innovators with their works solely transported through cyberspace comprise an international electronic publishing milieu.[12] The products of these information suppliers are accessible by every user of the World Wide Web through the Internet. In fact, we live in an age in which anyone with a computer (an instrument that was created to execute computation functions, by the way) and a modem can instantly begin circulating his or her very own creative wares to the world.[13] Yet the content's legitimacy, the corroboration of sources, precision, and candor all may be taken with a grain of salt: An increasingly distrustful audience of readers, listeners, and viewers has grown suspicious of being duped by those who toss authenticity aside in their fervent attempts to gather a throng of trailing believers.

Under the guise of relevancy and integrity, they offer alarmingly problematic reporting on Web sites that directly compete with online appendages of respected ventures. The "sound-bite culture" that some people are rushing to substitute for newspaper reading may be devoid of context and history. That's the opinion of media studies instructor Peter Steven at Toronto's Sheridan Institute of Technology. Speaking of some independent news purveyors, Steven contends, "They encourage immediacy, speed and first impressions as the prevailing news values. In most cases they emphasize breadth at the expense of depth of information."[14] Rushing to feed material online, such entrepreneurs often are without the experience, training, talent, commitment, and sufficient staff to meet the demand for in-depth news coverage. It's an indictment that doesn't appear to be going away.

Based on the traffic rankings in March 2013, the 15 most popular news web sites and their estimated unique monthly visitors (meaning individual computers that clicked on one of its pages)—and verified by a handful of skillfully qualified outfits charged with performing measurement functions—were:

1. Yahoo! News (110,000,000)
2. CNN (74,000,000)
3. MSNBC (73,000,000)
4. Google News (65,000,000)

5. *The New York Times* (59,500,000)
6. Huffington Post (54,000,000)
7. Fox News (32,000,000)
8. *The Washington Post* (25,000,000)
9. The *Los Angeles Times* (24,900,000)
10. Mail Online (24,800,000)
11. Reuters (24,000,000)
12. ABCNews (20,000,000)
13. *USA Today* (18,000,000)
14. BBC News (17,000,000)
15. Drudge Report (14,000,000)[15]

You will observe that only four newspapers made it into the top 15 news sites, only one of those into the top five. For many newspapers, the news hasn't been stupendously—or even moderately—joyful of late. The leading search company in cyberspace, Google, earned *profits* of $1.4 billion in a recent year. This compares with Gannett's—the leading news company's—total *revenues* of $1.4 billion *in the same year*, netting just $58 million in *profits*.[16] What's wrong with this picture? It's indicative of a tremendous slide that newspapers have witnessed during this century as a time-honored business model fades little by little before its practitioners' eyes.

In 2010, for instance, a Pew Research Center study disclosed that 35 percent of Americans relied on newspapers as a method of keeping informed about national and international current events. For the first time ever, in spite of this, the newspaper readers were surpassed by 40 percent who were turning to the Internet to satisfy some or all of their quests for information about what's taking place in the world beyond their doorsteps. Perhaps even more astoundingly, the Pew analysis found that 70 percent of Americans—twice the proportion reading the newspapers—were still dependent upon television for their daily dose of current events.[17]

This data comes in a day in which we are continually told that the TV news audience is evaporating. A survey in 2000 conducted by Stanford University found that video's share of the American psyche was eroding speedily. New media, and particularly the Internet, were infringing on more and more people's time, affecting numerous diversions.

(TV viewership, readership, and face-to-face interactivity were all shrinking. The pollsters attributed their findings almost altogether to a steadily growing presence of the Internet in people's lives.)[18] That leaves some to ponder: Just how many out there are getting *any* news on a regular basis today?

In the meantime, of the trio of leading methods mentioned for informing the population (newspapers, Internet, television), three out of five recipients who haven't yet reached their 30th birthdays have commonly selected the Internet as a prime (and possibly their only) source for staying abreast of current events.[19] This revelation is almost certain to send shock waves through anybody who is currently working for newspapers or in TV journalism. It is but one more acknowledgment of a trend that has been gathering momentum at least since the turn of the century. The signs portend a very different outcome for the news junkies of successive generations.

To the uninitiated it may come as a surprise in the meantime that the depth of most online news searches isn't all that striking. Another Pew inquiry reported that—for a conventional news site—a visitor ordinarily devotes no more than three minutes and four seconds to accessing all the material available there. The comparison with the average paper-and-ink media reader doesn't come off well, with the latter group typically engaged for up to 40 minutes daily.[20]

As a result, to an advertiser hoping to score big gains in building the brand of a consumer commodity the casual visitors to an online news site plainly pose whatever value they represent to the advertiser in diminished terms. But one preservationist still notes that not quite all is lost here, arguing that not every tracker can be painted with the same brush. Though apparently not in the majority, some exceptions exist:

> By contrast, some visitors are highly engaged with a site, including those who come to the home page of a news site, the way they once picked up the newspaper on their front doorstep. They tend to browse the site with care, staying longer and returning often—a much better target for a branding campaign by a major advertiser willing to pay more to reach the right people.[21]

By no means are any of these the sole indications that the traditional news sources are in serious jeopardy. A couple of *Washington Post* journalists, Leonard Downie, Jr. and Robert Kaiser—collaborating on an introspective into the industry early in this millennium—confidently noted: "There is no disputing the fact that newspapers are no longer the ubiquitous, pervasive news and advertising medium they once were." The pair went back to 1964, the era in which both had launched enduring careers with the *Post,* to observe that 81 percent of American adults were then recurring newspaper readers.[22]

Yet the last time daily newspaper circulation rose was in 1984, at which time it reached 63.3 million.[23] During the final decade of the 20th century daily readership fell by 15 percenage points, from 52.6 to 37.5 percent.[24] In a span of about a third of a century (since 1964) the audience of the daily newspapers in this country plummeted nearly 45 percent!

Young readers declined far more. Another survey found that—toward the end of the previous century—just 19 percent of those comprising the bracket of 18-to-34-year-olds in the United States traditionally consulted a daily newspaper. With the growing proliferation of distractions to interest the age cohorts, would we be far off base to anticipate that the 19 percent could have fallen further in the intervening years? According to Downie and Kaiser, projections like this are more than just a tad unsettling. They alleged with these figures, "Conceivably, newspaper readers would steadily die out."[25] That's not a heartening contemplation!

Speaking of newspapers, *USA Today* columnist Rem Rieder claimed: "Young people avoid them like they were flip phones."[26] And get this: only 9 percent of that 19 percent *actually trusted* the information presented to them within those pages to have any genuine credibility! Wow. (Strictly as an aside incidentally, lifelong scribe Philip Meyer, a journalism prof, proclaims: "Newspapers that operate in places where they are trusted do better than newspapers in other places."[27] He's referring to circulation, advertising, revenues, and influence by other measurement sticks.) In still more insight on today's youth, Internet blogger Alan Mutter, a media consultant specializing in joint journalism-technology ventures, advises that "the phone and the tablet are their windows on the world." According to Mutter, the current generation of youthful digital partisans "can't be bothered to drag around paper, CDs, or books."[28]

4. The Only Thing Constant

Writer Joseph Epstein offers a couple of notions about youth's increasing lack of appreciation (tolerance maybe?) for print journalism in the contemporary age:

> According to one ... the young, having grown up with television and computers as their constant companions, are "visual-minded," and hence averse to print. Another theory holds that young people do not feel themselves implicated in the larger world; for them, news of that world isn't where the action is. A more flattering corollary of this is that grown-up journalism strikes the young as hopelessly out of date. All that solemn good-guy/bad-guy reporting ... for them, is so much hot air. They prefer to watch Jon Stewart's *The Daily Show* on the Comedy Central cable channel, where traditional news is mocked and pilloried as obvious nonsense.[29]

Anybody up for *Saturday Night Live* perhaps? All of this provokes a slant on textual journalism that more mature adults may have universally failed to grasp.

In 2011, the Audit Bureau of Circulations confirmed that just 44.4 million of the total households in the United States were receiving a daily newspaper.[30] That occurred in a land in which the number of citizens had soared from 235.8 million residents in 1984 (cited earlier) to 312.8 million at the end of 2011, an increase of 77 million.[31] With about 26.8 percent of U.S. households subscribing to a daily paper in 1984, that impetus was diminished by almost half in the intervening years, as just 14.2 percent were paying customers in 2011, indubitably a demoralizing whack.

And as if that weren't bad enough, newspapers have experienced yet another—and potentially far more disastrous—blow to their foundations in the 2000s. U.S. dailies saw their advertising revenue peak at $49 billion in 2000. But within a decade, by 2009, that figure had tumbled to $28 billion—an alarming deficit of 43 percent of what is universally considered to be most papers' chief source of income.[32] Yet one year later (in 2010) advertising revenues were even lower, possibly only as much as $25 billion.[33] And don't be misguided into thinking that as online traffic has burgeoned online advertising has kept pace. It has not. From ads appearing on newspaper sites, just $716 million was added to newspapers' coffers between 2005 and 2010.[34] That doesn't begin to offset the losses.

In practice, the emergence of booming online activity has introduced new threats to the revenues that traditionally have gone to the paper-and-ink media. Since going on the Web in 1996 for instance, the ever-expanding Craigslist has been wiping out newspapers' once-reliable classified advertising income.[35] Bleak trends are in the forecast. A 2012 Pew Research Center report determined that for every dollar they earn digitally newspapers lose $10 in print revenue.[36] It's one more "Bad Day at Black Rock" for the longtime print sources that are updating what's happening, yet another nail in the coffin.

In the meantime scads of American dailies have vanished, particularly afternoon papers and journals that competed in markets with stronger papers. It makes little difference that these disappearing acts reliably went about performing their expected functions in acceptable and sometimes-extraordinary manners. They're simply missing from the landscape of the Information Age. Why has this happened?

"The simplistic answer," ex–*Chicago Tribune* newspaperman and UPI staffer Charles Madigan explains, "is that the Internet, with its immediacy and its zero-dollar cost of entry, swept in to make newspapers seem every bit the nineteenth-century institutions they are." While that has played a role, he alleges, it is "maybe not the central role."[37] The possibilities of suspects that Madigan cites contain a few cultural factors and even some media philosophy itself:

> In an America that seems stripped of leisure time, where young women pound their laptops even as they sip their lattes at Starbucks, and where a vast collection of gizmos has evolved to help everyone multi-task, there may be no time left for a quiet hour during the day for reading a very low-tech account of what happened yesterday. Newspapers evolved in an era in which the definition of news was something like this: "What happened today that didn't happen yesterday, dressed up and delivered tomorrow." Today news is something that happened an instant ago. A collection of media developments that began in the mid-twentieth century with the arrival of television network news also cut into the market for newspapers. Radio—all news and all the time—had its impact....
>
> The thought that there is an authoritative source for anything has fallen under a wave of unchecked, unreported, and unprofessional babbling on the Internet, where no one reviews credentials or facts and the wacky and the wise march hand-in-hand right into the laptops, handheld devices, and living rooms (and basements too) of America. One part of this new culture defines itself in opposition to what it calls the MSM (Main Stream Media) and delights in its own hyperbole—passionate, factless in many cases, and in some bile fueled.[38]

4. The Only Thing Constant

As gloom and doom continues to envelop the trade, is the handwriting of newspapers' future on the wall? Could the consequences be broadened to include other forms of print media as well? Time certainly will tell, but the prognosticators suggest that the matter will remain unsettling to the purists who persist in holding to traditional structures as the sole means of conveying details of current events. That was so 20th century, many of those observers believe. The newsprint form just may be going the way of the rooftop TV antenna, the eight-track tape deck, and the automobile CB (citizens band) radio.

The problem is exacerbated by the fact that, as news industry analyst and newspaperman Ken Doctor points out, readers aren't receiving all the news that was fit to print in an earlier interval today:

> It's not your eyes that are deceiving you. We're getting less news.
>
> There are simply far fewer people bringing it to us. Overall, America's daily newspapers have shed about ten thousand newsroom jobs in the last decade, well down from the 2001 peak of 56,400.[39] While we can sympathize with the 45,000 or so journalists who remain under stress in U.S. newsrooms, how do we begin to comprehend the loss of their reporting, of their community knowledge?
>
> Newspapers have been sliced and diced down to near-brochure size. Almost a hundred of America's dailies are no longer daily, an oxymoron if there ever was one. Many stories are never covered. There are simply fewer reporters available to cover them.
>
> So we know less. How much less? We don't know exactly, but we do have some indications. Over the last five years, U.S. newspaper companies have cut their newsprint usage 40 percent. Figure that half of what has been cut is ads and half news. So the 20 percent cut in newsroom staff is about matched by a 20 percent cut in news reporting....
>
> In short, we don't know what we don't know, but we do know we know less than we used to.[40]

As just one example of what is transpiring, in the five-year period from 2006 to 2011 *The Baltimore Sun* reduced the number of stories it regularly presented for readers' attention by a third.[41] The venerable old paper dates to 1837, a bastion of celebrated journalism excellence within its regional geographical boundaries.

Another bystander with plenty of reason to know what's going on in the mass media, Stephen Shepard—whose professional pedigree is linked to editorial posts at *Newsweek* and *Business Week,* the presidency of the American Society of Magazine Editors, and the deanship at a university journalism school—offers his "take" on the suffering that is stemming from contemporary media's reduced attention to detail:

> Critical issues—from education to the courts—are not covered as well as before, or even at all in some communities. In many places, there are no reporters keeping an eye on city hall or the state capitol, a traditional watchdog function of the press. In Senate testimony in 2009, David Simon, the former *Sun* reporter who created the hit HBO show *The Wire*, put it bluntly: "It is going to be one of the great times to be a corrupt politician."[42]

A perplexing and sobering uncertainty in all this remains: "Where is the Internet going to get its information if the newspaper in your town goes out of business?" Something to ponder there, as blogger Paul Gillin stipulates, "The information [that] people expect to find for free online has to come from somewhere, and ... the institutions that provide it are in peril."[43] Gillin's assessment in 2012 contrasts with that of *Washington Post* reporter Paul Farhi five years earlier. The capital scribe rebuked media accounts of the looming fall of newspapers, calling them "greatly exaggerated, if not flat wrong," and claimed that "newspapers may have the best chance of any of the old media to survive in a new-media world."[44]

Beyond this finely honed conjecture, Farhi argued that newspapers will triumph over any rivalry generated by the blogosphere: "For all their self-infatuation and all their ... criticism of the Old Media," Farhi says, "many bloggers would be out of business without the traditional media. Blogs draw their lifeblood from the raw material served up each day by conventional news organizations." Well, yes, and isn't that the point?

In 2005, when Farhi's observations appeared, paper-and-ink's durability seemed a little more certain. While advocating going with the flow, which presumably includes electronic transmission, he exhibits an unyielding perception that newspapers invariably will be around to overcome their competition. That doesn't appear to square with proclivities nearly a decade later, however.

As troubling conditions loom and multiply—the extensive contributions of newspapers now plainly on an endangered species list—will the substantial volume of information they have provided to freethinking and opinion *always* be there? Ex-newspaperman James O'Shea argues the point that much of what we know—and need to know—starts with intrepid newspaper correspondents. "Although many newspaper staffs have been thinned," says he, "a dwindling core of journalists still file into courthouses, police stations, legislatures, and government agencies to report on the people's business. While news aggregators on the Internet boast snazzy websites and fresh content, if you peel back the surface, you'll find that most—if not all—of their content is based on a newspaper report."[45]

Obsessing over the passing of some venerated musical performers of yesteryear, a country music tune inquires, "Who's Gonna Fill Their Shoes?" The same may be pondered now. Eric Alterman expounds on the potential loss: "It is impossible not to wonder what will become of not just news but democracy itself, in a world in which we can no longer depend on newspapers to invest their unmatched resources and professional pride in helping the rest of us to learn, however imperfectly, what we need to know."[46]

Referring specifically to the wing of journalism pertaining to newspapers, Charles Madigan, introduced earlier, references it as "the business" in a treatise he edited surveying the disintegration of that grand old institution. He writes: "The business sits, after all, at the intersection where truth and trouble collide, and that is a risky place. It searches every day for the doom and the delight that define life. It tells sad, happy, pointless, profound stories. It is inconceivable that it would disappear, but not inconceivable that to save itself it will change so much you may not recognize it."[47]

French classical author Francois de la Rochefoucauld (1613–1680) said it well when he penned an idiom that has since acquired a semblance of immortality: "The only thing constant in life is change." Legions of journalists will corroborate that, based on many years of experience. Nothing in their profession remains static very long. And that reality seems most definitely applicable to the course of typeset communications in the days ahead.

5

Supply and Demand

In the opening decade to the 21st century, many Americans transitioned from their long-established practices of acquiring news from predictable wellsprings of information to consulting the diverse new sources that were proliferating. There arose the perception that news could be effectively retrieved virtually anywhere at any time. As that decade played out, the replacements prompted a couple of perceptive media observers, Bill Kovach and Tom Rosenstiel, to offer an estimate of what was transpiring:

> Some imagined that this would scatter the audience to a million new places for news, including blogs and articles by citizen journalists, and substantially away from traditional news values such as journalistic objectivity, the idea of the journalist as an independent broker who has verified the news that is published and who offers multiple points of view.... This notion ... isn't really what has happened in journalism. When it comes to news, the reality ... [is that] Traditional online news sites got bigger, not smaller.[1]

In 2009, the Project for Excellence in Journalism (PEJ) certified that—just two years earlier—the nation's ten largest newspapers could boast an aggregate of 19 percent of U.S. circulation. That same year (2007) those same ten journals supplied 29 percent of the audience of newspaper Web sites. A year later the 700 leading online news and information sites witnessed a respectable 7 percent rise in viewership. That may have seemed like something to crow about until one realizes that the 50 prime Web sites run by newspapers and/or TV stations experienced a 27 percent rise in traffic that year.[2]

Is this a telltale harbinger of things to come?

Subsequently, in 2010, the PEJ confirmed that of the foremost 200 American news sites then available online approximately four out of five were "legacy" news sources (tied to established print or TV media) or combinations of those venerated news disbursers. In addition, the PEJ said that 83 percent of Web traffic then pursuing the news focused on the aforementioned four out of five electronic news suppliers.[3] It was just another way of authenticating the country's dependence upon the known, the unfailing, the generators of current events. In them we have consistently expressed our almost unparalleled confidence.

A well-versed media observer, Ken Doctor—a man who in earlier years devoted much of his professional livelihood to newspaper writing, editing, and management—identified a powerfully influential core group of international news and information providers, which he labels the *Digital Dozen*.[4] Describing these as "news-producing companies," Doctor says the trade considers them "multiplatform" distributors. Indeed, they ship news to consumers wherever, whenever, and however the recipients desire. Does this sound familiar? They work in print, on desktops and laptops, iPhones, BlackBerries, car displays, gas station screens, cable television, and a surfeit of added outlets.

Doctor brands this elite cadre as the unassailable leaders of the pack. Yet he acquiesces on one point: The number in his combine isn't quite precisely an even dozen participants. His count actually cites 16 parent firms (some suppliers are invested in more than one medium, thereby posting a still higher figure). But Doctor is convinced that, as time elapses, mergers and consolidations will trim the ultimate quantity to about a dozen. Here's the list of the global players he envisages as dominating the creation and delivery of online news on a permanent landscape:

Newspaper-Based Firms
 The New York Times
 The Wall Street Journal
 USA Today
 The Washington Post
 The Guardian (UK)
 The Telegraph (UK)
 Times Online (UK)

Broadcasters
 NBC
 ABC
 CBS
 BBC (UK)

Cablecasters
 MSNBC
 CNN
 Fox News

Wire Services
 Associated Press
 Reuters

Radio
 National Public Radio

Financial News and Information
 Financial Times (UK)
 Bloomberg

Many savvy media types will swiftly identify these players. (The four leading U.S. newspapers, for instance, appear in a recent list by circulation of America's top 10 daily newsjournals in this order, top to bottom: *The Wall Street Journal, The New York Times, USA Today, The Los Angeles Times,* the New York *Daily News,* the *New York Post, The Washington Post,* the *Chicago Sun-Times, The Denver Post,* and the *Chicago Tribune.*)[5] Few could argue seriously that any of them might not have formidable chances of figuring prominently in whatever outcomes transpire in the delivery of news and information to consumers of succeeding generations.

All of these (radio, television, newspapers, otherwise) have demonstrated incredible measures of resolve, energy, imagination, and innovation—when coupled with sound financial traction—that will let them reach most of their quests. Doctor summarizes: "Though we think of their brands by their legacy roots—television, newspaper, radio—by 2015, I think the winners will all be known to us as big news brands associated strongly with all forms of taking in the news—reading, viewing, and listening.... They are gingerly dismantling their old businesses, while engineering new ones."[6]

In spite of all the bad press for the media in general from time to time, there is in this land an overwhelming confidence in what we are acquainted with and trust and have therefore counted on for enduring periods. At one time at least a solitary representative of the media (the late TV anchorman Walter Cronkite) was widely touted as "the most trusted man in America," a symbol of that faith. Our collective allegiance to news Web sites under the aegis of long-established (and, in many cases, well-respected) news generators can be nearly taken for granted, and it may be. It is a solid testament to an ongoing affirmation that when those particular sources deliver the news most of the time we can take it to the bank.

If it was not for the traditional, reputable legacy purveyors of news, in fact, we'd be in an awful fix. Hard-pressed to know the truth, we'd be left to our own ruminations, floundering in our stupor, wondering what is really going on. Upon those sources rests the bulk of practically all the authentic news we get, including much that is "borrowed" by a multiplicity of news blogs and other online sources. As noted already, the latter rely mainly on the recognized print and broadcast media for

5. Supply and Demand

their story ideas, if not the sometimes-altered material they originate themselves.

There is simply no getting around the fact that basic journalism prevails in this country because there are still authentic investigative reporters on the job, people who ferret out the truth—whose entire careers and livelihoods are dependent upon their successfully digging up the facts and transferring them into communicative forms for transmission through diverse means. There awaits a hungry audience, anxious to answer the presumptively lingering question: "What happened?"

It's that other 20 percent of online news disseminators that has materialized in recent years that gives us reason for pause. They challenge the dependability and—at times—the integrity of the Web sites that Americans most consistently turn to for news and information. And their numbers are rapidly increasing. Many independent news Web sites go about their tasks in responsible fashion, seeking to provide truth without opinionated twists on current events. They work quickly and intently, similarly to the organized media that sponsor electronic editions. It's telling the difference between these sites and their less reliable counterparts that can create problems:

> Of course, the Internet provides a lot of information of dubious value and origin. Anyone with a computer, a modem, and an axe to grind (or an agenda to promote or a product to sell) can create a credible-looking Web site and publish "news" for a global audience, right alongside the news provided by the world's established news providers.... How can a news consumer tell what's reliable? It's not necessarily easy, and it makes going online potentially hazardous.[7]

Among the nation's news junkies—those seemingly "obsessed" with keeping up with breaking news—so profoundly prominent have news Web sites become that journalism prof John V. Pavlik of Columbia University has ascertained: "When visiting a Web site, a viewer often first checks when a site was last updated and, if this hasn't occurred recently, moves on to another site. Software robots even automatically alert 'netizens' (citizens of the Internet) when a favorite news site or story has been modified."[8]

How's that for applying instant technology?

There is no dearth of suppliers in meeting the burgeoning demands of surfers for reliable news in digital form. The devil is sometimes in the details, however. A trustworthy Web site one has discovered can become a real "find"—and thereby a "keeper" worth returning to again and again and again.

6

The Bad News Is

How many times have you heard the expression "I have good news and bad news for you"? That phrase is frequently followed directly by "Which do you want first?" It may be little or nothing to start sweating over unless, of course, you're hearing it from (a) your teenager or spouse who's been out driving your car, (b) your tax accountant, (c) your superior at your place of employment, or (d) your physician.

Recently it was the latter for me, a skin cancer surgeon who returned to my operating room following a procedure. He had removed a basal cell carcinoma after which he read the report of a pathologist who analyzed the discarded tissue. The surgeon announced: "I have good news and bad news for you."

The good news, he allowed, was that what he had set out to eradicate had been successfully excised. The bad news, he added, was that he had discovered a second and potentially more threatening squamous cell carcinoma. It had gone undetected until he went to remove the original. Subsequently he purged the latter—the one we hadn't known was there—and later that day returned with a favorable report on that one from the pathologist, too. It was a reminder that in almost every circumstance in life there is a silver lining. The operative word (if that's a good term in this application) is *almost*. Not every encounter turns out as well as this one did.

Take newspapers, for instance, and particularly the kind in print. The good news is that most of them are still on the job—still delivering good and bad news to subscribers and single-copy purchasers every single day (except, of course, in places where they are no longer distribute in hard-copy form every single day). In due course, furthermore, it may turn out that if that portion of the industry should capsize and go belly-up only the tangible structure and its delivery scheme need to be altered.

Many times the substance itself can be rescued. Think of it like a caterpillar shedding its original outfit in order to convert into a butterfly. The transformation isn't the end but the adaptation of something altogether different. So it could be with the venerable newsprint journal.

While other chapters of this text underscore the possibilities for newspapers that make the shift from paper to pixel, it's the bad news—to be highlighted in this chapter—that offers an impetus for publishers, media conglomerates, and groups of investors to consider a transition. The personal computer, the laptop, and an escalating host of mobile devices that deliver the Internet have paved the route for newspapers to leap onto the rolling digital bandwagon. The reasons that the electronic engagement holds such appeal to printed newspapers are legion. And actually that's the bad news. There's plenty of it to make a convincing case.

Let's start with the graying of America and its unmistakably weighty implications on readership. It's a huge factor now in what's transpiring at the dailies and weeklies that are still producing the bulk of their work in a pen-and-ink mode. Ex-newspaperman Alan D. Mutter, currently a Silicon Valley consultant in corporate initiatives and new media ventures that engage both journalism and technology, identified some figures early in 2013 that could be disturbing to the status quo:

- Only 6 percent of people in their 20s and 16 percent of 40-year-olds routinely read newspapers, compared to 48 percent of people over 65.
- Only 29 percent of the U.S. population read a newspaper regularly in 2012, down from 56 percent in 1991.[1]

Only a few years earlier a study fostered by Adweek Media and the Harris Poll disclosed the alarming detail that 10 percent of Americans *never read any newspaper* at all. And when it comes to age groupings the trend is even more pronounced and unsettling. Among Americans between the ages of 18 and 34 pollsters found that just 23 percent indicated that they read a newspaper of some type "almost every day." Another 17 percent, meanwhile, said that they *never* read one. And there was a third category of 60 percent of respondents within that rising age cluster that could be classified as comprising a rather broad "occasional" readership faction. Those subjects indicated that their news reading habits wavered between a "few times a week" and an even more disconcerting "few times

6. The Bad News Is

a year."[2] Their replies were not just unsettling; they were demoralizing, suggesting a tendency that doesn't bode well for the future of the medium.

Writing in *The New Yorker* in 2008, Eric Alterman declared that the average age of a newspaper reader in the United States is 55. More recently, in 2013, the Pew Research Center reported that in a study it had conducted not long before, fewer than 10 percent of respondents under age 30 said they read a newspaper within the previous 24 hours. Conversely, almost 50 percent of those above 65 years of age had done so. Pew noted that three-fourths of America's newspaper readers are now over the age of 45. It further pointed out that just 39 percent of U.S. citizens comprise the segment of Americans who are older than 45. Beyond that, "that group is getting older and dying while the under–45s are not."[3] A few years ago, a *Chicago Sun-Times* columnist announced matter-of-factly: "Newspapers aren't dying; our readers are."

A letter that appeared in a major U.S. daily late in 2013 from a woman who had recently celebrated her 80th birthday is typical of the fervor that age group demonstrates for its newspapers across millions of enduring lifetimes:

> I know in an age of bloggers, e-mailers, tweets and other fascinating ways to avoid newspapers and to keep my brain "sharp" I should be learning newer ways to find out what is going on.... I know I am expected to be conversant with all kinds of alternative media. But I cling to my daily newspapers like a baby to its pacifier ... I can't be weaned off.
>
> If you are in your early life, you don't get it. You were brought up with computers and megabytes and windows and all that jazz.
>
> You don't think you are missing anything. I don't believe that.
>
> You are missing relationships with local media collectors and distributors of news, with men and women who can give you fast feedback on your point of view and distribution of that point of view to the muddled masses yearning to be free of anything that has the word gigabyte in it.
>
> So this is a love letter to a newspaper that has always been on my front porch in the morning and always will be.... It lands at my house like clockwork unless a tornado or a fire interrupts its publication.
>
> ...My only complaint is that it has begun to feel like a paper napkin owing to that alternative media. Save me from these obsessive alternatives. Newsprint, live on![4]

"One thing is clear," the Adweek Media–Harris Poll concluded. "The era of Americans reading a daily newspaper each and every day is coming to an end."[5]

What does all this mean? Alan Mutter lamented: "At some point, the newspaper audience may contract so severely that (a) publishers cannot attract enough advertisers, (b) publishers no longer enjoy the economies of scale necessary to print profitably, or (c) both of the above."[6] Bloggers such as Bill Hoffmann, commenting for Newsmax, have perpetuated Mutter's assumptions. As he reiterated Mutter's figures, Hoffmann offered a bleak outlook for newsprint's future. "The time for the industry to pivot from print to pixels appears to be running low," he quotes Mutter. "In the meantime, none of us is getting any younger."[7]

Said *Newspaper Death Watch* blogger Paul Gillin: "Few advertisers want to reach people over the age of 50, and almost no one wants to reach 65-year-olds. People in that age group live on fixed incomes, have no children at home and very modest spending needs. They buy very little. Yet this is the core audience newspaper publishers have to sell to their advertisers."[8] (While that estimate is generally true, you'll recall that the evening TV news on the national hookups is absolutely saturated with commercials for pharmaceuticals, insurance and sexual performance enhancements for the elderly. How so if there isn't a receptive audience for them?)

Before we completely swallow all of the falderal about the aging of print newspaper readers and the consequences for the future, consider for a moment the sheer possibility that there might be more than one side to this tale. You know what they say about "no good deed goes unpunished?" Mutter's invective painting a preponderance of newsprint readers as elderly, irrelevant to advertisers, and therefore comprising the final remnants of a once-proud legacy of the newsprint faithful, has been gamely disputed. And not so by just a casual critic of the trade but by one of Mutter's most venerated contemporaries.

Tom Rosenstiel, who was quick to respond to Mutter's discourse, is executive director of the American Press Institute. At the same time he's a member of Poynter's national advisory board as well as a venerated author and journalist. Following the release of Mutter's comments, Rosenstiel replied in a Web-circulated rebuttal:

> By Mutter's analysis, roughly three-quarters of newspaper readers are now over age 45. That, according to his calculations, is up dramatically from half in 2010—a graying of newspaper readers by 50 percent in two years.
> He based his analysis on data from the Pew Research Center that I was involved in producing from summer 2010 and summer 2012....

The problem is, the analysis doesn't reflect reality.

First, the numbers don't track with any commensurate significant drop in newspaper readership in the Pew dataset. In the survey conducted in June 2012, 49 percent of adults said they read a newspaper "regularly," the same percentage as in 2010. If you take the narrower number, the percentage of adults who read a newspaper "yesterday," there is a slight change, a drop from 31 percent in 2010 to 29 percent in 2012, but nothing that would support the kind of dramatic structural shift Mutter estimates. Nor do recent circulation figures suggest it.

Mutter attempted to estimate the percentage of print newspaper readers by age cohort by comparing the Pew Research data with Census data. But the Pew data was a sample of adults. He compared that to the population overall, including children. So his percentages are not comparing the same populations.

The market research firm Scarborough Research produces analysis that covers the ground Mutter was trying to walk—the percentage of newspaper readers by age group. Scarborough's data, which is based on a large sample of some 200,000 people, also find, like Pew Research's data, relatively minor change in two years. According to that Scarborough data, 68 percent of the people who said they read a print newspaper "yesterday" were over 45, compared with 66 percent in 2010, a slight drop but also not an irrelevant one given long-term trends.[9]

So is this good news in the middle of the purportedly bad news? It may depend on whose interpretation of the figures one selects. In all fairness, however, it creates some uncertainty that (a) there is a mass of old people out there clinging to their printed news journals who in some curious way are potentially obstructing their local papers' abilities to shift into digital overdrive; and (b) readership is down so far for so many leading U.S. dailies and weeklies with print editions that forcing a collapse of their operations is a threatening next step. At least, it all sounds pretty ominous. Could it really be that bad?

Rosenstiel goes on to cite more sources that insinuate that the graying of print's readership may not be quite as pronounced as some authorities have a tendency to imply. He concurs with Mutter that "developing digitally native products" is the newspaper's real future. At the same time, Rosenstiel cautions his audience: "As we navigate our way, we need a cold, clear and accurate eye on the present and a discussion that avoids the Pollyannaish or Apocalyptic."[10]

The bad news, in this case, just might not be quite as foreboding as we have customarily imagined. If all of it is relative to one's perspective, maybe this is a bit of good news in fact.

But the next concern for printed news journals unquestionably is all about bad news—and in spades: declining revenues. The greatest sting is being felt from the sharp curtailments in the advertising budgets of commercial enterprises that in large measure used to faithfully underwrite their local newspapers. Now much of that revenue source has gone dry or is down to a mere trickle as more and more retail and manufacturing organizations turn to other venues to allocate their marketing dollars.

The severity of the situation was quite evident in a summary jointly issued early in 2013 by Aquent and the American Marketing Association. It spelled out the foremost emphases in which marketers expected to *decrease* their focus (disbursements) in 2013.[11] They are given in percentages.

Reductions in Marketing Allocations for 2013

Newspapers—32%
Consumer magazines—28%
Radio—24%
Trade magazines—22%
Television—21%
Out of home—15%
Events/trade shows/virtual events—14%
Video games—12%
Direct marketing—9%
Podcasts—9%

The biggest loser was newspapers, with one in three marketers planning to decrease spending there throughout the year. Joining newspapers in the cellar were consumer magazines, radio, trade magazines, and television, all of which were expected to realize cuts of more than 20 percent. The real winners, in the meantime, were mobile media, social media, and marketing automation. More than three-fourths of marketers planned to increase their spending in those three arenas. For that reason you can put another checkmark in the digital column. It's unquestionably more tangible evidence of which way the wind is blowing.

Another downer for newspapers, of course, is the continuing drop in circulation, cited in several localities throughout this text. Then there are the severe cutbacks on staffing (about a third of editorial employees in the newsrooms in a decade), also referenced numerous times, in order

6. The Bad News Is

for publications to stay above water. None of it is an omen of good times to be. Adding to all of it is a proliferation of competing start-ups vying for the same audience's attention: "The struggles of the daily newspaper will continue as Americans have more and more ways to find the news content they need and want."[12] As these periodicals seek ways to get their content to people and to make money in doing so they are being threatened on all sides by forces seemingly determined to bring them down and in some cases to supersede them.

In 2009, *Time* magazine's Douglas A. McIntyre, reporting on behalf of 24/7 Wall St., projected "the 10 most endangered newspapers in America."[13] His reference was specifically to the newsprint editions. The imperiled collection there included the following journals, listed in numerical order, most endangered first:

1. The *Philadelphia Daily News*
2. The Minneapolis *Star Tribune*
3. *The Miami Herald*
4. *The Detroit News*
5. *The Boston Globe*
6. The *San Francisco Chronicle*
7. The *Chicago Sun-Times*
8. The New York *Daily News*
9. The Fort Worth *Star-Telegram*
10. *The Plain Dealer* (Cleveland)

In presenting this catalog coupled with precise reasons for each of the dismal projections, McIntyre elaborated:

> 24/7 Wall St. has created a list of the 10 major daily papers that are most likely to fold or shutter their print operations and only publish online. The properties were chosen on the basis of the financial strength of their parent companies, the amount of direct competition they face in their markets and industry information on how much money they are losing. Based on this analysis, it's possible that 8 of the nation's 50 largest daily newspapers could cease publication in the next 18 months.[14]

All of these journals were saddled with significant economic problems. The reasons for their individual appearances on that endangered list included descriptive phrases like "advertising falling sharply," "could survive if its rival folds," "no serious bidders," "strong competition," "unlikely that it can merge [with a rival]," "[must] make tremendous cost cuts," "no chance of competing with [its opposite]," "fighting for circulation and advertising," "not owned by a larger organization," "could easily lose millions ... no chance of recovering," "competes with a larger paper in a neighboring market," "[must] shut down or become an edition of its rival," and "in one of the economically weakest markets in the country."

Despite the dire predictions with ominous-sounding clouds hanging overhead, as this is written in late 2013—almost five years beyond when those grim prognostications originally surfaced—all ten of the publications on the list remain in business. All ten produce simultaneous paper-and-ink and digital versions. In the intervening time, nonetheless, two of those ten news journals have reduced their home deliveries of newsprint editions to just three days weekly (including the *Detroit News* and *The Plain Dealer*). That's a route that a rising segment of pundits expect to see widen across the industry in the not-very-distant future. (For much more on this see the chapter that follows.)

And with their financial woes worsening, any of these papers—along with many more U.S. dailies that are hanging by a thread—could become casualties at any point. It would seem that they could cease publishing their newsprint versions fairly easily. Worse, however, they could stop publishing altogether (including the pixel incarnations) as some have done, and so reported elsewhere in this volume. Newspaper owners are, frankly, looking for white knights bearing shining armor and sitting atop great steeds who are ready to ride in and rescue their faltering properties. If those saviors fail to appear with feasible plans for a quick resuscitation, it's virtually certain that still more once-distinguished nameplates will be joining some that have departed already. They left the scene because they were unable to cope any further as viable commercial ventures.

Several of these, maybe from this list and from other survivors still holding on, could easily be gone before the third decade of the 21st century arrives. While naming names may not be advisable in this matter, the fact that many major newspapers are in deep financial chaos is troubling enough to a trade whose mission has always been to *report* the news rather than to *be* the news.

7

Out of the Hybrid an Oxymoron

Like many other sources cited already, the Poynter Institute, headquartered in St. Petersburg, Florida, and given to maintaining excellence in journalism, painted a rather bleak picture of the industry it represents in early 2013.[1] Noting that publishers and broadcasters are seeking survival in an age in which traditional media is fractured by a growing obsession with electronic transmission, which—at that juncture—offered inadequate revenues for sustaining news operations, Poynter's Rick Edmonds candidly observed:

> As readers and advertisers dive headlong into the mobile era, the outlook for news companies remains difficult. For much of the past 15 years, news organizations have been forced to trade print dollars for digital dimes, as revenues from print and television evaporated far faster than digital revenues have grown. Now, things may get even worse: News may be entering the era of mobile pennies.
>
> …
>
> …News remains a tiny player in a digital market dominated by Apple, Amazon, Google, Facebook and a handful of other tech giants that are far stronger financially and, in many cases, technologically. Even as their revenue picture darkens, news organizations have little choice but to invest time, personnel and resources in the proliferating spate of digital and mobile platforms their readers are using.[2]

For a moment, think of some pairs of quantities that are so demonstrably aligned that—in our common perception—they cannot be freely interrupted or disjoined. Here are a few such examples:

The sun rises and the sun sets.
The winds blow from hot to cold.
The rains come and the rains go.
The sea rolls in and the sea rolls out.

The seeds are planted and the crops sprout.
The forest is dense and then it is barren.
Life begins and eventually ends.

A sense of order and the reliability of recurring cycles offer contentment in sustaining our sense of stability and security. Except in rare instances, for which there is often a plausible explanation, the consistency of nature's logical pattern isn't frequently violated.

Since time immemorial, print journalism has been such a durable presence in society that many people would have difficulty imagining its termination, much like the phenomena of natural experiences. But as it turns out, the things that man creates never come with an infinite shelf life.

In this case the reference pertains to the daily newspaper of the paper-and-ink variety, the operative word being *daily*. As we have witnessed several times already, the substance of the paper's habit-forming routine has been steadily slipping. In a rising number of provinces within contemporary times the daily news journal actually has been disappearing altogether. And now it seems that, for the newsprint media still with us—including some of it that appears to be on life support—a practice that many Americans thought was sacrosanct is shaken to its very foundations. It turns out that the joining of *daily* and *newspaper* has progressed into a myth more than an absolute.

The first signs pointing in this direction materialized in 2009. That year a handful of formidable fortresses of daily print journalism announced that they would limit their newsprint publications to something less than a generally standardized seven-day week (or fewer days if entrenched in six- or five-day cycles). For local readers of the pooled *Detroit Free Press* and *The Detroit News,* for instance, a prime early example of this tactic, it meant a reduction from publishing seven days to just three for the conventional porch-thrown issue. (Here's something else to think about: Is the term *conventional* still apropos in referencing newspapers now if comparing the form's contemporary replicas with those of their storied pasts? Think about content, size, staff, and territory served.)

Since 2010, the Motor City's *News* has printed Monday through Saturday editions but delivered those papers to homes in the Detroit metropolitan district only on Thursday and Friday. In the meantime the "skinny" issues are available for purchase at newsstands every day. On Sunday a section of the *News* is bound into the *Free Press* for delivery to residential subscribers. An online version of the latter mode is touted to the significantly populous market as "available each morning by 5:30 a.m." This digital edition has replaced the seven-day home-thrown edition.[3]

Those Motor City readers may have fared somewhat better nevertheless than the long-standing traditionalists subscribing to *The Christian Science Monitor*. In 2009, *Monitor* patrons lost four of the five days of their customary newsprint edition, which many had been receiving for a lot of years. Only the Saturday copies survived. That's in addition to a daily Web-based incarnation of the highly respected news journal. Those who had long ago cultivated an appreciation for the habit and feel of a newsprint mock-up suddenly witnessed the *Monitor* being effectively reduced from a business week daily to a weekly. Unless they exhibited the capability, desire, and resolve to capture the electronic rendering, from then on they were out of luck.

Adios, au revoir, auf Wiedersehen. Good night!

For newspapers once referenced as *dailies*—including several with enduring legacies that cover a handful of genuinely mega-size urban markets—let us make no mistake: Occurrences like this one are clear indications of a mounting trend that is rapidly catching fire in the trade. We had better be getting used to it, in fact, if we haven't already. If this innovation hasn't caught on yet in your neighborhood just give it a little time. The chances are rising that it could be instigated in the not-too-distant future. In many places it may be a foregone conclusion. There is very little territory in the United States that will completely escape the exercise of reducing newsprint dailies into something appearing less frequently in driveways and mailboxes and on front porches. That is if, indeed, the paper-and-ink model survives anyway.

This isn't going to occur ubiquitously overnight. But as more and more success stories are recorded, as newspaper readers get used to transitioning to a new form, and as publishers save more and more money by implementing the changes, it will be difficult to reverse a rolling bandwagon that is gaining rapid momentum. If we can look ahead for a decade or more it's possible we may view a landscape for paper-and-ink news journals that will be quite different from anything we have been accustomed to in the past.

Terming it "a movement," media analyst Ken Doctor is persuaded that we are right now seeing "the beginning of the end of the seven-day weekly." By 2015, he says, many more newspapers will have leaped upon the publishing reduction bandwagon. "Newspaper companies tend to move as a herd," he asserts.[4]

A Spring 2012 report released by the Pew Research Center comprised of the responses of 38 U.S. news executives not only is revealing but also could be classified as riveting. It suggests that—most likely by 2017—the bulk of American newspapers embracing the paper-and-ink model will be dominated by "less frequent" publication schedules. "Maybe just on Sunday," the Pew data concludes.[5]

In a few years, according to Ken Doctor, "a lot of people, especially young people, will be amazed that trees were actually cut down to produce a daily newspaper." Referencing this current era as the "Digital Decade," he is almost adamant in a conviction that by the conclusion of the present decade we will be experiencing "digital heavy, [with] a little print."[6]

> The financial logic driving reduced frequency, which has been discussed as an option for years, is that print advertising is now concentrated on Sunday (nearly half the total) and a few weekdays. The few advertisers on Mondays, Tuesdays and Saturdays might be persuaded to switch schedules to the remaining print days, the theory goes. And as print advertising continues to fall, readers also may be more satisfied with three substantial print editions a week.[7]

Doctor claims that 85 percent of the revenues of most newspaper companies are attributed to print advertising. The print days that are retained by a newspaper become the market days, he notes, the ones advertisers prize most. Many times Sunday yields more than 50 percent of a newspaper's advertising income, Doctor attests.[8] Meanwhile another media analyst—John Morton, who writes a column about newspaper economics for the *American Journalism Review*—sheds a little more enlightenment on the topic of print days:

> It's a fact that most newspapers don't make money every day.... They tend to lose money on Mondays and Tuesdays, and some lose money on Thursdays and Saturdays, depending on the market. So what's good financially,

although it's very bad for journalism, is not to publish on those days. It's sad, but I'm afraid we'll see a lot more of this going forward.[9]

This news arrives in spite of gargantuan newspaper holding companies' repeated declarations that have disavowed such intents for the journals gathered under their corporate umbrellas. Motivated in recent years by sharp declines in advertising and circulation, they have been on a cost-cutting tear in modern times while seeking to spur profits in what has been a generally poor economy. They have been implementing the startling and rather drastic paring of their budgets mainly at the expense of several targets.

Included are a reduced workforce embracing both professional journalists and support personnel; maintenance, presses, paper, ink, storage, transportation, utilities, and miscellaneous overhead; and, at the same time, content—almost invariably content, with some angry protestations from readership to the contrary. In spite of the business concerns pertaining to survivability and a capacity for newspapers to continue to make a profit, the subscribers themselves are asking more pertinent questions that are critical to their own particular interests as consumers:

> Some readers are most interested in a different bottom-line: Will their local paper remain a valued source of news and accountability journalism? Does the industry still hold top chair at the table in deep coverage of national and international affairs, its investigative fangs still sharp? Or has that role passed on to a networked agglomeration of digital efforts ranging in scale from potent new entities like Politico and ProPublica, to bloggers, to citizen observers?[10]

These are among the unanswered questions that could have a powerful influence upon the future of American newspapers in whatever forms they may be dispatched in the years ahead. An aggregator, for the uninitiated, is a Web site that links users to other Web sites, you may remember.

Typical outlays for paper, ink, printing, and delivery have been estimated to consume about 30 percent of a newspaper's most common expenditures.[11] In the meantime, for some media moguls, making promises they cannot or will not be able to keep has been a habitual hallmark, to the disenchantment of growing numbers of their subscribers and employees. To be certain, there is an inherent danger built into all these transitional prospects. The course they travel is itself mined with the nagging possibility that public reaction could be so vociferously rebellious and readership losses so great that they negate whatever anticipated benefits might be derived from the adjustments and curtailments:

> By cutting back on print publishing, newspaper executives are betting they can wean loyal customers and advertisers from their daily print newspaper habit, while at the same time driving them to their own Web site. Some industry analysts warn that readers raised on a daily newspaper appearing at their door will lose a sense of loyalty if it arrives only a few days a week. It is like having CBS and NBC going dark on nights when they do not sell much advertising.
> "It is risky because you do invite readers to go elsewhere," said Craig Huber, an independent research analyst with Huber Research Partners. "It might drive more loyal print readers away from the newspaper as they're looking for a consistent place to get their news seven days a week."[12]

Another source pinpointed the loss of advertising as the principal fly in the ointment that is driving the disruption of the nation's newspaper-reading habits:

> At most newspapers, advertising is concentrated on several days, often Wednesday, Friday and Sunday. On the days when it's light, the papers lose money. Rather than subsidize those skinny cash drains, why not use the money to bolster the paper's profitability and invest in a digital future?
> The risk, of course, is driving off the remaining print customers. Media consumption is very much a matter of habit. If there's no paper on Tuesday, or if you have to forage to find one at a newsstand (and it's a thin edition with very little in it), you might begin to question why you're still getting it at all. And while the future may be digital, newspapers are still heavily dependent on print advertising.[13]

Despite such perilous warnings of imminent danger, by 2010 nearly 90 U.S. dailies had discontinued their newsprint editions at least one day per week, with many of them omitting hard-copy editions on multiple days of each week.[14] Whether the subscribers wished to move to the Web to continue attaining their news from a time-honored provider, many times they have been given little or no choice in that decision. Particularly is this true if they wanted to continue receiving it five, six, or seven days a week. And some papers have even abolished their print editions altogether.

The *Seattle Post-Intelligencer,* the oldest reporting citadel (founded 1863) in its city, steeped in journalistic tradition, banished newsprint completely in 2009 when it evolved into a wholly online entity.[15] A few companies took even more drastic measures. After establishing a proud heritage that went all the way back to 1859, Denver's *Rocky Mountain News* celebrated its sesquicentennial in 2009 by shuttering its operation totally to divest itself of further financial vulnerabilities.[16] Other journals made threats that they seemed perfectly capable of carrying out should circumstances fail to improve.

On June 26, 2013, the owner of New Jersey's largest daily, Newark's *Star-Ledger,* with a weekday circulation of 340,778 and Sunday circulation of 432,040, issued an ominous warning: If the union printing the paper did not negotiate responsibly within three months, the enterprise would have little choice but to close its doors forever on December 31, 2013.[17] One option for maintaining the paper might be to outsource the printing if talks break down, the owners said.[18] At the time such a mandate hardly seemed like idle chatter, however, to those who would be most directly affected by it, including the employees, readers, and advertisers.

"Such blunt threats are not an uncommon [reality] in the newspaper business these days," Jim Bettinger, director of the John S. Knight journalism fellowship program at Stanford University, acknowledged. The Hearst Corporation had extracted major concessions from the union representing its editorial and commercials workers at the *San Francisco Chronicle* only after promising to sell or close that journal without them.[19] Given such final outcomes, the reduction to fewer published days in paper-and-ink models may be—for some purists—a still more acceptable alternative.

Of the journals moving the original configuration to something less than a time-honored six- or seven-day week typifying the terrain, many of the inked issues are surfacing not more than two or three days weekly. As previously noted, their normal print days are the ones most preferred by advertisers. And most now include a Web-based edition that is offered on assorted days, often as many as seven weekly if publishing daily had been part of a newspaper's former pedigree.

In the meantime, by mid–2013, nonetheless, the majority of papers hadn't yet joined that chorus but were intensely observing every aspect of it. Not only are those publishers comparing costs and savings, but they also seem to be just as interested in how advertisers and the public in general are responding to the switchover wherever it is being introduced. All of the raw data they can amass on the results of other papers' changes will help them eventually decide whether to dip their toes into the pond and—if they do—to determine how many toes, when, and under what circumstances.

North Carolina novelist Thomas Wolfe famously stated that "you can't go home again."[20] Once a choice is made to reduce the number of days a paper-and-ink news journal will be circulated to subscribers, any attempt to renege on that commitment at a future date could leave a paper in chaos. With a paper suddenly viewed as indecisive, an abrupt U-turn may open a wedge for an existing or start-up newsprint or Web-based rival to capitalize on the hesitancy and make hay on the paper's former turf. This comes at a further price as the conversion back to a home-delivered vehicle will be expensive.

If indeed a newspaper's glory years are visible only in its rearview mirror, its likelihood of actual survival may be dubious. It's important therefore for a publisher to *get it right* before making any public pronouncements. Any subsequent reversal could do more harm than good. In that case a sizable segment of the reading audience might just move on, losing interest and confidence in the publisher as well as the product itself.

Nevertheless, a mounting cluster of newspaper owners that serve markets ranging from small and intermediate dimensions to genuine megalopolis levels has made the transition already. These pioneers accepted the supposition that "less is more" for their paper-and-ink models. Trimming days from the enduringly standardized, perhaps even repetitious daily publishing blueprint is the norm for a proliferating faction within the industry.

At the vanguard of the move away from daily publication is an outfit run by the heirs to the media empire amassed by newspaper magnate Samuel Irving Newhouse, Sr. (1895–1979). The Newhouse unit operates under the trade banner of Advance Publications, Inc. (API). Due to its extraordinary and expanding connection with the still innovative pursuit of limited editions, API—which owns 33 dailies at this writing (2013)— requires a more extensive analysis than other entrepreneurs of the ilk.[21] API's reputation, participation, and reaction have provoked a lot of stir both inside and outside of the media in general. Because of the commanding position that the firm occupies in the evolving trend, it is detailed to some considerable extent here.

Born in New York City, Newhouse (né Solomon Neuhaus)—the son of a Russian Jewish emigrant—began to make his mark on publishing early in life.[22] In 1912, at age 17, he was given the assignment of rescuing a failing *Bayonne* (N.J.) *Times* by the paper's owner.[23] Can you fathom that? By age 18, Newhouse had retired the paper's indebtedness and seen it turn a profit. When he was 21, his annual salary was inflated to $30,000. And by the early 1920s he was personally buying several more struggling newspapers.

In each case he applied the ingenuity he had exhibited earlier in turning around the Bayonne journal. He shed operating expenses while concurrently escalating advertising and circulation attempts. A couple of years after purchasing the *Staten Island Advance* in 1922, Newhouse incorporated the Staten Island Advance Company, the nucleus of his future publishing fortune. That nomenclature stuck for a quarter century, to 1949, when the firm renamed itself Advance Publications, Inc. That moniker stands today.

In the middle of the 20th century, Newhouse and two sons, Samuel Jr. (nicknamed Si) and Donald, began implementing an aggressive posture that was to create a radically expanded company.[24] It resulted in added newspaper holdings and considerable media diversification. Among API's copious acquisitions over three decades were *The Oregonian* (Portland, 1950), the *St. Louis Globe-Democrat* (1955, which API shuttered in 1986), Condé Nast Publications (embracing a handful of popular national magazines, 1959), *The Times-Picayune* (New Orleans, 1962), *The Plain Dealer* (Cleveland, 1967), Booth Newspapers (Michigan dailies in Ann Arbor, Bay City, Flint, Grand Rapids, Jackson, Kalamazoo, Muskegon, and Saginaw, in addition to *Parade* magazine, 1976), and Random House (book publishers, 1980).

At the time of the founder's death at 84 in 1979, Advance Publications was the third-largest newspaper chain in the United States, maintaining an ongoing circulation that exceeded three million readers. By that point the firm owned 31 news journals, seven magazines, five radio stations, six TV stations, and 15 cable TV systems. In the years since there have been more acquisitions and diversifications of its expansive business. At one time or other API's active magazine inventory consisted of more than a dozen acclaimed titles. Among them have been *Architectural Digest, Bride, Condé Nast Traveler, Glamour, Gourmet, Gentleman's Quarterly, House & Garden, Mademoiselle, The New Yorker, Portfolio, Self, Vanity Fair,* and *Vogue*. Several of those legacy slicks are still fashionably trendy today.

For API, the move to reduce the number of days of the week that a newsprint edition of one of its newspapers is issued began in 2009. Wherever the concept has been implemented thus far it has been coupled with a commensurate expansion into a daily Web-based presence. What this means, according to media analyst Ken Doctor, is that the firm is "acknowledging that daily print has ended its lifespan."[25] *The Ann Arbor* (Mich.) *News* was selected as the guinea pig for what has become a mounting pack of former dailies joining those ranks, all marked by the "fewer than seven days" motif. In instituting the digital-first strategy in Ann Arbor—a pattern repeated elsewhere numerous times—API reduced its hard-copy issues to home subscribers to two days weekly.

In theory, said *The New York Times,* the Ann Arbor experience "may offer the best insight for what is ahead" with a few years of post-implementation then under its belt. In actual practice, Advance dissolved *The Ann Arbor News* and rebranded it as AnnArbor.com, a Web site that distributes a newsprint edition on Thursdays and Sundays. API doesn't release financial data for its individual news entities. But the Audit Bureau of Circulations noted that in March 2009 Sunday circulation for AnnArbor.com was 54,207. In March 2012, it was 34,923, a plunge of nearly 36 percent.

It should also be noted that Advantage holds a benefit—an "advantage," to be sure—over some competing media corporations that may ultimately pursue a similar course. API properties generally aren't unionized, freeing the owner of an additional layer of issues that papers with unions invariably encounter at times to their detriment.[26]

Typical of the Ann Arbor newsroom upheaval that occurred in the aftermath of the emblematic shift from paper to pixel is the career adjustment experienced by Geoff Larcom, a 25-year *News* veteran. Larcom was part of almost half the newsroom's staff of about 45 journalists—reporters and editors—dismissed within the first three years of the conversion. When his $60,000-a-year post was wiped out Larcom was invited to return to the online edition at a salary of $45,000. As perhaps one of the luckier scribes to be sacked, he preferred an alternative and joined the Eastern Michigan University ranks in media relations.[27] Not all of the newspaper hires caught in the transitory dilemmas precipitated by the swings from newsprint to electronics are believed to be faring nearly as well. Interviewed by *The New York Times,* Larcom offered some perspectives in the wake of the revamping of a durable Ann Arbor print journalistic heritage, alongside another Wolverine State industry observer:

> The more noticeable changes have been in its content. Mr. Larcom noted that while the Web site AnnArbor.com had improved, the Web site and paper lost columns, features and investigative pieces.
> "The dot-com is a much more news-hit-directed entity," Mr. Larcom said. "It wants to get news up that will direct traffic. You don't get a broad feel for the town...."
> Charles R. Eisendrath, director of the Knight Wallace Journalism Fellows at the University of Michigan, said that the quality declined so much that he no longer subscribed and did not need to read the paper at work.
> "Is AnnArbor.com discussed much in Ann Arbor? No. Is it an authority? No," Mr. Eisendrath said. "I don't trust anything that is done on the cheap."[28]

Everything seemed to be progressing reasonably well with API's objective of moving some of its newspapers into the "less is more" model by trimming back on the print edition while increasing its daily online presence. That is, until the outfit hit a snag in the spring of 2012. In one fell swoop it unveiled its plans to sharply curtail the publishing schedules of four leading regional newspapers it owned that are situated deep in the heart of Dixie. Although there was no particularly disturbing dustup over the revelations that the firm's trifecta of Alabama journals—*The Birmingham News, The Huntsville Times,* and Mobile's *Press-Register*—had made the concessionary list, a fourth paper not far away in the Pelican State nevertheless precipitated an outburst of boisterous and sustained fury.

In effect the publishing conglomerate inadvertently created a public relations nightmare for itself. It was wholly unprepared for the vociferous rage that was unleashed against it in New Orleans. That was the result when API made it clear in May 2012 that—the following September—the Crescent City's widely heralded bastion of journalistic excellence, *The Times-Picayune* (*T-P*), was to be reduced to a mere newsprint (footprint?) figment of its former robust self. The paper-and-ink edition would be circulated three days weekly instead of seven while an online edition would fill in at times between and be offered daily. The action was to leave New Orleans as America's largest metropolitan center without a daily newspaper in any conventional sense.[29]

> Why New Orleans? The paper was in better shape, editorially and financially, than other Advance properties. And New Orleans lags well behind other cities when it comes to Internet connections.
> Says Kevin Allman, editor of the city's all-weekly *Gambit,* "New Orleans people want a daily printed paper thrown on their porch that they can open over coffee. At a time when we're told that no one wants that, that's very much what people want here."[30]

"New Orleans has a much stronger newspaper reading habit than most places and will be affected by reduced printing," protested media analyst John Morton in reaction to API's announcement. "This is going to reduce the connection between the paper and the reading public. Just how serious those consequences are, we don't know. But there's sure to be consequences."[31] In a way his assessment seemed like a premonition of an ominous future.

Advance defended its decision as a matter of getting out in front of a general transition in the industry. By implementing the new system *The Times-Picayune*'s owner noted that it would be able to slash the uncontrollably increasing costs it experienced on a legacy pressroom, paper, and delivery. At the same time its local Web site, NOLA.com, was to receive the focus of its news and growth activities and would be continuously available to patrons on myriad platforms.

In summary, for its long-term survival, the company intimated that there wasn't any other alternative readily available to it. But in reality it seemed that most Orleanians weren't buying any of it. Reported one national journalist: "The result was a public relations disaster that Advance was ill-prepared to counter. Battered New Orleans, which had seen the paper as a lifeline in the post–Katrina era, erupted in outrage. It also didn't help that the company had launched a digital-first foray with a website that was universally derided."[32]

The transition was, according to a Web site, nothing short of "a fiasco."[33] Not since 2005 when Hurricane Katrina roared across that extensive landscape that is served by the *Times-Picayune*—leaving horrendous destruction in its wake—did the coastal community see anything proportionately approaching the storm of protests that was unleashed. Subscribers, civic and political leaders, professional journalists, and the general population residing throughout the lower halves of Louisiana and Mississippi were left reeling. Many registered the most vehement, clamorous remonstrations they could muster against API.

Surprisingly, the firm itself appeared to have given little thought to how its judgment would be received. In a community that was clearly dependent upon a venerated daily boasting the *Times-Picayune*'s sterling reputation, the downsizing seemed virtually unthinkable. To the locals it confirmed how little they mattered to the big newspaper owners calling the shots affecting them in far-off New York City. The issues inherent in the subscribers' lives were perceived as being of little concern to those operators. Of course such decisions regarding a newspaper's publication—in whatever communities around the country they might affect—were going to be fraught with the potential danger of similar public reaction.

In distant Louisville, Kentucky, for instance, a letter writer to its local paper abhorred the new tactic occurring in newspaper circulation: "In my native Alabama, the newspapers in Birmingham, Mobile, and Huntsville, three major cities, have recently been reduced to three-day-a-week publication, and their contents are far less rich than they once were.... I challenge every current subscriber to make a ... gift of a subscription ... to someone who would be sad if our newspaper, with its long and worthy history, were to go the way of Alabama."[34] Could there be more readers beyond the places where print reduction has been implemented already who harbor a tinge of distress over a once-robust publishing style that's plainly diminishing as a newer, contracted one catches on?

Not surprisingly, Randy Siegel, Advance's president for local digital strategy, certainly would have preferred that API's intents had been received differently in New Orleans. Outlining the history of his firm's seeming preoccupation with digital delivery, in a published interview he explained:

The company's newspapers, like papers everywhere, were steadily losing readers and advertising dollars to computers and tablets and mobile phones. And there was no reason to think that would ever change. All of the growth opportunities were on the digital side. Even though the papers weren't on the verge of going out of business, it was time to change the "trajectory" of the company.

"If you just ride out a decline, that's not a path to survival," he says, adding, "Perpetuating the status quo was not an option."

And to compete effectively in the digital world is not cheap. So this, he says, was the money question: Do you publish daily newspapers that bleed cash three or four or five days a week when you need capital to invest in digital?

Siegel hastens to add that while the focus will be increasingly digital, Newhouse sees newspapers as an important weapon in the company's information arsenal for quite some time. "Print will be a big part of the picture longer than the pundits predict," he says....

While newspapers have found digital dollars hard to come by, Siegel doesn't believe that will always be the case. "Digital revenue growth potential is unlimited," he says.[35]

In another interview, Siegel addressed the company's approach to the big picture in a more comprehensive manner:

"The people who think we have a one-size-fits-all plan don't understand what we're doing.... We're always reviewing our operations and thinking about the future of our local companies. And our local executives in each one of our markets are carefully studying local conditions and working on strategies to respond to the changing economic circumstances in this increasingly digital environment."[36]

To counter API's decision limiting *The Times-Picayune* to three newsprint issues per week while possibly soothing the rumpled feathers of many seemingly dispossessed Orleanians, a family of enterprising journalists living nearby saw a chance to capitalize on the Big Easy's media turmoil. David Manship, at the helm of *The Advocate*, the daily circulated in Louisiana's capital city of Baton Rouge, about 75 miles northwest of New Orleans, announced that his journal would come to the disenfranchised city's rescue. Establishing a news bureau in downtown New Orleans, said Manship, *The Advocate* would fill in the gaps as the *T-P* faded from daily home delivery. And as local *Advocate* subscriptions and advertising grew, so would the scope, content, and size of the New Orleans edition.

More journalists would be added to provide more and more locally originated stories. "We still believe in the printed newspaper every day," Manship said. "We don't doubt the importance of digital—we have a website and an app; we even have an e-edition, so we feel like we are there. We just felt like the people of New Orleans were very strong toward their reading of the *Times-Picayune* seven days a week. So we thought we'd step in and fill the void."[37]

Shazam! It was an answer to everybody's prayer, with of course the exception of Advance Publications, Inc. Nine months after its inception on Crescent City streets, *The Advocate* was reaching 22,000 homes and individual purchasers.[38] Before the launch Manship had felt an eventual 20,000 subscribers would make it a practical embarkation.

In May 2013, prosperous New Orleans financier John Georges acquired *The Advocate* from the Manship clan.[39] The new publisher installed a couple of *Times-Picayune* veterans to run *The Advocate* who had been unceremoniously dumped by API. In early going Georges evidenced as fervent a commitment to the success of the dual-city newsprint formula as that demonstrated by the Manships, if not even more.

At the time he took over the paper, rival owner Advance announced that it expected to recapture some of the journalistic footprint it had abandoned in the Big Easy. It was adding a tabloid edition on Monday, Tuesday and Thursday—three of the days on which it no longer published—although the tab (known as *TPStreet*) wouldn't be home-delivered but sold at newsstands. All of this set the stage for an escalating Battle of New Orleans II while distinguishing the market from others in the United States. The precedent-setting changes may be merely the tip of an iceberg that in short order may witness unique publishing patterns emerging in urban centers throughout the nation.

Advance's Web sites have posted strong traffic numbers. Applying search engine optimization and supplementary processes, it claims its heavy reliance on digital has been thriving financially. According to another observer of the trade, however, "The sites remain clunky in design and technology, and news coverage is notably thin with, for example, high priority local beats that seem to be covered by part-time freelancers."[40] Among *The Advocate*'s New Orleans hires, Kari Dequine Harden, a former *T-P* reporter, in an open letter to *T-P* management claimed that the *T-P* maintained "the worst news website known to man."[41]

In 2013, with about 75 newspapers in its portfolio, almost half historically having been issued daily, Advance was stepping up its realization of the bold hybrid paper-and-pixel strategy that it initially introduced in 2009. In February 2013, for instance, *The Patriot-News* at Harrisburg, Pennsylvania, and *The Post-Standard* at Syracuse, New York, increased the momentum by joining API's select circle of non-daily newsprint performers. In early April 2013, readers of *The Plain Dealer* (*PD*), serving Cleveland and much of northeastern Ohio—with 311,605 as its average total circulation in March 2013, easily making it the Buckeye State's largest news journal—learned that by late summer that year it, too, would enlist in Advance's swelling chorus of three-day-weeklies.[42] It would be home-delivered on Sunday and "on two days yet to be named," according to the preliminary announcement.

API explained that to effectively compete in the digital age, the *PD* would continue to be released seven days weekly, although "subscribers no longer will enjoy seven-day home delivery."[43] To readers without benefit of desktop, laptop, or mobile devices, it could mean the necessity of purchasing a piece of electronic equipment or appliance—or making arrangements for using one—or being regularly separated from the daily newspaper. Of course this is true in any market in which the limited hybrid model is instituted, regardless of the paper's ownership. The *PD* also expected to lay off a third of its newsroom staff, editor Debra Adams Simmons acknowledged.

The changes occurring in Cleveland's proud journalistic heritage in the spring of 2013 were being acutely scrutinized perhaps 2,500 miles to the west of that Ohio conurbation that hugged the southern shores of Lake Erie. In the nation's Northwest alongside yet another mighty body of water, the Pacific Ocean, the professional journalists and long-time readers of *The Oregonian*—Portland's historic hometown daily—found little cause for rejoicing. That paper is another residing in the communications arsenal of Advance Publications, Inc., that dominates a midsized American market. The events transpiring at a few of the properties of that media behemoth had led some *Oregonian* employees to think that their destiny was sealed and they were living on borrowed time. As it turned out, their fears weren't at all misplaced:

This new reality was hard to imagine in the newspaper's Southwest Broadway offices a decade ago.... The *Oregonian* reached its zenith in quality: five Pulitzers, and eight finalists for journalism's top award....

The *Oregonian's* circulation numbers—like those of many large dailies—have spiraled, falling by a third since 2002. These declines, and abandonment by advertisers, have already triggered big changes.

The newspaper offered buyouts, cut pay and—violating its longtime pledge to full-time employees—laid off 37 people, mostly from the newsroom, in 2010. Other layoffs throughout the company have followed.[44]

The 2012 declaration about the future of New Orleans' *Times-Picayune* had prompted reaction from the West Coast, leaving some Portland wordsmiths and support staff shaking in their boots. "In the newsroom, the announcement in New Orleans shattered any illusions," a blog conceded.[45] Speculation implied that it was but a matter of time until API's sharp paring knife reached Oregon's largest metroplex for additional rounds of cuts. Said one unidentified *Oregonian* source: "We are living with the reality that any day might be the day when the people from Jersey walk in."[46]

Actually, they didn't have to wait long following the squeeze notice in Cleveland. On June 20, 2013—less than a week before Advance's largest paper, *The Star-Ledger* in Newark, learned of its prospective shutdown (which wasn't yet a "done deal" but a seemingly authentic possibility)—the same owner gave the "Big O," as the Portland paper is known in the trade, the bad news: On October 1, 2013, home deliveries would be reduced from seven to four days per week—on Wednesday, Friday, Saturday, and Sunday.[47] While the Big O would continue to be published daily, readers would have to purchase copies from local newsstands or retailers on the other weekdays. Nonetheless, there would be a daily Web presence available.

To institute the changes about 100 positions would be eliminated. Advance promised to maintain a newsroom of "more than 90 reporters, which is what we have today." One informant cited an epoch between 1993 and 2009 when the Big O's newsroom reached a peak of 400 members: "If the paper does maintain its present staff size, it reflects the move to digital. There is some irony in this: *The Oregonian's* strongest suit has been a talented staff of reporters and editors; its weakest link has been its web site, OregonLive.com."[48]

All of the babble regarding alterations in the publication schedules of some of the major U.S. newspapers suggests how swiftly change is occurring within the trade. During the second decade of the 21st century the uncertainties provoked by sometimes sudden stunning announcements are underscoring that a massive state of flux exists. Some of the pillars of the house are structurally standing on quicksand, seemingly unable to stabilize and project a semblance of security. Industry observers on the outside can see it while those on the inside whose careers are being threatened by persistent upheaval feel it.

Lest anyone think that the trend toward reduction in newsprint copies is purely an American journalistic phenomenon, incidentally, it should be noted that some of our continental neighbors to the north are following in this train as well. In the spring of 2012, only a few days after API revealed its intents for the papers it owned in Birmingham, Huntsville, Mobile, and New Orleans, Canada's Postmedia chain announced a similar strategy for several of its biggest urban papers.[49] The firm owns dailies in most of the dominion's foremost metropolises, including Calgary and Edmonton, Alberta; Vancouver, British Columbia; Ottawa and Toronto, Ontario; Montreal, Quebec; and Regina and Saskatoon, Saskatchewan.

Postmedia declared that the *Calgary Herald*, the *Edmonton Journal*, and the *Ottawa Citizen* would no longer publish Sunday editions. Sunday advertising was expected to be shifted to the Saturday and Monday issues. Furthermore, the publisher revealed that it would cease publishing Monday newsprint editions of its nationwide journal, the *National Post*, during the summer months. To reduce printing costs, it already had been experimenting with that plan earlier. In an interview Postmedia CEO Paul Godfrey disclosed that he was "seriously considering" the possibility of permanently ceasing publication of the *Post* on Mondays. Postmedia said it would install paywalls at many of its newspapers after instituting the model on a trial basis at Montreal.

The English have also begun investing in the concept that fewer paper-and-ink editions makes good economic sense. Johnston Press, with origins dating to 1767 and currently proprietor of roughly 170 British news journals—the UK's second-largest newspaper publisher, incidentally—has funneled a handful of its daily properties into weeklies.[50] Now running with a greater page count, the firm has positioned itself to become a more "platform-neutral" operation. It's doing so with daily electronic updates of Web sites in addition to increased use of iPad apps.

Johnston's revamped model was inaugurated in 2012 at five of its newspaper properties: Halifax's *Evening Courier*, the *Northamptonshire Evening Telegraph*, the *Northampton Chronicle & Echo*, the *Peterborough Evening Telegraph;* and Scarborough's *Evening News*. If this works out satisfactorily, we may anticipate that it will spread to other countries on the Continent and, not unthinkably, to Australia and New Zealand as well. It would seem, quite frankly, only a matter of time until the trend could be leaping across more international boundaries and over more oceans. With local modifications it could be headed for global implementation.

Despite the steadily growing momentum toward scaling back a publication's number of issues, there are some major newspapers and publishing chains that—as of mid–2013—have refused to adopt the reduced deliveries of their papers. Thus far they have demonstrated that they believe there are better ways to be profitable than printing only on days that attract the most advertisers.

Robert J. Dickey, president of community publishing for Gannett Company, which owns 83 newspapers, including *USA Today*, and is presently the nation's largest newspaper-holding body, expressed some observations on the topic. He still sees demand from readers for a print product that they can read every day. It would take substantially more readers turning to digital subscriptions for a three-day-a-week plan to tempt Dickey to alter the business model pursued by Gannett, he said. "Those seven days build a reading habit," Dickey allowed. "I want to know from the consumers [that] they're less interested in a newspaper because they're going to use their tablet or PC at the office."[51]

He's not alone in his sentiments. There's a chorus out there who are singing a different tune from those who would interrupt the flow of information from its long-accustomed schedule:

"We think the experience our readers have first thing in the morning with their cup of coffee is very important," said Patrick Talamantes, CEO of McClatchy, ... at the 2013 convention of the American Society of News Editors.

Talamantes said there's a "zero percent" possibility in the next five years of cutting back or eliminating daily publishing at any of McClatchy's 30 daily newspapers....

Other executives—Gracia Martore, CEO of Gannett; Mark Thompson, CEO of The New York Times Co.; and Katharine Weymouth, publisher of *The Washington Post*—also downplayed the strategy of reducing print schedules.... "We're not contemplating it," Thompson said. "Demand for the printed product remains incredibly strong."

Martore said that the fast-changing natures of the news industry and of technology make forecasting difficult. "The downside of cutting (down on) days or other models is that you're getting people out of their habit," she said. "I can't predict (the publishing strategy). Five years ago, there wasn't a tablet. I feel highly confident we're going to have a printed product."[52]

But a segment of the industry obviously believes that the impetus may be running in the opposite direction. That could be due to the enormous response that innovation often generates. For whatever the reason, cutting back on newspaper delivery is gaining more interest. Some oracles believe it's only a matter of time before it is accepted widely.

"Print is dying the death of a thousand cuts," an assessment of the modern trend advocated.[53] According to media economist Ken Doctor, the newspaper downsizing development is part of a "forced march" movement towards digital. Although driven by the incredibly acute reductions in print advertising, neither online advertising nor paywalls are filling the gap that remains—at least not yet. "Even the *New York Times* subscription model, which is one of the most successful in the industry, is not producing enough revenue to make up for that ongoing revenue decline," acknowledged one informant.[54]

All of this raises a question worth pondering: Should the cutbacks and layoffs and paywalls instituted at places like *The Times-Picayune* and Postmedia's former dailies, now weekly journals, fail to stem the tide of mounting losses, what happens next? There really are no easy answers to that one. Not just an industry but the readers themselves will be anxiously watching the outcome if all of this transition should diminish into that.

8

You Get What You Pay For

For a long while newspaper publishers had resisted the notion of raising their prices for home deliveries as well as the single-copy purchases of their product at newspaper boxes and retail establishments. At least they didn't do it by very much or very often. A fear of losing readers was a prime factor in their deliberations. Only when the out-of-pocket expenses inherent in the actual production and delivery phases such as presses, paper, ink, trucks, fuel, storage, maintenance, taxes, utilities, and insurance rose beyond all justifiable means for coping with a losing battle any longer were the owners finally persuaded to ask the general public to cough up a few more bucks.

In recent years a quarter's increase at a time for a daily copy was commonly considered to be generous, whether it covered the actual costs involved or not. Those onerous fixed production and delivery charges nevertheless—conservatively estimated to be anywhere from 65 to 75 percent of a paper's *real* expenditures—continued to escalate.[1] They simply remained a persistent thorn in the flesh of frustrated publishers.

"In effect, publishers conditioned Americans to get their news for far below the cost of production," observed the shrewd ex-editor of the *Los Angeles Times* James O'Shea. "Readers paid little for newspapers and they wanted it to stay that way. The economics were quite democratic; publishers delivered the news to everyone usually for less than a dollar. The media subsidized the cost of delivering the news with revenue from advertising."[2]

A vicious cycle had been created in the process. If more money was needed to maintain the journalistic side of the house the business side had to bring in more revenue. Most of the time a paper was first and foremost reliant upon advertising to keep a good thing going. Newspaper companies actually preferred to raise the rates for which they sold space before digging into their readers' pockets a little deeper. It was a system that had been in place pervasively for decades. But the intervention of the Internet was to have profound consequences on that method of budgeting for revenue in time.

In an insightful little book that addresses both reporters and the general public in regard to media's upheaval and transformation in the modern era, journalist-educator John Pavlik explores the implications of the changes derived by the arrival of cyberspace. His assessments were penned at the turn of the century, just as professional journalism was beginning to fully approach the very precipice of those pioneering electronic methods in implementing its assignment.

Pavlik's readers possess the ability today of looking back across an expanse of nearly a decade and a half to witness how well—or how poorly—those landmark innovations performed. At the same time they can see how the journalists that were linked to them reacted. Keeping the lapse of time in proper perspective, read what he says in regard to the realities of the trade's financial prospects:

> Profitability for most online news operations may be many years off.... There are several reasons.... First, despite the wide growth of the Internet, a majority of people in the United States still lack Internet access at home.... Second, the business model for online publishing is still taking shape ... and it is unrealistic to expect most online news ventures to have struck upon a workable profit model at this stage. Finally, ... it is critical to recognize that not only are online news ventures new businesses selling new products but the entire medium of the Internet is less than a decade old (as a medium of public communication). Compare this to ... *USA Today,* a newspaper introduced in 1984. *USA Today* was a new entrant in a medium three hundred years old. The basic business model was already established. Yet it took *USA Today* ten years to become profitable.... How can anyone realistically expect online newspapers to return a profit in less than a decade?[3]

Of course, in the intervening time we know that most people in the United States did acquire Internet access at home—at least, those who wanted it and could afford it. The business model for online publishing is still languishing in some places, but the third obstacle Pavlik mentioned—the hint of public suspicion surrounding the Internet—seems to have been vanquished by the majority of the nation's denizens. The resistance that once existed ("try it, you'll like it") simply isn't a factor for most people in whether to surf the Web, to seek answers to questions, to expand their knowledge, to comment on current issues, and even whether to shop online. We've come light-years since the Internet was introduced. And we've made significant strides in finding formulas that may one day make online journalism highly lucrative.

Media industry analyst Ken Doctor recalled that on one occasion ex–Knight Ridder news syndicate CEO Jim Batten admonished a pool of the firm's chief news editors: "The institution of American journalism owes more to the institution of the department store than the First Amendment." And subsequently, as department stores folded, consolidated, and substantially curtailed their advertising budgets newspapers bore the sting of those actions in brutal fashion. "In this new era, we will end up getting the journalism that we as a society and individuals pay for," allowed Doctor.[4]

> The Internet age has given readers and journalists alike unbelievable new tools to produce and distribute the news, and to read it anywhere and everywhere, and from the greatest diversity of sources imaginable. That promise remains, even as a mundane, but fundamental, question persists: Who is going to pay for the creation of high-quality news?[5]

The answer may not be as simple as it at first seems.

In an analysis released by the Newspaper Association of America in April 2013, the grimness of the industry's health was plainly exposed without any hint of attempting to gloss over it. In the same account a method for possibly reversing some of the trend was evidenced. According to *USA Today*, reporting some of the details:

> The study underscores what a huge mistake it was for the industry to give away its content on the Internet for all of those years. Now about 400 papers are charging, and many more, including *The Washington Post*, will start doing so this year. "The key is the metered paywall (which allows readers to access a number of articles before they have to pay), and it works," [media analyst] Doctor says. By 2015 he believes such arrangements will be the default position for newspapers both in the United States and elsewhere.[6]

After *The Wall Street Journal* became one of the first periodicals in America to begin charging subscribers for its electronic edition in September 1996, five months following its commencement, circulation of the pixel publication plummeted overnight. Roughly 90 percent of its almost 700,000 free riders instantly vanished.[7] As long as the computerized incarnation had been available to them without charge the readership had found the news source attractive. But when a fee was added to that blend many of those regulars simply lost their fascination for a compelling pioneering exploit.

Never mind that most of the departing "viewers" were quite likely investing hundreds of their hard-earned dollars annually in the media at the very same time: This occurred in the form of other hard-copy newspapers, magazines and newsletter subscriptions, cable television, pay-per-view television, video rentals and purchases, books, movies, online services, and on and on and on. It seemed like when the matter of coughing up a few bucks more for news coverage came up many were no longer eager to persist with an innovative delivery system that they had been getting for free.

The *Journal*'s backers hardly appeared miffed by this turn of events. On the contrary, Neil Budde, the online edition editor, considered the loss of more than 600,000 readers to be almost a godsend, according to one report. In the process of banishing the "freeloaders" (our term, not his), Budde acknowledged that the operation "gained a loyal following of users." A large segment of the base who literally subscribed to the electronic edition was not buying the *Journal*'s newsprint form and did not do so then. Another plus occurring just about the same time was this: "The electronic edition attracts an audience with an average age in the upper thirties, not in their fifties as the printed version does."[8] Good news for advertisers and the *Journal*, too.

Pay versus free—it's a provocative topic that has never gone away, and continues to surface wherever newspapers are looking for a method of keeping their heads above water. The debate over whether to charge for their services has been raging among pixel presses for two decades, since the first one began doing so about 1994.[9] Although *The Wall Street Journal*'s decision a couple of years hence gave real impetus to the movement and many other key publishing organizations have followed in its line, such decisions have not resulted most times without considerable debate and even wrangling among owners and management as they weighed every conceivable outcome stemming from the deliberations. It's never been particularly easy, for instance, to get people to shell out money for a service they have been accustomed to receiving gratis. There are many dimensions of that which generate pluses and minuses on a range of issues.

8. You Get What You Pay For

The unmistakable question that begs an answer in all of this may be put thusly: Why not charge for the online editions in the first place? The palpable response is that the potential clientele is being stimulated by goodies for which it will one day have to pay the piper or lose that privilege to which it has become accustomed (or possibly entrenched). Call it *cultivation*. The readership is being spoon-fed until, it is hoped, it cannot satisfactorily get along without the product, one for which there is going to be a fee in the future.

Some papers proceeded on a sampling basis, allowing non-subscribers to view certain documents and data that might entice them into the spider's snare. It let them go just "so far" but no more without offering up some recompense. The *San Antonio Express-News'* Ian Murdock summarized the particular lure in his rather astute observation: "We need to have enough value for the subscribers, but enough eyeballs for the advertisers."[10]

Although many online newspapers are charging their customers today—in fact, it is now the accepted norm—that wasn't always true. As recently as 2000, a study conducted by Princeton Research Associates determined that 89 percent of respondents in that inquiry had *never* paid for news or other information on the Web. Free was still very much the name of the game. And 83 percent in their analysis said they were unwilling to pay *anything*.

Meanwhile, as recently as 2010 journalism advocates Robert McChesney and John Nichols argued that attempts to get the public to cough up any recompense for what they acquired online would take the Internet precisely in "the wrong direction." Fostering class inequities and stifling creativity where cited as drawbacks of paywalls for electronic news. "There is little reason to believe that a paywall system could actually work with consumers," they said.[11] In that posture they echo the sentiments of *Editor & Publisher's* 2010 Editor of the Year, Steve Buttry, a digital transformation specialist with roots deeply embedded in several major midwestern newspapers. Buttry is convinced that charging for content is "doomed to failure."[12]

It should be noted that their collective expressions—and those of many other recognized scholars—were surfacing about five years ago. That was then and this is now. A rising understanding and appreciation of the finished products shipped through cyberspace has occurred in the intervening time. Certainly online news has flourished during that period. The public's confidence in the output has trended upward. Increasingly readers aren't as reluctant now to shell out a few coins to retrieve what they believe to be something of value to themselves as they once were. The well worn cliché "you get what you pay for" would seem to be more and more germane with the mounting valuation as the newshounds go searching on the Web.

Ex–*Time* editor Walter Isaacson, whose history includes considerable exposure to the news delivery arena—he was CEO at CNN prior to assuming his similar post as CEO of the nonpartisan educational and policy studies Aspen Institute—demonstrates some proficiency here. Back in 2009, he predicted dire circumstances for the news industry if the then-dominant online business model of giving away content persisted. Isaacson wrote: "It is now possible to contemplate a time when some major cities will no longer have a newspaper and when magazines and network-news operations will employ no more than a handful of reporters."[13]

The former newspaperman (*The Sunday Times* of London and *The New Orleans Times-Picayune/States-Item*) cited a Pew Research Center study in 2008 showing that more Americans got free news online that year than those buying newspapers and magazines. "That's not a business model that makes sense," he declared. Observing that newspapers and magazines have traditionally relied on three sources of revenue—newsstand sales, subscriptions, and advertising—Isaacson said the "new" business model was dependent on only the latter supplier. He added:

> Henry Luce, a co-founder of TIME, disdained the notion of giveaway publications that relied solely on ad revenue. He called that formula "morally abhorrent" and also "economically self-defeating." That was because he believed that good journalism required that a publication's primary duty be to its readers, not to its advertisers. In an advertising-only revenue model, the incentive is perverse. It is also self-defeating, because eventually you will weaken your bond with your readers if you do not feel directly dependent on them for your revenue.
>
> ...
>
> I love journalism. I think it is valuable and should be valued by its consumers. Charging for content forces discipline on journalists: they must produce things that people actually value…. The need to be valued by readers—serving them first and foremost rather than relying solely on advertising revenue—will allow the media once again to set their compass true to what journalism should always be about.[14]

8. You Get What You Pay For

If the news media needed an incentive for charging consumers for the paper and pixel output that it produces, is there one you can think of that's better than that?

Note: The succeeding chapter presents a more intensive examination of the paywall system, which for some years had been rejected by the majority of U.S. dailies. Currently it is considered by many estimates to be one of American newspapers' most promising and redeeming maneuvers. Despite this growing acceptance, its practice is not universally upheld by every respected analyst of the trade. As time elapses, some heated voices that have long been opposed to the implementation of paywalls have been relaxed and have reversed their chorus of protests nonetheless.

9

Paywalls: Like Hitting Pay Dirt?

Building upon the foundation laid in the previous chapter, let us now explore the theory of the paywall in greater depth. Its significance in the present era as well as the future must not be missed. The paywall is increasingly helping to underwrite the nation's daily and weekly news journals by partially blunting the perennial revenue losses they encounter. While this is not an end-all solution to that dilemma, the impact of the paywall is certainly far too crucial—too potentially significant long-term—to be overlooked or shortchanged. Thus let us take a close look at this key element of a publisher's income that few newspaper readers had encountered until recent years.

A paywall is a technique that inhibits Internet users from retrieving certain specified material that is residing on Web pages. Any would-be accessing parties must pay to obtain whatever it is that they are after.[1] As a result the paywall directly torpedoes any notion of acquiring something without initially exchanging something else for it. In this case, the reader is shelling out a few coins. The "free ride" doesn't exist any longer wherever a paywall is implemented.

In the spring of 2013, it was reported that 33 percent of the nation's 380 daily newspapers at that time (127 in total) either had instituted a paywall already or had a strategy in the works for such a future undertaking. This is probably just the tip of the iceberg as more and more papers try to think of a justification for *not* following suit. Meanwhile, Poynter's Rick Edmonds cautioned: "A corollary to asking readers to pay is giving them a news report that's worth it in an era where free options are abundant."[2] There are some strings attached to paywalls, you may be sure.

A recent analytical work examines the surprising sluggishness of

9. Paywalls: Like Hitting Pay Dirt?

newspaper publishers in embracing the paywall over an extended period. ProPublica executive Richard J. Tofel helps his readers comprehend how some of this foot-dragging and seeming reluctance played out.[3] He traces the still fairly brief history of online paywalls before citing a variety of reasons that prompted newspaper owners to open themselves to the notion of charging for their digital wares. Tofel, with an impressive résumé that includes some newspaper-publishing experience, appears eminently qualified to examine the issue's diverse facets. He explores publishers' demonstrated laggardliness that seems mystifying now; after all, the pattern of charging for the product and services that they provide had long ago been established. Why should an innovative transmission system make any difference?

Slowly but surely more and more owners adopted the idea of instituting paywalls following a protracted period of indifference and even complete resistance. Having championed a pay-as-you-go structure since the inception of newspapers, those journals—and their proprietary overseers—bring to mind an advertising slogan of a generation ago that some readers may recall. The tagline of the commercial was "Mrs. Butterworth, why did you wait so long?"

Tofel poses the question, "How, as a visitor from another planet might ask, did a large industry that had successfully charged customers for its product for more than a century come to decide to give that product away and thus threaten its very existence?" Before answering that query he visits a business model of newspapers that—in his opinion—"has been broken, irretrievably."

Furthermore, Tofel is convinced that "the era of newspapers as the dominant form of journalism" is over in this nation. That role has been taken over by organizations including public radio, local broadcast or cable television, and emerging nonprofits. Says Tofel: "The newspaper business was led—led itself—into fundamental error, the error of giving away its content, what some have termed the 'original sin' of digital publishing."

Before we continue to explore the reactions to paywalls, it should be properly noted that there is more than one type of paywall currently in use. On the one hand, *hard* paywalls permit little or no access to content without considerable recompense.

On the other hand, *soft* paywalls present greater flexibility in what an interested party is able to view without subscribing beforehand. This might include an ability to choose free content and/or it might include a limited number of—for example—articles, based on a daily, weekly, or monthly basis. Some newspapers offer online content in combination with distribution of a Sunday newsprint edition at a lower price point than online access by itself.[4]

Paywalls have provided added revenues to help publishers in defraying the costs of creating online content. Yet there is a second and possibly equal or even greater benefit to organizations that are putting them into use. Paywalls boost the number of print subscribers a newspaper may verify, and sometimes significantly so. This not only gives newspapers bragging rights in regard to their total circulation figures but, more important, also increases the number of potential exposures to an advertiser's message. This of course affords the net effect of increasing the ad revenues, which provide a publication's most reliable revenue stream.

Poynter's Bill Mitchell concludes that for a paywall to spawn sustainable income, "new value" in online content (such as adding innovative ideas, improved quality, and so on) must be implemented by newspapers. For customer acceptance, there must be obvious evidence that payment is warranted for heretofore free content prior to the initiation of a paywall.[5]

In the meantime, a host of paywall detractors as well as advocates have emerged in contemporary times to prolong the controversy over that mechanism. At least one Web site proffered the names of several on both sides of the issue:

> Experts who are skeptical of the paywall model include Arianna Huffington, who declared "the paywall is history" in a 2009 article in *The Guardian* [UK]. In 2010, Jimmy Wales (of Wikipedia fame) reportedly called *The Times's* [UK] paywall "a foolish experiment." One major concern was with content so widely available, potential subscribers would turn to free sources for their news. The adverse effects of earlier implementations included decline in traffic and poor search engine optimization.
>
> Paywalls have become controversial, with partisans arguing over the effectiveness of paywalls in generating revenue and their effect on media in general. Critics of paywalls include many businessmen, academics such as media professor Jay Rosen, and journalists such as Howard Owens and media analyst Matthew Ingram of GigaOm. Those who see potential in paywalls include investor Warren Buffett, former *Wall Street Journal* publisher Gordon

9. Paywalls: Like Hitting Pay Dirt?

Crovitz, and media mogul Rupert Murdoch. Some have changed their opinions of paywalls. Felix Salmon of Reuters was initially an outspoken skeptic of paywalls, but recently expressed the opinion that they could be effective. Renowned NYU media theorist, Clay Shirky, was initially a skeptic of paywalls, but in May 2012, wrote, "[Newspapers] should turn to their most loyal readers for income, via a digital subscription service...." Paywalls are rapidly changing journalism, with an impact on its practice and business model, and on freedom of information on the Internet, that is yet unclear.[6]

Incidentally, the influential Warren Buffett, one of the world's most affluent human beings—cited in numerous discourses—is a figure worth hearing from on many levels. Recently the Oracle of Omaha has become particularly optimistic about small-market news journals. Only a few years ago he pooh-poohed those enterprises' prospects for their "unending losses," stating that he wouldn't buy them "at any price." But the financier has altered his tune in the intervening time. More recently Buffett announced, "It's almost unnatural how much I love newspapers."

The billionaire's change of heart has been revealed in a tangible way through Buffett's longtime investments in *The Washington Post* stock and his purchase of *The Buffalo News* in 1977, of his hometown *Omaha World-Herald* in 2011, of 63 Media General dailies and weeklies in 2012, and of the *Tulsa World* and the Greensboro (N.C.) *News & Record* in 2013. He's thought to possibly be looking for more, similar opportunities.

Those following recent industry trends surely won't be surprised by one of the decisive factors Buffett identifies in determining his "sound investment" strategy:

> One reason that Buffett is more bullish on the future is the advent of charging for digital content. He thinks newspapers—his own in Buffalo included—made a huge mistake by giving away their material for so long. He praises Walter Hussman, Jr., the owner of the *Arkansas Democrat-Gazette* and an early paywall adapter, for his sagacity.
>
> Hussman's motivation was not simply to make money but to protect the core product: Why would people continue to buy the paper if they can get all of the content free? That's Buffett's rationale, too. "I'm not interested in the Internet for money. I'm interested in preventing the erosion of print." He adds: "I could kick myself for not figuring this out earlier."
>
> While community newspapers are dwarfed by Buffett's big-ticket holdings ... his enthusiasm for them is palpable. And he clearly believes that if you buy the right ones, and run them properly, they remain sound investments

as well as objects of affection. "If we go down, we're going down with a big news hole," he says.[7]

One of the leading exponents of the paywall strategy—though once a practicing nonbeliever—is *The New York Times*. In April 2012, that celebrated newspaper instituted a modified paywall system. Nonsubscribers were then entitled to receive up to 10 free articles per month instead of a previous 20.[8] In 2011, Felix Salmon had depicted the *Times'* metered paywall as "not only soft, but porous." At the time it permitted access to any link posted on a social media site and up to 25 free articles per day if they were pursued through a search engine.[9]

Said the Pew Research Center: "The model is designed to allow the paper to 'retain traffic from light users,' which in turn allows the paper to keep its number of visitors high, while receiving circulation revenue from the site's heavy users."[10] Wikipedia added: "Though the success of a metered paywall would create revenue for the newspaper and increased freedom for the public, the profitability of the metered model has yet to be sufficiently proven."[11]

But it since has!

In October 2012, *Adweek*—applying the latest figures from the Audit Bureau of Circulation (ABC)—reported that by increasing the paywall's rates and limitations six months earlier *The New York Times* surpassed all other major U.S. dailies in increasing its circulation during the period.[12] The advertising and marketing trade publication attributed the *Times'* phenomenal growth to greater digital application. Total daily sales jumped to 1.6 million within the time frame, a rise of more than 40 percent.

Meanwhile the *Times'* digital circulation more than doubled during the previous year to 896,352. That resulted from a hard-hitting drive to expand the paid digital subscription base by promoting the paywall plans. The increase in digital circulation caused online daily subscriptions to exceed the print version then set at 717,513. Sunday circulation rose sharply, too, to 2.1 million subscribers in the same period, up an astonishing 27.7 percent.

All of these figures appeared on the heels of some just-as-shocking numbers released by ABC on March 31, 2012. At that time it announced that the *Times'* average weekday circulation had skyrocketed some 73 percent in the 12-month period just ended.[13] The unparalleled growth rise, according to the Web-based *Capital,* occurred after the news journal began charging patrons for unlimited access to its Web site and e-reader editions. The unusual thing is, of course, that—in this circumstance, at least—by demanding compensation for the services it rendered the *Times* had experienced a gargantuan leap in paid circulation. It was simply the antithesis of what many observers of the business just might have anticipated.

Near the end of 2012, the Poynter Institute took note of how well the newly inaugurated paywall plans were affecting the widespread newspaper-publishing business:

> With the fast adoption of paywall systems, paid digital has risen to 15.3 percent of the total [of America's dailies], compared to 9.8 percent in the 2011 period. That means print numbers are falling by roughly an equal amount.
>
> That change is not surprising given digital pay plan trends. More than 300 papers now charge for digital, with 70 of Gannett's 80 community papers making the switch and McClatchy's 30 just beginning a similar roll-out.
>
> So digital-only subs [subscriptions] are on the rise. Plus the many papers that offer a bundled subscription including print and several digital platforms can count users on each of those additional platforms as new circulation, so long as the digital option is accessed once a month.
>
> At the same time, many publishers—including Gannett and *The New York Times*—are raising print subscription rates. They are accepting some loss in circulation numbers to get equal or greater revenue.
>
> Finally, the new digital packages often allow Sunday-only subscriber access to all digital versions, shifting some print readership from daily to Sunday. So Sundays have been showing better results for several reporting periods....
>
> ...
>
> Included in the paid totals are digital replica editions and copies sold on e-readers....
>
> Also there is a category for "branded editions," allowing clusters like MediaNews's San Francisco holdings or the *Chicago Sun Times* and its suburban papers to be combined for reporting purposes.[14]

Is the paywall at last *pay dirt nirvana,* finally hitting the mother lode required to maintain the news journals of America indefinitely? Not by any means. Indisputably, however, it will impact the practicality of sustaining those outfits' presence in the foreseeable future—in pixel as well as paper manifestations, as their owners so choose. Industry analyst Rem Rieder, who pens a popular media column in *USA Today,* offered his readers some perceptive impressions of the paywall and its assistance in keeping the U.S. newspaper trade's pens fertile. In the same analysis he issued a stern warning that in exchange for coughing up the dough subscribers hold high expectations for a certain value of return on their investment.

In the meantime, you can chalk up another exponent for the promise extended by the paywall:

> Charging for digital content is not a panacea, a way to obliterate all of the financial challenges that have plagued traditional news outlets with one bold stroke. It's not likely to bring in enough revenue to make up for all that has been lost. Regional and local news outlets are signing up far fewer customers than the [New York] *Times.*
>
> But it is an important weapon to add to the arsenal. Now the search is on for Revenue Streams No. 3 and No. 4 [No. 1 is advertising]. Many news outlets are hoping that providing marketing services for local merchants will occupy one of those slots.
>
> While charging for content represents an opportunity for legacy news outlets, it also brings with it a significant challenge. *The New York Times* has lined up all of those digital subscribers for a reason: It has terrific content, something that a great many people want enough to pay for. Same for *The Wall Street Journal,* which has been comfortably nestled behind a paywall since 1997....
>
> Cable TV proved long ago that people will pay for something they were used to getting for free—if it was good enough. The same will be true for news websites. Sadly, many news organizations have cut back so severely that there just isn't that much quality content left....
>
> The key, as is so often the case, will be delivering the goods.[15]

Yet another ongoing *USA Today* media contributor, Michael Wolff, interjects his "take" on newspaper circulation after segmenting the audience by age alignment. His prognostications might as well be interpreted to fully embrace the implementation of the paywall as a "recovery" fee. Identifying older subscribers as "the people who actually read newspapers," Wolff points out that this group maintains "little price sensitivity" whether they are receiving their content electronically or in newsprint editions. He notes that while higher prices generally discourage younger readers, "they don't read newspapers, anyway."

The journalist distinguishes between the individual age cohorts: "Older readers, on the other hand, seem willing to pay anything to hold on to what they're used to. A paying audience (old codgers or not) is no small thing," Wolff elaborates.[16] Ultimately they may have to trade in their newsprint models for digital replacements. But they've long been accustomed to the established practice of paying for the commodities they purchase.

The paywall, it would appear, is destined to be branded as a lasting feature of online journalism.

10

An Endangered Species

In the midst of all the deliberations surrounding the viability of news journals in newsprint format, there is a legitimate question being raised in some circles about the sustainability of newspapers in *any* configuration any longer. A limited number of probably well-intending oracles would lead us to believe that a cessation of all that has come and gone before is utterly inevitable. They would forgo the paper edition as well as the pixel conception that many sages view as the natural savior of the medium.

For these doubters, *the best of times*—as Charles Dickens referenced life in *A Tale of Two Cities*—is history. It's toast, finished, over and done with—pick a metaphor of your liking. The American newspaper is on its way out of mainstream practice and usefulness and doesn't have a prayer for any long-term permanence.

Period.

In a particularly punishing invective that signifies the palpable limitations of the newsprint product, online blogger Seth Godin rags on everything from wood pulp to printing presses, typesetting machines, delivery trucks, and newsstands on the street. "Years and years after some pundits began predicting the end of newspapers," he stresses, "the newspapers themselves are finally realizing that it's over. Huge debt, high costs, declining subscription rates, plummeting ad base: will the last one out please turn off the lights?" Is Godin's estimate mere hyperbole or a right-on evaluation?

Godin cites a bevy of competing digital sources that supply all one can perceptibly need. In his opinion the alternatives are done as well as, if not perhaps better than, the print dailies they seek to replace. At the same time, those sources are available without tying their patronage to any notion of furnishing the news as a single one-size-fits-all package.

10. An Endangered Species

One may go to where his specific interests lie without being bombarded with stuff that doesn't offer fulfillment. Godin complains: "Newspapers took two cents of journalism and wrapped it in ninety-eight cents of overhead and distraction."[1] Like so many of the trade's complainers, he summarily dismisses what has gone before and purports that it's time to move on.

Acknowledging that "nobody should relish the demise of once-great titles [newspapers]," *The Economist* nevertheless was rebuking the trade's defenders as long ago as 2006. "The decline of newspapers will not be as harmful to society as some fear," the global newsweekly proclaimed. Labeling the industry "an endangered species," it further observed: "The business of selling words to readers and selling readers to advertisers, which has sustained their role in society, is falling apart." The periodical predicted that although "newspapers have not yet started to shut down in large numbers, it is only a matter of time. Over the next few decades half the rich world's general papers may fold."[2] Will it actually take that long?

There are some outspoken critics who would undoubtedly second the motion. Blogger, consultant, and media entrepreneur Mark Potts is one. "Journalism does not equal newspapers," said he, "so the death of newspapers doesn't mean the death of journalism. It just shifts it to myriad other media types." Potts insists that even if newspapers should disappear, "there will still be people wanting news and information, and people wanting to provide it, and businesses who want to reach customers. All those ingredients are unchanged."[3]

Yet another confirming voice belonging to blogger Clay Shirky similarly admonishes: "Society doesn't need newspapers. What we need is journalism. For a century, the imperatives to strengthen journalism and to strengthen newspapers have been so tightly wound as to be indistinguishable. That's been a fine accident to have, but when the accident stops, as it is stopping before our eyes, we're going to need lots of other ways to strengthen journalism instead."[4]

And one of the most riveting statements on the topic was offered by San Francisco mayor Gavin Newsom, who later became his state's lieutenant governor. He once told a magazine reporter that if the *San Francisco Chronicle* went out of business "people under 30 won't even notice."[5] The notoriety provoked by that remark led Newsom to add later that he was speaking of the paper's physical manifestation only. Nevertheless, it seemed telling.

Perhaps the initial evidence of a crack in the industry's hold on tradition and longevity will occur for real when some major U.S. metropolitan municipality is left with no foremost local newspaper whatever. Writing in *The New York Times* in 2009, reporter Richard Pérez-Peña attributed that looming calamity to expressions from economists and newspaper executives alike. Collectively they exclaimed that it was "only a matter of time, and probably not much time at that," before a leading American city found itself bereft of a long-standing published news source. The journalist quotes industry analyst Mike Simonton, a senior director of Fitch Ratings, who predicted that "all the two-newspaper markets will become one-newspaper markets, and you will start to see one-newspaper markets become no-newspaper markets."[6]

> "It would be a terrible thing for any city for the dominant paper to go under, because that's who does the bulk of the serious reporting," said Joel Kramer, former editor and publisher of The Star Tribune [Minneapolis] and now the editor and chief executive of MinnPost.com, an online news organization in Minneapolis.
>
> "Places like us would spring up," he said, "but they wouldn't be nearly as big. We can tweak the papers and compete with them, but we can't replace them."[7]

Reporter Pérez-Peña goes on to identify a handful of examples of places that could be potential candidates for the questionable honor of being "the first big city without a large paper."[8] (A few years back one CNN ideologue professed that San Francisco might qualify for that dubious "honor."[9]) Most of those ventures or their owners are in bankruptcy now or have more cumbersome economic woes. Their issues principally include falling advertising and circulation revenues while experiencing rising payrolls, production, distribution, and still added miscellaneous overhead expenses.

Buzz Woolley, an affluent San Diego businessman and at times outspoken adversary of his city's *Union-Tribune,* is one of the chief instigators of the Internet news site VoiceofSanDiego.org. In spite of that circumstance he nevertheless allowed: "I can't imagine what civil society would be like [without that paper]. I don't want to imagine it. A huge amount of information would just never get out."[10]

Even blogger Seth Godin, whose rant saw little excuse for newspapers to persist, admitted that when the sports, weather, book and restaurant reviews, ads, and opinion pieces are banished from the newspaper, all of which may be supplied by independent Web sites, there is at least some cause for alarm remaining. "What's left is local news, investigative journalism and intelligent coverage of national news," said Godin. "I worry about the quality of a democracy when the state government or the local government can do what it wants without intelligent coverage. I worry about the abuse of power when the only thing a corrupt official needs to worry about is the TV news. I worry about the quality of legislation when there isn't a passionate, unbiased reporter there to explain it to us."[11]

No need for a newspaper? Indeed!

"The problem is this," blogger Tony Rogers explains. "There are many things newspapers do that simply can't be replaced. Papers are a unique medium in the news business and can't be easily replicated by TV, radio or online news operations."[12] Rogers outlines five things that are lost when newspapers die: large news staffs, beat reporters, comprehensive and in-depth coverage, investigative reporting, and journalists who have empathy for the people they write about. All five are indubitably tied to the personnel who staff the large newsrooms that have traditionally been characteristic of major daily newspapers. The loss of those assets can be crushingly devastating to a community, he admonishes.

Not everyone agrees on that point however.

Jeff Jarvis, director of interactive journalism in the graduate journalism school at the City University of New York, thinks the death of a newspaper should result in a profusion of far smaller online news sources.[13] They should supply no less coverage than a newspaper did, Jarvis believes. Although those digitally conceived providers might be viewed as less than polished at times—and rightfully so—they would be competitive just as well. Furthermore, they would serve to put the quietus on a seemingly out-of-control power trip accorded many newspapers in their communities—a role they have habitually used to advantage many times over enduring periods.

Comments journalist Pérez-Peña: "No one yet has unlocked the puzzle of supporting a large newsroom purely on digital revenue, a fact that may presage an era of news organizations that are smaller, weaker and less able to fulfill their traditional function as the nation's watchdog."[14]

Likewise, in 2009 the *American Journalism Review* (*AJR*) reported on research conducted by Princeton University economist Sam Schulhofer-Wohl and a colleague, Miguel Garrido. It referenced the closure of *The Cincinnati Post* that had occurred recently at the end of 2007. The pair of researchers depicted some menacing clouds that were derived by the paper's exodus. The *Post* folded when its circulation tanked at 27,000. Yet even a publication as effectively weakened as that one had "a substantial and measurable impact on public life," those examiners maintained.[15]

Schulhofer-Wohl and Garrido believed the departure of that grande dame of Ohio River journalism that had serviced not only its namesake city but correspondingly several northern Kentucky suburbs (under the banner of *The Kentucky Post*) precipitated some weighty outcomes affecting the area's residents. Its absence, they insisted, "lowered the number of people voting in elections and the number of candidates for city council, city commission and school board.... It also increased incumbent council and commission members' chances of remaining in office." The duo's inquiry concluded: "When there were fewer stories about a given town, its inhabitants seemed to care less about how they're being governed."[16]

Although Schulhofer-Wohl took pains to point out that their study wasn't definitive and had been conducted during what could be termed an uncommon election cycle in 2008, he allowed: "For the extent that we can extrapolate, we can say that local coverage is something the newspapers uniquely provide, and when people don't have it, they're much less engaged."[17]

Corroboration of the findings about lower voter turnout during elections also surfaced independently in the discoveries drawn from a study ordained by the University of Chicago's Booth School of Business. Associate professor of economics Matthew Gentzkow and his colleague Jesse Shapiro confirmed that once a leading newspaper in a region has gone out of business local elections can be powerfully swayed by the absence of a substantial number of voters who might have been at the polls previously.[18]

The *AJR* persisted, incidentally, in offering some disturbingly probing questions related to the effects a metropolitan community experiences when it's suddenly left without a reputable and influential paper-and-ink journalistic footprint. Particularly deep is the impact in an area in which people have placed their collective trust in the medium for multiple decades.[19]

> These attempts to quantify newspapers' impact on public life come as a handful of major American newspapers close and others barely cling to life. The unsettling possibility looms that some big cities could lose their sole remaining daily newspaper—and that the public won't care. If the dead-tree edition of a newspaper falls in a crowded media forest, will it matter, except to the journalists who work there? Are newer, hipper online news outlets poised to fill the void? What, if anything, will be irrevocably lost?[20]

At the Massachusetts Institute of Technology, economics and political science prof Jim Snyder linked with Stockholm University economist David Strömberg to undertake another intriguing pursuit.[21] The pair's inquiries netted some fascinating information pertaining to the national political climate. The twosome learned that members of Congress who had garnered boatloads of newspaper coverage for their activities performed them with far more gusto on behalf of their constituents than did their colleagues who received less generous exposure by the printed press. Members with enhanced publicity were found to be funneling considerably more of the federal largesse to the territories they represented back home than did the other camp. In addition, they testified at greater numbers of committee hearings while at the same time casting fewer votes in altogether partisan blocs than did their compatriots who regularly received reduced limelight from the print media:

> Pollsters at the Pew Research Center for the People & the Press have exposed an alarming disconnect between newspapers' role in civic life and the public's appreciation of it. A Pew survey ... of about 1,000 adults found that only 43 percent of Americans say losing their local newspaper would hurt civic life in their community "a lot." A mere 33 percent said they would miss reading the local paper a lot if it were no longer available.
>
> "In our media surveys, you get the sense that many people don't recognize the source of their news, especially when it comes to online news," says Carroll Doherty, Pew's associate director. "They may be following a link, they may be forwarding a link, they may be on Facebook and click on a link. People may be getting more information from newspapers than they realize."[22]

In the meantime, there are plenty of media analysts who are convinced that any talk about shutting down America's dailies is terribly overblown and premature. Philip Meyer, emeritus journalism professor at the University of North Carolina and author of *The Vanishing Newspaper* (University of Missouri Press, 2004), proclaims: "I don't think we're heading toward a no-newspaper trend."[23] Of course, it might be well to keep in mind that a decade has elapsed since those words were penned.

Referencing 1,422 U.S. dailies still publishing in 2009, media analyst and *AJR* columnist John Morton averred: "We never hear about, say, 1,350 of those newspapers, almost all of which are profitable ... but they're not out on the edge of a cliff, either."[24]

Nonetheless, the Poynter Institute's Rick Edmonds, a media business analyst, anticipates deepening compression within the industry, ultimately becoming a recognized hallmark of the trade: "The most typical scenario is that we will continue to have newspapers in major cities, but they're going to be a good deal smaller and there will be diverse [media] players, some of them that have been around for a while and some of them brand-new." Edmonds acknowledges that the downsizing is visible already. He cites instances such as the fact: "Almost all metro papers have pulled back from their coverage of the more distant suburbs."[25]

Adds scribe Rachel Smolkin in the *American Journalism Review*: "For newspapers' survival to matter ... the core of the new [business] models must remain the same as the old: the dedication to illuminating stories and rich storytelling, the commitment to serving democracy."[26]

Just for the record, in case you're wondering, in mid-2013 *Ad Age*, a type of bible of the marketing trade, released the names of the five best and five worst U.S. cities centered on denizens' daily print newspaper reading habits. Though overall print newspaper reading fell nearly 20 percent between 2001 and 2012 according to Scarborough, a leading research entity, the disparity didn't occur evenly across the country. Some journals still boasted strong print readership figures, for example. In certain localities, particularly in regions bordering the Great Lakes and in the Northeast, print readership sometimes hovered close to 50 percent in 2012 compared with 35.7 percent nationwide.

Scarborough found that the U.S.A.'s strongest and weakest print newspaper audiences among adults resided in the following locales and subscribed to the publications it identified here:

America's Best Print Newspaper Readership Among Adults

Pittsburgh, where 19 percent of adults were said to read the *Post-Gazette,* 12 percent devour the *Tribune-Review,* and 9 percent say they peruse a daily digital newspaper.

Albany, New York, in a tie with **Hartford/New Haven**: 17 percent of adults read Albany's *Times Union* every day while 12 percent access newspaper Web sites there. In Connecticut, 17 percent of adults read the Hartford *Courant,* 5 percent *The New York Times,* and 11 percent daily newspaper Web sites.

Cleveland, with *The Plain Dealer* claiming 20 percent of daily adult print readers while another 10 percent accessed the Web. *Note:* These figures were based on newsprint delivery seven days weekly, which have since been reduced to a maximum of three days per week for home delivery.

Buffalo, Honolulu, New York City, and **Toledo**, all co-equals for fifth place.

America's Least Print Newspaper Readership Among Adults

Atlanta, where 13 percent of its adults read the print edition of *The Atlanta Journal-Constitution* daily. Concurrently another 11 percent of that age grouping read newspaper Web sites each day.

Houston in a tie with **San Antonio**: The *Houston Chronicle* is the top print read in that city at 18 percent of adults, while the Web gains 9 percent of lookers. The San Antonio *Express-News* draws 19 percent of adult print readers as 8 percent peruse a newspaper Web site.

Las Vegas, with 24 percent in the adult age range who consult the printed *Las Vegas Review-Journal* as 8 percent focus on a daily newspaper Web site.

Bakersfield, which boasts 22 percent of its adults reading the print edition of *The Bakersfield Californian* while another 6 percent access a daily newspaper Web site.[27]

For an endangered species, newspapers are surely facing a perilous time. Misjudgments could lead to dire consequences. "There is not yet a major city without a newspaper," the authors of the Pew Research Center's Project for Excellence noted in a recent annual State of the News Media summary. "But that could be coming soon."[28]

A skeptical reporter for *The Bristol* (Conn.) *Press,* Steve Collins, maintains that news blogs that are popping up all over "can't possibly provide the breadth of a local paper." He asserts: "Everything that the community knows about itself, it learns from the newspaper. It's going to be a shock when there is no way to find that out."[29]

Reporting what local institutions are doing, ferreting out corruption, and fending off legal challenges to public information will be among the losses occurring without a viable alternative to newspapers, *The Spokesman-Review* of Spokane, Washington, injects. If it should dwindle down to that, the northwestern journal insists, "[T]he demise of newspapers goes beyond the sadness of journalists losing their jobs. It darkens democracy."[30]

Borrowing on entertainer Allen Funt's tagline at the conclusion of every *Candid Camera* television show, "Don't be surprised if somewhere, sometime when you least expect it," some great American metropolis is no longer going to be able to tout having a daily (or several times weekly) news journal as one of its sterling identifying assets—neither printed, digital, hybrid, or any other format. That hasn't occurred as of this writing at the close of 2013. But once that bridge is crossed—and I think there's a fair chance it eventually may be—will that open a floodgate of replications by more publishing firms that figure the public will embrace life without a paper's presence?

How terribly unsettling for scores of reasons for those directly affected should it ever come to that.

11

Cutting to the Paper Chase

For all of the cyberspace wizards who proclaim that the future unfalteringly belongs to the world of electronics, there remain some people who are steadfastly convinced that the compositions of yesteryear will be around in the tomorrows to be. Among them are certain newsprint connoisseurs who are convinced that any approbation afforded the electronic edition of the daily newspaper has been vastly overstated. Although they may be naysayers to the nth degree, can we be absolutely, positively certain that they are wholly off the mark and out of touch with reality? And in the meantime, just how far might the horizons of the rabid advocacy crowd of Web-affirming fanatics extend anyway? There's obviously a differing of opinion on this topic. A few souls hold extreme positions on either side, incapable—so it may seem to a middle-ground contingent—of concurrently accommodating more than one point of view.

In earlier chapters the concept of the paper-by-pixel model has been introduced in all its glory. This chapter's theme is the *original* form, however—the hard copy that for so long has been the standard incarnation of the accepted news journal. If we acknowledge the presumption that it will persist, how might it cope with an ever-increasing fascination with so much that is now so digitally oriented? What might the press run of the future be like if there is one?

Industry observers, including Leonard Downie, Jr. and Robert Kaiser, have expressed their views on the matter. While the daily paper may appear in a reduced form, frequency, and dispersion system, these seers presume that there will still be a need for a newsprint form with tangible pages that may be held in one's hand.

Apparently forever:

Newspapers in Transition

The history of new media is instructive: radio did not eliminate newspapers; talking movies did not destroy radio or newspapers; television did not obliterate radio, newspapers or movies. For nearly a century, Americans have made room for and taken advantage of new technologies without turning away from old ones that are still useful or fun....

News does not grow on trees, and raw data is not the same as journalism. Some bits of data—ball scores, stock prices, weather conditions—are interesting in their own right, but most data and facts become useful to people only when they are organized, put into context, evaluated and digested. And of course much important information is not readily available but must be dug up by resourceful investigators called reporters.

Improving technology has already made more and more information available to each of us, and will continue to do so. But more is not necessarily better. We think that the more raw information there is available, the more consumers will need professional journalists to sort through it for them, find the wheat and reject the chaff, organize the important information in an easily digestible form, check to be sure it's accurate and display it in a way that reflects its importance. Journalists make sense of things—that is their function. A data-rich world, all interconnected by the Internet, will generate a great deal of confusing information that won't be useful until someone makes sense of it.

In other words, even when amazing, still-unimagined new gizmos make the transfer of information fast, easy and fun, the art of journalism will still be necessary. We're convinced that people enjoy a news product that provides a coherent overview of what is happening in the world—like a good newspaper.[1]

Other voices have been raised in fervent protest to those who would ballyhoo that we're about to see the ink dry on the last press run. They argue that the day of the newsprint news journal has not passed and that, indeed, it will remain with us for quite a while, if not permanently. *Recruitment Advisor: The Digital Publisher's Guide to New Revenue* offered this explanation in the spring of 2013:

> Digital news delivery is rapidly becoming the standard, but that doesn't mean that print is dead. Other platforms that were supposed to be obliterated by technological progress, like radio, cinema, and printed books, are still around and still popular. Print journalism is definitely changing, but it is likely to continue to have an important place in the American experience for a long time to come.[2]

The same blog suggests five reasons why print newspapers will survive:

1. They're still great for local community news.
2. They're embracing more platforms.
3. They are mining online demographic data to their advantage.
4. The industry is gradually figuring out paywalls.
5. Print will be seen as a valued extra.

In 2012, the founder of the *Newspaper Death Watch* Web site (http://newspaperdeathwatch.com), Paul Gillin, expressed his opinion that—while print newspapers will always be with us—"there will only be five major metro dailies left by 2025, maybe a little sooner."[3] He didn't identify them.

But in a similar revelation, the Annenberg School's Center for the Digital Future at the University of Southern California did.[4] On December 14, 2011, it released a report of a study it had conducted, maintaining that—sometime prior to 2017—just four major dailies published in the United States would continue to produce a print edition. They were *The New York Times, USA Today, The Wall Street Journal,* and *The Washington Post.* Local weeklies will also persist, Annenberg officials believe.[5] Although no other major metropolitan and national dailies were cited, center director Jeffrey Cole added that—with newspaper circulation floundering—"we believe that the only print newspapers that will survive will be at the extremes of the medium, the largest and the smallest."[6]

As far back as early 2008, the matter of life-and-death for the newspaper itself was a topic of genuine absorption for columnists then seeing the handwriting on the wall. One such wordsmith, Alex Alben, whose topical pieces on technology, media, and politics turned up frequently in *The Seattle Times,* may have offered a hint about the sustainability of the newsprint edition. He advocated that "newspapers will survive by doing what they do best." And that clearly provided implications for the hard-copy version.

Alben allowed: "The strength of newspapers is that they are trusted sources of information and that they cover local events in a way that a national news organization can't. In the next decade [through 2017 by his interpretation], we will continue to see local dailies shrink their national and international coverage, while they concentrate on what they do best—covering local beats of City Hall, crime and culture."[7]

And their shrunken presence might just resemble the county seat weeklies in the days of yore, still filling what would be a major void in community-oriented journalism if they weren't there. They themselves might evolve into a daily presence on the Web but maintain the true aura of a local weekly—or Sunday and one weekday in print—to inform their neighbors of the events and happenings and news of prime interest to them. In a way it might be like a return to the days of yesteryear.

In the meantime, a different Web source reaffirmed an earlier clue to why the printed news pages you hold in your hands aren't likely to disappear anytime soon. Referencing the enormous competition that journalism has spawned in recent years—including that which is on- and off-line—a blogger proclaimed: "The reason that newspapers are here to stay is that those [other] sources lack credibility." He persists:

> A study conducted at the University of Miami found that readers often distrust online news sources, believing that they don't get the facts right as often as print newspapers do. This is because the two types of sites have different goals. The print newspaper has a reputation to maintain. There's a reason that there are corrections daily on the back of the front page. Not to mention that print newspaper employees are paid primarily for reporting the facts correctly. Providing correct and detailed information is essential to help people know the truth and make educated decisions.
>
> The times are changing, but the news landscape is evolving to cope with the short attention spans of readers. The hurricane of free online news won't knock down newspapers for good.[8]

Another strong factor hinting at print's longevity is accentuated by the associate director of the Pew Research Center's Project for Excellence in Journalism (PEJ), Mark Jurkowitz. In 2012, Jurkowitz observed: "Shifting too quickly from print carries a risk. An average of 80 percent of total newspaper revenues still comes from print advertising." He cited a then recently completed investigation in which the PEJ discovered that for every $11 in revenues they took in from print advertising newspapers collected just a dollar from digital ads.

"There's a powerful argument to be made," Jurkowitz conceded. "How can we disregard the piece of our business that is still paying the bills and signing the checks? That makes the transition harder," he assured. And it's an awfully compelling rationale for maintaining those print editions in the years ahead.

Although many others are contributing to an ongoing dialogue surrounding the viability of a sustained newsprint edition, it's clear that a portion of those voices are absolutely convinced that these journals are worth preserving in their original form. In this sector's collective opinion, the newsprint brand is here to stay. Some major influencers, previously considered, that have helped determine their thinking include these assets:

1. Newer technologies do not preclude that old ones must be replaced.
2. People routinely depend on newsprint for information about their communities while national and international reportage is increasingly dispatched to multiplying alternative sources.
3. Sentimental attachment to print editions surrounding special occasions locally will probably take many years to be vanquished, if ever.
4. Printed newspapers have long maintained their reputations as widely trusted and reliable news sources.
5. The newspaper business still remains overwhelmingly dependent on newsprint advertisers to underwrite all of its activities, no matter how its newsworthy contents are circulated.
6. A dedicated bloc of the reading audience is passionately committed to a long-standing love affair with the paper edition. Interrupting those readers' normal habits would dislodge some forever if the form went away.

A preponderance of active deliberation on the matter of retaining a paper format for the news dailies and weeklies of American journalism is currently open to a few other interpretations. Yet the fact that a steadfastly faithful segment of the readership is so firmly entrenched in maintaining newsprint's permanency cannot be overlooked in any serious discussions. To some extent it is this loyal audience who have established U.S. newspapers as the resourceful repositories that they have been esteemed as. While this audience's numbers may be shrinking, this valued faction remains significantly large enough to wield a big stick and to figure prominently in whatever debates will determine the consequential fate of the newsprint edition.

In this crucial transitory period, the question of the hard copy's disposition will likely be settled in more and more places. Within five years—and surely ten at the outside—we'll probably have a better handle on whether, or even if, the possibility of holding newsprint in one's hand is to be a foregone conclusion or a fading memory.

Newspapers, it seems, not only serve the nation's readers with the latest dispatches of information but also supply handy covers for the floors of birdcages. Should the hard copies eventually become extinct the reading habits of millions will be altered just as the habitats of millions of our feathered friends will be disturbed. If the readers lose their newspapers, the birds follow in pecking order. More than one species may feel the effects if the newsprint editions go away.

12

Are We Missing Anything?

A disclaimer is in order at the beginning of this chapter. Before any temperatures rise or blood boils, be assured that the author is cognizant that the Internet frequently offers an immeasurable wealth of information on virtually any topic one may pick to explore. We're mindful of the reality that when, for instance, one seeks current news on the Web a solitary search may produce multiple sites, articles, documents, data, tables, lists, images, illustrations, and other extraneous matter that may be relevant to the original quest under pursuit.

At the same time—after discovering that far more time has been invested in the activity than one initially intended—there still may be a disconnect at the point of extracting valuable details that pertain to the fundamental expedition. Not just overlooked, the material never may have been available online (except in replicas of hard-copy newspapers where all-inclusive stories appeared).

The point is—for many newspapers that are still about excellence in journalism (including paper and pixel models)—those patrons opting solely for Web sites sans resourceful newspaper coverage miss a whole lot. Equally disconcerting is the fact that, on many occasions, "they don't know that they don't know." It has to be distressing to the newspapers and journalists that take justifiable pride in the comprehensive work they deliver every day.

* * *

One of the incredibly disappointing outcomes that has resulted from the swing to electronic journalism is the confirmation that this transition appears to be producing informational illiterates in its wake.

These are ordinary citizens who are bereft of some of the knowledge and skills that could help them cope with the pressures inherent in a modern society. Lacking extensive knowledge in current events, they may be unable to contribute very much of universal consequence in the way of constructive thinking in governing themselves, as one example. Without sufficient background information, they are likely limited in their ability to offer some help, as they are no longer well versed in local affairs beyond a mere rudimentary awareness of current events.

While they may obey the laws of the land and pay their taxes to various governments, they have little credibility for indulging in much of anything beyond the surface issues that affect their neighborhoods. One major reason is because they know so little of substance. They may even feel inadequate in attempting to interact responsibly with other citizens on pursuits that could upgrade the quality of life about them. Imperiled by a lack of little more than surface knowledge, they experience an even worse dilemma: The fact is, many of them don't realize how little they know in the first place—or, if they do, they don't seem to care about what they're missing. It's a circumstance that's proliferating. And alas, the shift to cyberspace just may be vigorously stoking the furnace.

It wasn't supposed to be this way. When we looked upon the World Wide Web, many saw it as a provision for far more detail than newsprint could ever begin to record. And although there is categorically more information available on the Web than most average readers have time to absorb, a great deal of its matter is a far cry from the efforts that painstaking, dedicated print journalists had put into their news coverage in the heyday of newsprint's exclusivity. The insightful choice morsels often added to stories resulted in more comprehensive accounts of what was happening beyond people's doorsteps. After reading them, patrons often ruminated for a while over some of the tidbits they found tucked into their newspapers, savored them, and formed more intelligent reactions to what they had encountered because they had acquired more information.

A couple of practiced print veterans, *The Washington Post*'s Leonard Downie, Jr. and Robert Kaiser, became convinced that the better U.S. dailies are considerably more *ambitious* than their media peers. The duo offers an assessment of the modern newspaper:

12. Are We Missing Anything?

Their public service is to bring a rich, detailed account of yesterday ... to their readers every day, an account that enables citizens to remain in touch with numerous aspects of contemporary life in their community, country and world. A good paper explains big events and puts them in context. Beyond that, a newspaper keeps watch on the powerful people in its immediate neighborhood, checking constantly for competence, honesty, candor and all the other qualities that citizens hope for in the people who run the institutions they depend on.[1]

Meanwhile, in referencing the monumental nightmare that befell our country on September 11, 2001, Downie and Kaiser observed:

Television gave Americans immediate access to the news, but the journalism that provided the information essential to understanding what had happened was done primarily by newspaper stories....

...Newspapers still do most of the original reporting. In America's towns and cities, the local newspaper sets the news agenda. A few major newspapers do the same for the national news media. Of all the participants in the news business, none is remotely as committed to covering news as the country's daily papers.[2]

Today's contemporary newspaper may seem like it's behind the time in reporting what Americans have already been tipped off to by means of diverse electronic media. Those sources report the attention-grabbing breaking news almost instantaneously. This possibly appears to make the news journals unwieldy, unacceptable, and maybe even unnecessary at times. Despite such sweeping generalizations, however, no other news delivery organism consistently demonstrates equal resolve and even capacity, for instance, for ferreting out little gems of information for its accounts. This includes topics that are both extraordinary as well as trivial in nature.

Even long-standing broadcast journalist Dan Rather recognized a rival medium's unique contributions and wasn't intimidated when he needed to call a spade a spade. In August 2001, Rather recounted an address by President George W. Bush in which the chief executive proclaimed his intent to permit restricted medical research using embryonic stem cells. In his inimitable style, Rather followed that announcement with this imploring explication: "It's the kind of subject that frankly radio and television have difficulty with. It requires such depth into the complexities of it. So we can with, I think, impunity recommend that—if you're really interested in this—you'll want to read in detail

Newspapers in Transition

one of the better newspapers tomorrow." The veteran CBS newsman "got it," for, plain to viewers, he trusted the print journalists to tell them the details that some of his viewers could be seeking.

"The future of newspapers, it seems to me, will be in the sort of careful reporting that only a product as *slow* to come together as a daily newspaper will allow," said journalist Paul Oberjuerge in the blogosphere. "We never will have anything remotely like our grip on the audience that we did in the 19th century. But perhaps we can attempt to be the honest, fair, accurate and thorough arbiter of events in the 21st century."[3]

The enormous background that newspapers supply on any given subject can be absolutely priceless. Were the journalists who are involved in the investigative pursuits suddenly to be removed from the scene, as I have noted many times, much of what they furnish predictably would be left unsaid. That would result in depriving inquiring minds of substantive details to help them seize upon complex matters more completely and to establish more accurate opinions about what's happening. To date, no other medium has exhibited a proclivity for filling in the gaps as comprehensively, suggesting that there is still no substitute for what newspaper purchasers pay out their money for in the first place.

While there's some of this appearing in material currently provided on the Web of course, many newspapers—whether they appear in paper, pixel, or hybrid embodiments—hardly begin to have as many paid reporters and correspondents digging out all the enticing details that characterized most leading newspapers only a few years ago. At the same time, the profusion of electronic updates and pithy mentions on the countless platform options is frequently resulting in more and more mentions but less substantial information on a given topic. Especially is this true when these electronic updates and mentions on platform options are compared with many newspaper accounts on the same precise subject.

The discerning screen addicts may literally be asking themselves just how much of what's available on a handheld device is really all that newsworthy—or merits the time and attention they have devoted to tracking it and maybe even scanning through numerous articles or postings related to their search topic. Though at times they are quite satisfied with their finds, it still comes at the cost of skipping the normally invalu-

12. Are We Missing Anything?

able insights of fixated newspaper reporters whose intent is to turn up as much as they can on the pursuit they have undertaken. The depth of their impressions continues to linger for a while among many in that audience. Modernization aside, the older source still has much going for it.

In the meantime, some Americans have decided, it seems, that no news is good news. In a biennial study of U.S. news consumption habits the findings of the Pew Research Center in autumn of 2012 certified some rather startling revelations: Some 29 percent of Americans who hadn't yet reached their 25th birthday responded that they get no news from digital news platforms. Included were cell phones and social networks as well as traditional news platforms (such as newspapers, radio, and television). This is four percentage points beneath the disclosures issued after a similar Pew study conducted a couple of years earlier.[4] It's also indicative of a depressing trend that has significant implications for the nation's future.

Perhaps it isn't all that surprising that more people under age 25 receive their news from digital sources (60 percent, actually) than from the standard long-established sources (just 43 percent). What may be more disturbing, however, is that Pew investigators found that for people in this young adult age grouping some 76 percent rely upon Facebook or another social networking site *for some or all of their news* (italics mine). In the meantime, 71 percent depended upon a mixture of available sources, perceptibly being somewhat cautious and discriminatory.

The dual factions (social networking and multiple originators) reported by Pew would seem to suggest that there is considerable overlap in the dual groups. Yet these figures clearly hint that younger Americans—most of them (theoretically, at least) high school graduates and perhaps many college graduates as well—are turning to nontraditional sources in large numbers for their "news." This reaches well beyond the enduring "establishment types" like newspapers, magazines, radio, broadcast and cable television, and the Web's foremost dispensaries of conventional news.

The Pew survey found that only five percent of those Americans under age 30 admit to closely following reports that embrace politics, political figures, and Washington actions. Just 12 percent in the age bracket read a daily newspaper. That's even with *The New York Times* included, which rather surprisingly reaches 32 percent of readers under age 30 (or about one in three), the highest percentage tapped by any newspaper in Pew's analysis.

A leading New England newspaper publisher, Martin C. Langeveld, whose journalistic incumbency extends back three decades, offered what appears to be a plausible explanation for younger Americans' migration away from the conventional communications enterprises. At the same time it provides a reasonable interpretation of contemporary American culture:

> Back in the 1970s and early 1980s, publishers noticed that younger people weren't reading newspapers as much as their elders.... And, the philosophers among us said, "Look, when these kids grow up, get married, buy houses, have kids in school, and pay taxes, they'll read newspapers because they need to know what's going on." And indeed, some of them did. But the experience since the 1970s is that each succeeding age cohort reads newspapers less than the prior cohort.... Nothing the industry has tried to do has made the slightest dent in these inexorable trends.
>
> The industry now tends to point to the Internet and to suggest that it is both the problem and the opportunity—younger people read newspapers less because they get their news online, but the industry is benefiting from rapid growth in online readership and revenue.
>
> Hold on, though: the age-cohort readership trends started in the 1960s, not in 1995 or so when the online readership started to make an impact. This problem has been a long time coming.... Around 1970 the nation was still fairly monolithic in its readership habits—all age groups were heavy newspaper readers with rates ranging from 70 to 76 percent.
>
> Here's my theory of what happened to that solid franchise. Go back to the Great Depression of the 1930s. Everyone was in the same boat; the country was unified in its interests and concerns; although there were different political viewpoints, everyone read newspapers and listened to radio to know what was going on. Few had time or resources for anything but mainstream interests and pursuits. This continued through World War II, the Korean War, the early stages of the Cold War, and the Vietnam War. But the Baby Boom generation changed the game. With greater prosperity and less international turbulence to worry about, interests began to diversify enormously from the 1970s right through the current decade. It was a luxury we could afford—more cable channels, more movie screens, more books and magazines focused on more niche interests, more sports franchises, more highways to go to more malls, more resorts and more entertainment venues, more exotic foods on supermarket shelves, more diversity in every possible direction.
>
> Daily newspapers can no longer reflect all this diversity in their pages. The idea of a single mass medium that everyone in a community or metrop-

12. Are We Missing Anything?

olis would want to read is no longer logical, any more than we are all likely to watch the same television programs or tune to the same website or radio station.

The web, of course, has only accelerated this trend of diversification into niche interests. It was not the cause of the decline of newspaper readership, but it's not the solution, either.[5]

Publisher Langeveld has much more to say on this topic in a later chapter of this text.

Coincidentally, Pew Research discovered that more and more TV news watchers are extending a pronounced tendency of recent years in which Americans turn away from their TV sets. While local television is still commanding as a key news source, the percentage of people paying attention to the small screen has plummeted. Nowhere has this happened as piercingly as it has among younger adults. Is this any surprise? In 2006, some 42 percent of adults under 30 got their news from television. In 2012, just 28 percent of those age cohorts turned to video for news, a decline of one-third of that crucial audience.

Pew affirms that its data indicates that the coverage most people go to television for—weather, breaking news, and traffic reports—is "up for grabs." As the small screen diminishes, its turf is considered "ripe for replacement by any number of web- and mobile-based outlets."[6] It's confirmation that manifold media are losing their once-enduring loyalties, and particularly so among younger Americans.

Some media pundits, politicians, and others with clearly vested interests in this province have expressed a few doubts over the direction the country's youth is pursuing. By favoring chat rooms and blogs and social media exchanges, the collective youth culture is turning its back on the traditional news sources. As a consequence the durably consistent professional news readers and writers of past ages have been replaced by a new set of interpreters.

Although youth have greatly expanded their horizons in their quests for current events topics, they have done so by blithely dismissing the security that normally follows the standard-issue performers. Whether youth recognize it or not—or whether it matters at all—lost is a genuine sense of responsibility, credibility, consistency, objectivity, and inclusivity that traditionally accompanies the realizations of committed, venerable news providers. It's an arsenal not easily replaced. The principal determinants of youth's "knowledge" about world affairs have been radically altered. A whole lot of reliable information encountered in previous generations may be missing. As vocalist Peggy Lee used to wistfully inquire in melody, "Is that all there is?"

Even more chillingly perhaps, where does this leave us as we ponder the nation's future?

One of America's earliest chief executives, James Madison (1751–1836; U.S. president 1809–1817), advocated a well-informed constituency: "Knowledge will forever govern ignorance, and a people who mean to be their own governors must arm themselves with the power which knowledge gives."[7] One of the pervading themes of a U.S. Commission on Reading report that was released to the public fervently advocated the opinion that "reading is important for the society as well as the individual."[8] The panel called for increased measures to improve and encourage the nation's reading habits in order to bestow a more broadly informed culture.

In 2013, research studies conducted by *Consumer Reports* disclosed that "people who regularly read the newspaper reported higher levels of happiness [than those] who watched lots of TV."[9] In the meantime modern journalism professor Philip Meyer was warning his protégés: "If we're all attending to different messages, our capacity to understand one another is diminished."[10]

One of the bona fide concerns the country may encounter down the road isn't that we're not reading from the same page any longer; it's that we may not be, very possibly, reading from *any* page—either in newsprint or online or from a handheld device. At least, we may not be relying upon reliable intellectual wellsprings. These sources have traditionally initiated practical answers to thorny issues through comprehensive information. Once older leaders die off, what sources will provide the answers required by tomorrow's best minds that are seeking to govern themselves? If the culture persisted in turning its collective backs on sources that have been proven reliable and invaluable to previous generations how well will those denizens be equipped to meet the challenges they face?

There is more data that has recently surfaced indicating that what was once a fairly solid affirmation for respected news media is now skating on very thin ice. In research conducted among more than 2,000 adults in early 2013, the Pew Research Center found that fully three out of ten Americans (31 percent) have deserted a specific news outlet "because it no longer provides the news and information" that they had come to expect.

Significantly, the majority of those individuals are liable to both consume and subscribe to the news; they are among the best educated, most affluent and eldest members of that study group. Aside from these characteristics, those who left a trusted news source included more men than women and more Independent and Republican than Democratic voters. A third of the former two political persuasions stopped relying on a news outlet, while only a quarter of Democrats did so.

Finally, the "primary concern" of those who gave up on an outlet was "loss of perceived quality" over an earlier time frame. "Fully 61 percent … said stories were less complete than they had been versus just 24 percent who complained there were too few stories," said Pew's researchers.[11] This, of course, may have something to do with the financial crunch in which established news media companies have been pushed in this millennium. As I have already noted elsewhere, it has resulted in layoffs of thousands of qualified professionals and necessitated some service cutbacks that have also netted some disturbing consequences.

If one boldly dismisses the established news providers to solely rely upon other sources that report without demonstrated track records—the kind normally associated with responsible journalistic efforts by seasoned news-gathering organizations—the results may be lagging. In 1597, Sir Francis Bacon was among the early theorists to testify: "Knowledge is power."[12] Knowledge may penetrate human beings in myriad ways. Pixels and paper are two carriers. The methods that individuals select for receiving the news aren't usually nearly as critical as the sources that originate the information. It's a choice that ultimately may supply the key in attaining an edge.

13

An Alternating Landscape

In 2013, the Newspaper Association of America (NAA) released statistics for the industry. The data compared the most recent year's figures (2012) with those of the previous year. The results of that report furnish a bird's-eye view of current trends and prevailing circumstances:

> Overall, total revenue ... declined by 2 percent in 2012 from a year earlier.... U.S. newspaper media took in $38.6 billion in 2012 compared with $39.5 billion ... in 2011....
>
> ...While advertising revenue continues to decline—down 6 percent in 2012—several other categories of newspaper media revenue are now growing. Circulation revenue grew 5 percent in 2012 while a host of new revenue sources not tied to conventional advertising ... grew by 8 percent. These ... include ... digital consulting for local business and e-commerce transactions, [and] now account for close to one-in-ten dollars coming in.... They are significant enough ... that NAA has begun to collect detailed data about these revenue categories and track their trajectory ... for the first time.
>
> ...Approximately $6 billion [is] in additional revenue, $3 billion ... not counted before and another $3 billion that did not exist a few years ago, comprising about 16 percent of all newspaper media revenue in 2012.
>
> ...
>
> The overall composition of newspaper revenue ... has thus also changed.... Circulation now makes up 27 percent of total newspaper media revenue, new revenue sources 8 percent, digital advertising 11 percent, niche publishing and direct marketing 8 percent, and print advertising 46 percent.
>
> ...
>
> NAA projects that of the $38.6 billion in total revenue in 2012, $18.9 billion came from print advertising, $3.4 billion from digital advertising, $2.9 billion from advertising from direct marketing/niche and non-daily publications, $10.4 billion from circulation and $3 billion from new revenue sources. In 2011, of the total revenue of $39.6 billion, NAA projects $20.7 billion came from print newspaper advertising, $3.2 billion from digital advertising, $3

billion from direct marketing/niche and non-daily publications, $10 billion from circulation and $2.7 billion from new revenue sources....

Combined digital revenue (from circulation, advertising, e-commerce, digital marketing and other sources) made up 11 percent of total revenue in 2012....

The 5 percent overall growth in circulation revenue was the first gain in this category ... since 2003. Within that total ... digital-only circulation revenue grew 275 percent; print and digital bundled circulation revenue grew 499 percent.... More organizations ... bundling print and online into combined access subscriptions [saw] print-only circulation revenue declined 14 percent.

Within the 8 percent growth in new revenue sources, revenue from digital agency consulting for local businesses grew 91 percent. E-commerce revenue grew 20 percent.

Mobile ad revenue ... less than 1 percent of total revenue, doubled (up 100 percent)....

When revenue from print, digital, niche and delivery of preprints outside of newspapers are combined ... total advertising revenue made up 65 percent of overall revenue in 2012. Within that figure, traditional print newspaper advertising fell 9 percent and now makes up 46 percent of total revenue. Digital advertising increased 5 percent and now makes up 11 percent; pure-play digital advertising (digital only) increased 20 percent.[1]

In the most recent year with published data available (2012) the NAA's revenue stream composition for newspaper media shows the following breakdown:

Print newspaper advertising—46%
Circulation—27%
Digital advertising—11%
Non-daily/niche/direct marketing—8%
"New" revenue—8%[2]

What does all of this actually mean?

It confirms that print advertising is continuing to spiral in freefall fashion while digital sales keep climbing. At the same time various supplementary revenue sources provide room for optimism.

The NAA figures highlight a still powerfully exalted enterprise that is visibly transitioning its revenue strategies. Moving from one that was predominantly based on advertising and circulation income, it has now embraced a course with virtually unlimited possibilities, calling for some creative thinking. Caroline Little, NAA president and CEO, observed in 2013: "America's newspaper media are transforming themselves. In virtually every community they serve, newspapers have the biggest newsrooms, the best-known brands and significant audience market share. Now they are building on those to find new ways to serve audiences and local businesses."[3]

Breaking out of a mold that has held for more than a century, newspaper publishers—now often embracing the *media* organizational term and the wider territory it implies—have taken some innovative steps to deal with their plight. To some, this could be viewed as an act of desperation. To others, perhaps it might resemble treason. But to forward thinkers, it's a strong indication that as times have changed much of the trade is changing with them. It must do so to survive, to continue to be viable, competitive, and profitable. By enlarging its scope to include a diversity of entrepreneurial activities, the media giants are repositioning themselves to deal with the unknowns that are just ahead.

Around the turn of the century, Leonard Mogel—with publishing and writing pursuits that allowed him to be on the cutting edge of an extensive mix of media interests—cited a trio of generators that have characteristically netted most newspaper advertising revenue: *retail*, including display ads from department stores, food chains, and other local merchants with goods and services to sell to the public; *general*, which is display advertising for national marketers with commodities or brand names that is distributed on a countrywide scale; and *classified*, made up of small locally placed ads listed by categories such as "Employment," "Apartment Rentals," "Home Sales," and "Automotive Dealers."[4]

A few reflections from enduring journalists Bill Kovach and Tom Rosenstiel will lead us to contemplate how advertising figures into the media (and the newspaper trade in particular) at a time in which electronics is heavily influencing it. Those analysts touch on the subsequent upheaval that all this transition has produced:

> When numbers from their new and old platforms are combined, many traditional media venues are seeing their audiences grow. The crisis facing the news industry created by technology has to do more with revenue. The technology has decoupled advertising from news. Many advertisers no longer need the news to reach their audience—be they big-box retailers with their

own Web sites or individuals posting apartments for rent or bicycles for sale on Craigslist. At the same time, the Internet has turned out to be a poor delivery system for the kind of display advertising that financed news gathering in the twentieth century. News delivery for the past century benefited from a happy accident. A commercial system (advertising) subsidized a civic good (professional journalism). That system is now ending.[5]

As we can see, the digital shift has profound implications for news-publishing enterprises' primary revenue source, advertising. (Advertising has traditionally contributed about 80 percent of the newspaper freight in the U.S.[6]) That steadfast mainstay that bankrolled so much of the print media in the 1900s has been dramatically altered with the shift from paper to pixel. As a result newspapers have had to adjust their thinking, moving in the modern age from an accustomed fortress of financing to seeking creatively diversified solutions—and some never before tried.

James O'Shea, who filled executive posts at two of the nation's premier dailies (*Chicago Tribune, Los Angeles Times*) for a while, detected trouble brewing in the revenue expectations by news journals several years back:

> On the surface, newspaper finances in 2006 didn't seem that bad; the real estate boom that fueled the subprime mortgage crisis was in full swing, generating huge amounts of real estate classified ad revenue. But help wanted and automobile classified ads, a crucial component of newspaper revenue, was in a free fall, partially because of the Internet and partially because advertisers were aware of newspapers' declining circulations. Were the real estate market to soften—something that was only a matter of time—newspapers would be in real trouble.[7]

Newspapers could cope with diminishing circulations by eliminating subscribers living great distances from their centers of greatest appeal—the people who were generally of least concern to the most advertisers in any case. By focusing on readers who resided in the essential districts most preferred by advertisers, papers could lower their paper, ink, print, storage, and delivery costs, sometimes substantially. At the same time, some papers bit the bullet in another way, discarding decades or maybe centuries of home delivery routines to opt for reduced distribution or sales in other ways. (For a more comprehensive examination of this maneuver, see chapter 7.)

The losses of advertising, however, were nonetheless devastating. Advertising income not only underwrote the bulk of papers' print budgets; it was expected to contribute heavily to their Web-based efforts at the same time. It wasn't the best of times; it was the worst of times. So much of the house was depending on servicing, satisfying, and sustaining those print advertisers. And so many of them were spending less and less, if not cutting out altogether, what they had been earmarking for newsprint with cyberspace becoming so relevant. Thus publishers were looking into every nook and cranny in their quests to slash their budgets. Staff layoffs supplied a great deal of it. But they asked themselves: Were there ways to attract new advertisers and to pacify traditional advertisers, too?

All of this was to have some profound effects on the way those publishers approached their businesses in the future.

14

Families in Distress

In August 2013, the durable overseers of *The Washington Post* made an unexpected declaration to their staff and to the public: After eight decades, the reins of their iconic, widely idolized magnum opus were about to be transferred into the hands of an entrepreneur without a track record in the trade. To at least a portion of the veteran journalists hearing that word it must have cut like a dagger thrust into the heart of an already perilously challenged profession. Allowed one, who claimed the outgoing custodians "survived Nixon but not the Internet": "If Hell froze over, pigs took wing, sheep fell from the sky, and snow blanketed Hawaii, it still wouldn't be as astonishing as Monday's announcement that the storied Graham family is selling *The Washington Post* to a billionaire online-retailing entrepreneur."[1]

With fourscore years of experience under its belt in running that venerated citadel of exemplary journalism—a paper and a period that is viewed in many circles as a mark of the nation's moral compass—the esteemed Grahams of the homeland's capital decreed an impending separation from the celebrated perch they had occupied for so long. Although by then publicly traded, their cherished enterprise—nevertheless the clan's most authentic asset—would be shifted to the responsibility of a capitalist whose coffers bulged with treasure that was derived primarily through electronic selling.

For myriad decades *The Washington Post*'s readers and staff had felt "safe" with the Grahams at the helm of "their" publication. These were not absentee managers, as some are branded, for they were in the office daily laboring alongside their employees, including some who were devoted friends of many years' duration. As they partnered with their staff, the Grahams attempted to imbue the "sacred trust" for which they appeared well suited as caretakers with the noblest standards of integrity that could be funneled into local, national, and international journalism.

Their output became a powerful symbol of their principles of decency and was frequently modeled by metropolitan dailies elsewhere, so several sources reported. "A robust and competitive *Washington Post* is essential to the long-term health of our family-controlled newspaper," inferred Arthur Ochs Sulzberger, Jr., chairman of The New York Times Company and publisher of its emblematical namesake.[2]

A vocational prodigy of his time, journalist James O'Shea, painted a pithy word picture of what it was like for the American breeds that experienced the good fortune of acquiring one or more newspapers as their principal source(s) of livelihood. In the environment in which they operated, one that has largely passed almost altogether, they sometimes approached their challenges with mixed behavior:

> The owners ... viewed themselves first and foremost as local *public service institutions,* part of a larger civic power structure that protected and guarded local standards and traditions. Of course ... some abused their powers and ... promoted particular political agendas. Some were downright scoundrels, and family ownership clearly had its pitfalls.... Those who could afford to acquire newspapers did so under the assumption that they'd make a profit, but the bottom line was just part of the equation. They were interested in getting out the news and in maintaining a powerful seat in their respective communities. Newspaper publishers were often fixtures of local arts, culture, and charity boards. Their responsibilities were huge.[3]

That exclusive coterie included several names that became widely recognized. Not limited merely to those who read them every day, their names were known to national political figures, major civic advocates, widely read journalists, educators, and others whose tasks included reaching over vast expanses to connect with local leaders in distant locales. Among the most readily respected U.S. newspaper-publishing families of the period were the Binghams of Louisville; the Chandlers of Los Angeles; the Cowleses of Des Moines; the Coxes of Atlanta; the Fields, Medills, and McCormicks of Chicago; the Grahams and Meyers of Washington; the Hearsts, Newhouses, Ochses, Pattersons, and Sulzbergers of New York; and the Knights of Miami.

To be certain, the surprise announcement that the Grahams and their kinfolk delivered in 2013 was accompanied by absolute astonish-

14. Families in Distress

ment from many sectors tied to the paper—shareholders, subscribers, staff, advertisers, critics, still other stakeholders, and the industry at large—all of whom were apparently caught off guard. At the same time, the masses in some quarters exhibited a spirit of optimism while genuine uncertainty prevailed in others. This wasn't just *any* newspaper, of course. It carries the torch of daily reportage in a geographical district that is occupied by the seat of federal government.

Jeffrey P. Bezos of Seattle, the *Post*'s new custodian, 49 at the time of the buy, made his mark as the founder, CEO, president, and chairman of the board at Amazon. Before launching that property in 1994, the man who was to be *Time* magazine's 1999 Person of the Year was a financial analyst at D. E. Shaw & Company, a global investment and technology developer. In the meantime, as a whiz kid for viewing mature businesses in innovative and unconventional style Bezos turned an online bookseller into the Web's foremost merchandising agent. One source dubbed Amazon "the world's biggest online retailer."[4] And he bought *The Washington Post* at a fire-sale figure ($250 million) without relying on his corporation for any shared financing. (On that purchase Bezos divested less than 1 percent of his net worth, reportedly $28 billion at the time.[5])

Once the word of that astounding acquisition became widespread, many in the trade expressed sincere optimism that the new owner might become an inspiration to an endangered species. "If there's somebody who can succeed, it's Bezos," affirmed *Post* associate editor Bob Woodward. (It may be recalled that, operating under executive editor Ben Bradlee, Woodward and colleague Carl Bernstein led the *Post* to a Pulitzer Prize for their intense scrutiny of Richard Nixon's crime-ridden White House.) Woodward persisted: "He's [Bezos] the innovator, he's got the money and the patience.... In some ways, this may be the *Post*'s last chance to survive."[6]

Shortly after making the announcement public, *Post* CEO Donald Graham, then 68, maintained: "The Post could have survived under the company's ownership and been profitable for the foreseeable future. But we wanted to do more than survive. I'm not saying this guarantees success, but it gives us a much greater chance of success."[7] There were some other industry analysts who took exception to Graham's indolent explanation at the time, however.

"Seven years of declining sales, triggered by an industry-wide advertising slump, ultimately pushed the family to sell," Bloomberg bloggers Nick Turner and Edmund Lee clarified. And Ken Doctor, media critic at Outsell, Inc.—and quoted many times in this text—believed: "It's kind of like the Grahams threw in the towel. They looked at the future, and they said, 'We can't see how to get from here to there, and we need someone who knows what to do.'"[8]

Even Don Graham confessed to a reporter that the sale of the *Post* was forced by "a declining newspaper industry and challenges too large for a small publicly held company to handle." The Alliance of Audited Media revealed in March 2013 that the *Post*'s weekday circulation had fallen 6.5 percent in one year, to 474,767. Meanwhile, Graham acknowledged that the paper's revenues had consistently waned for the previous seven years (2006–2012). He disclosed, "We had innovated and to my critical eye our innovations had been quite successful in audience and in quality, but they hadn't made up for the revenue decline. Our answer had to be cost cuts and we knew there was a limit to that."[9]

"The Grahams were incredibly proud of their family ownership," said former *Post* reporter Chip Brown soon after they announced their impending sale. "They fought to maintain family ownership. At the height of Watergate, when it went public, and they were possibly losing control, the Nixon administration came after them. They survived the Nixon administration, but they didn't survive the Internet."[10]

In the meantime the buoyancy already expressed persisted in some other quarters as well. Jim Friedlich, president of Empirical Media, considered the *Post* "well positioned" under Bezos "to take advantage of the promising trend of readers ... willing to pay for quality digital content." Friedlich added, "In both digital and legacy media, he [Bezos] has both the money and the vision to think big."[11]

Michael Moritz, a Silicon Valley financier who was instrumental in establishing the media giants Google and Yahoo!, predicted: "Compared with the cautious owners he is replacing, Mr. Bezos has an eye firmly on the future and will be prepared to take more radical decisions. Stopping the print edition of the *Post* entirely and combining its digital business with Politico, a political blog, are the kind of moves that might come next."[12]

Perhaps Bezos could also lead his symbolic bastion of quality press

14. Families in Distress

to acquire even more plaudits beyond those it has already garnered in its award-winning past. Given that, plus some resurgence in local interest and the full adaptation of digital technologies, the venture might persist as a continuing force in mainstream media. In doing so it would lengthen a heritage that dates back almost 14 decades to 1877. Time will tell how smart Bezos and the Grahams were when they struck their unforeseen deal.

That announcement, coming as it did on the heels of the sale of *The Boston Globe* by The New York Times Company in the same month to yet another affluent caretaker without a journalistic birthright, underscores once more—as the writer of Second Corinthians affirmed—that "the old has passed away; behold, the new has come."[13] The latest magnate over the *Globe*, John W. Henry, 63—who is also principal owner of the Boston Red Sox baseball franchise—offers a fascinating study that is just as mesmerizing as the acquisition of *The Washington Post* by Bezos. Henry, yet another multimillionaire like his contemporary, was born the son of Illinois soybean farmers. He established his legacy by successfully trading soybeans and other commodities early in his career. When he was in his twenties, one of Henry's innovative ideas resulted in creating an automated technique for managing a futures trading account.[14]

His ascension into the catbird seat at the *Globe*—along with several other secular wizards from the outside world who now occupy controlling posts at a few other metropolitan dailies—is confirmation enough that future attempts to discover traditional publishers among U.S. news journals may require more than perfunctory pursuits. It appears that there won't be any long lines wrapped around the newspapers' premises and saturated with practiced journalists of the old school. They're not among those awaiting a turn to offer up some extra cash for a vehicle that just might be withering on the vine and perhaps dying in the process.

"The big marketing challenge is getting readers to see the value in subscribing online," commented Boston University journalism professor Lou Ureneck. "Can John Henry do this? If he can get them to buy expensive beer and peanuts, maybe he can get them to put down a few dollars a month for their local newspaper. There's a lot more at stake here than a ball game."[15] (That costly beer and peanuts are among the concessions available to Red Sox patrons at the famous Fenway Park, where sold-out seats are now reportedly among the priciest in Major League Baseball. Of course, winning the World Series in October 2013, one of the storied team's most recent accomplishments, hasn't hurt the franchise—or its owners' deep pockets—either.)

Ureneck takes exception to the fact that Henry "paid more for his second baseman than for the Globe" ($100 million for second-baseman Dustin Pedroia versus $70 million in another fire-sale newspaper buy, which The New York Times Company had paid $1.1 billion for a couple of decades earlier). Maintaining profitability at the *Globe*, the Boston prof thinks, will require "digital products strong enough to attract paying readers." Says Ureneck: "Advertising, once a reliable source for print media, is a cheap commodity on the Internet. Classified advertising is a distant memory, ancient history. Maintaining newspapers, or more importantly the news organizations behind them, is going to be a long and difficult slog."[16] Did Mr. Henry know what he had bought?

Among commanding metropolitan U.S. dailies the current ownership trend is moving away from traditional journalism-oriented family-run businesses. Sometimes control of those papers has shifted to a few thriving innovators who made their mark in other disciplines (e.g., Bezos, Henry). On other occasions a handful of investors or publicly traded conglomerates with or without a strong media presence have added these journals to their often expansive portfolios. The latter groups in some instances appear to exhibit little authentic interest in the perceived long-term value of their possessions.

Bottom-line results are usually paramount in those situations. From time to time such acquisitions prompt some fiery feedback on the Web. *Variety* columnist Brian Lowry is among those who made the threat proffered by this modern stance the subject of a contemporary discourse:

> The super-rich have exhibited what appears to be a heightened interest in newspapers, including the recent sale of the Boston Globe to billionaire investor John Henry—who also happens to own baseball's Boston Red Sox—and Warren Buffett's acquisition of several smaller publications.
>
> "If it wasn't clear that newspapers have become trophies for the wealthy with an interest in journalism or power—or a combination of both—it should be now," wrote New York Times columnist Andrew Ross Sorkin.
>
> Yet the lingering fear is that while journalists dream of finding a Bruce Wayne—or in the case of the Los Angeles Times, an Eli Broad or David Gef-

14. Families in Distress

fen—they might wind up under the thumb of a Lex Luthor or some Bondian villain, eager to use these shiny new toys to pursue nefarious goals and world domination.

That's always been suspected of Rupert Murdoch, who has made little secret of the glee he derives from his newspaper properties, yielding benefits that go far beyond what they deliver to his balance sheet. It took the phone-hacking scandal at outlets in the U.K. to prod the mogul to spin his print-grounded holdings off as a separate entity from his entertainment assets, and even then, he couldn't bring himself to completely part with them.

More recently, word that the Koch brothers—well known for their conservative activism and backing of so-called Astroturf groups, which appear to be grassroots organizations but are often backed by wealthy benefactors—were circling media properties, including the [Chicago] Tribune newspapers, triggered renewed hand-wringing. The mere rumor that the oil and gas barons harbored interest in the [L. A.] Times prompted Courage Campaign, a California-based progressive organization, to vigorously begin lobbying against such a transaction.

Under this logic, what good is it if the press survives, financially speaking, should the tradeoff involve becoming mouthpieces for moguls intent on acquiring media strictly to level what they perceive as an unequal playing field with left-leaning news outlets?

Bezos doesn't fit that profile, but he does have disparate interests that could be advanced through the Post....

Still, given the wrenching changes and widespread layoffs that have strafed their industry, journalists find themselves in beggars-can't-be-choosers mode. And Bezos comes armed not only with deep pockets but an established presence in the digital world that has reshaped newspapers.[17]

Would those dual virtues be the saving grace? By the time you are reading this both Bezos and Henry will have most likely revealed something of what they intend to do with these newspapers. An entire industry, including some potential buyers of other major metropolitan dailies, will be closely watching their every move with these trendsetting journals to learn what tricks the new owners have up their sleeves. Essentially: What are they doing with the unique opportunities that are theirs? Is it status quo or something more innovative or possibly even menacing?

Another blogger who felt compelled to provoke fears in a foreboding treatise on the *Post*'s shift from the Grahams to Bezos—*The Progressive*'s Matthew Rothschild—wasted no time condemning it. The outcome, he declared, had far greater implications than the mere transfer of power through ownership. Noting that it wasn't simply the cessation of the Grahams' relationship with the stately old voice of Americana that they had controlled for eight decades, Rothschild proclaimed it "the end of an era of print journalism itself."

Continuing, he intimated that new owners would persist in downsizing the papers they bought in their efforts to make those journals more profitable at the expense of content and staff. As we have heard before, Rothschild cautioned: "This is not good for democracy. There are fewer and fewer reporters to keep track of our elected officials, and even fewer to keep track of the unelected rulers of America, the corporations that throw their weight around not only in Washington but in every statehouse across the country.

"Today, newspapers have become merely the playthings of the super-rich," he condemned. "In no case is the public interest being served by the scavenging of the carcasses of daily newspapers. We need public journalism, not private journalism. And ... we're going to need public support for it, too, or you can kiss your dreams of democracy goodbye," Rothschild concluded.[18]

In a *U.S. News & World Report* blog, political and foreign affairs scribe Susan Milligan also responds to the shift transpiring within the ownership ranks of the American newspaper-publishing industry. Specifically citing *The Boston Globe*'s transfer—and realizing that her analysis could apply to plenty of other markets—Milligan identifies a key advantage that the nontraditionalist tycoon who ascends to the top may have over a cluster of investors who acquire their trinkets largely for financial gain.

The New York Times Company, by the way, reportedly passed over several higher bids for the *Globe* when it settled on Henry's. Milligan appears to hint, for reasons she identifies, that they may have gotten it right. And for the sake of Bostonians in this case—and journalism's relevance in general—many professionals in the trade probably share in that hope:

> Newspapers were in their heyday when they were part of the community, local institutions that might have published stories that upset elected officials or businesspeople or sports owners, but which were a critical part of the region. The trend toward selling papers to people who are mainly interested in profit or dividends for shareholders has had a very damaging effect on the product and on the institution of journalism itself. A paper has a far bet-

ter chance of keeping its integrity being owned by a single rich person than being owned by a bunch of stockholders who would rather let a misguided war in Iraq go uncovered and unexamined than spend the money to send some brave reporters over there to see what's going on. Henry may not like some of the baseball coverage in the Globe, but both the Red Sox and the Globe share a powerful bond: they are both Boston institutions, and they survive only if people stick with them during the tough times. An owner who cares about Boston, cares about quality journalism and cares about the Globe is the person who deserves to buy it. That kind of person in fact, is the highest bidder.[19]

Wordsmith David Von Drehle helped *Time* magazine's audience grasp some of the historic landscape on which papers such as *The Washington Post* and a handful of contemporary collegial U.S. dailies were fixtures—all family-run operations of long standing through much of the 20th century and all dominating their local markets. In addition to presenting a comprehensive range of national and international news, their journalists were first and foremost local reporters. It was their task to keep the communities they embraced fully informed with explicit details on items of interest transpiring locally. And in the process of carrying out that assignment, the owners became very powerful and influential members of the business communities and social and political environments in which they operated. Here's some of Von Drehle's history lesson:

> What made the great metro newspapers great was a passing historical moment when dominance in the morning was a license to print money. While the *Post* is most famous for its Watergate reporting, that helped bring down a corrupt President, its power stemmed from a much earlier moment. In 1954, after years of effort and red ink, the paper's owners, financier Eugene Meyer and his son-in-law Philip L. Graham, finally bought out their last remaining a.m. rival. Owning the morning meant that the *Post* would thrive as afternoon newspapers fell to the competition of television news. Advertisers hoping to reach a broad Washington audience had no choice but to pay the *Post's* steadily increasing rates. While the Sulzbergers of the New York Times pursued an elite national audience, in cities across the country great fortunes were made in the morning, and some beneficiaries—the Chandlers of Los Angeles, the Coxes of Atlanta, the Knights of Miami, to name a few—poured significant shares into better journalism. None outdid the Grahams.
>
> A common mistake is to say that the Internet derailed this gravy train by giving readers the news for free. In truth, free news was nothing new. Publishers never made much money on the news. During some of the *Post's*

most robustly profitable years, subscribers paid as little as 20 cents a day for home delivery—far less than it cost to gather, edit, print and hand-deliver the news by 6 a.m.

The money came from the advertisers, from the individual classified-ad buyer eager to sell a used lawn mower, to the grocers and department stores and car dealers who bought page after page of costly display ads. The business was about collecting a mass audience for those advertisers, so publishers bundled all sorts of diverse content—from box scores to horoscopes, from coverage of debutante balls to news of distant war zones—into the most broadly appealing package they could muster, then delivered it at a loss in exchange for eyeballs.[20]

To imply or even conclude, however, that the Internet had little or nothing to do with fabricating the dire circumstances experienced by newspapers today—particularly of the prevalent, predominant newsprint variety—would certainly be a mistake. Had the Internet not arisen, of course, and taken away the classifieds and the display ads that suddenly had so many other places to appear (and thereby redirected corporate marketing budgets)—plus the magnetic attraction of all those flourishing platforms that surfaced in a frenzied electronic atmosphere at times feeding a collective public's insatiable appetite—would that not have heavily contributed to the derailment of the "gravy train?"

One would simply have to *not* "get it" to believe there's little or no connection. As has been pointed out numerous times already in this text, cyberspace has heavily twisted newspapers, greatly diminishing their prominence, circulation, advertising, delivery, power, and the dominion they had long enjoyed in the territory they served.

While repeating some of the aforementioned, a couple of *Financial Times* reporters explored the movement away from single-family ownership of U.S. news dailies and weeklies. Their dour appraisal of the outcome seems in line with those of a majority of discerning pundits:

> The industry has been convulsed as the heirs to the great U.S. newspaper empires have bowed out. Sellers have included the Chandlers (who said goodbye to 114 years of history at the Los Angeles Times) and the Bancrofts (104 years at Dow Jones, owner of The Wall Street Journal). Only a few— The New York Times's Sulzbergers (117 years and counting), the Hearsts and the Newhouses—are keeping the flame of a family dynasty alive.
>
> Along with newspaper mogul Rupert Murdoch, the buyers are a mixed bag of bottom-feeders, local influence-peddlers and aspiring national play-

ers. Asked why a crop of wealthy individuals would buy newspapers, Alan Mutter, an industry analyst, says: "I assume they have large fortunes they are trying to make smaller."[21]

USA Today's Rem Rieder contributes a few more names of prosperous financiers who have become the custodians of some American dailies in key markets during the modern era. Among those monikers: businessman Aaron Kushner, whose 2100 Trust acquired *The Orange County Register* in Southern California in 2012; a handful of local power players, including businessman George Norcross and ex–New Jersey Nets owner Lewis Katz, purchasers of *The Philadelphia Inquirer* and *Philadelphia Daily News;* billionaire Philip Anschutz, who picked up *The Gazette* in Colorado Springs; and local real-estate developer Doug Manchester, who bought *The San Diego Union-Tribune* late in 2011, now known as *U-T San Diego*.[22]

"The downside of course," said Rieder, "is the possibility that the rich dude decides to wield his new toy as a battering ram. Manchester in San Diego has been criticized for using his paper to advance pet causes in the unlamented tradition of William Randolph Hearst." And veteran newspaper analyst John Morton added: "While always hoping for the best, we mustn't forget that individual owners at times have been disasters for the readers of the newspapers they owned and misused." Rieder, meanwhile, who once worked under *Philadelphia Inquirer* owner Walter Annenberg, a well-heeled businessman who later became U.S. ambassador to Great Britain, said, "I saw this up close." Rieder allowed: "Annenberg used the *Inquirer* to reward friends and punish enemies. The names of people he didn't like simply didn't appear."[23]

In a recent year 71 daily newspapers in America changed hands in 11 separate transactions.[24] Despite the headlines that deal makers usually stimulate when they buy and sell major U.S. metropolitan journals, it's actually a couple of other classifications to which the bulk of financiers are attracted. Because they still govern most of the news gathering that transpires within their markets, it's the small and midsized papers that regularly appeal to the majority of investors now. Speaking in 2012, newspaper sales broker John Cribb shed a little more light on those dual categories of the trade: "I think the consensus is that the problems the mid- and small-newspaper industry has right now is 80 percent bad economy and 20 percent digital information issues." His comments offer still more affirmation that a portion of the ongoing dilemma in which the industry is embroiled is tied to online substance—including these journals' response, or insufficient response perhaps, to a range of cyberspace threats.

Taking a look ahead at the possibilities for newspaper ownership in America in the near term, what are the organizational and individual types that might be anticipated?

Earlier in this millennium a couple of lifelong journalists uniquely positioned to analyze the industry from their strategic geographical site noted that just one in five news journals in the United States could boast of local ownership any longer. Only remnants of an age virtually gone away still controlled the leading newsprint commerce in the towns in which they were published. "The best proprietors rose above parochial interests and encouraged tough-minded, independent reporting," observed Leonard Downie, Jr. and Robert Kaiser, veterans of *The Washington Post*. "Both good papers and bad ones had deep roots in their hometowns.

"No longer," the pair avers. "Today chains own 80 percent of America's newspapers.... Editors who once spent their days working with reporters and editors on stories now spend more of their time in meetings with the paper's business-side executives, plotting marketing strategies or cost-cutting campaigns. Chain editors now routinely have two titles: editor *and* vice president of a big corporation. Many editors of big papers are millionaires whose compensation is directly dependent on their papers' profitability."[25]

Many newspaper-owning families of long standing have found themselves in perennial distress, unable to rise above mounting financial pressures fostered by dwindling revenues derived by advertising and subscription sales. Cutting staff, services, coverage, delivery zones, and physical dimensions of the product (including shrinking the number and size of pages) has taken a heavy toll. For many aging families it's been too much. Prompted by a weakened economy and amplified by the public's increasing embrace of all things digital, plus additional relationship issues arising within some clans, prominent custodians of long standing have frequently felt the need to sell out. Regrettably, some have done so to the detriment of those most dependent upon them, extending to their subscribers and staff, as well as to local civic and political leadership.

14. Families in Distress

Platitudes of confidence are often expressed when making the announcements that the hometown journals are changing hands. Many times the departing overseers live to see a different outcome from the one they expected or hoped would be achieved, however. The papers that they may have treated as sacred trusts for the public's benefit may just become little more than pawns in the portfolios of behemoth conglomerates. With negligible or—worse—nonexistent concern for what has gone before, the new operators' shareholders maintain a single-theme objective: profitability—first, foremost, and beyond any and everything else. Whatever it takes to achieve that aim seems to become the prevailing business model, regrettably, in many metropolitan areas. As it turns out, the newspaper itself, no matter if it's in paper or pixel form, may become merely a vehicle to increase the coffers of its financiers. The family-run trust is virtually dead everywhere.[26]

Not all of these corporations are run in such a cold, calculating, and dispassionate manner, of course. There are exceptions to every absolute. Yet the contemporary trend toward absentee ownership hints at some traits that are inherent in diminishing those noble pursuits fostered by the conventional custodians of the past. Will a news journal managed for decades under the watchful eye of respected pillar clans of the neighborhood be viewed in the same way after a geographically distant tycoon buys the property?

As the strings that matter are pulled from great distances by people who may be pulling them for a string of media enterprises scattered across the U.S.A. at the same time, will the perception and the product remain unscathed? "A rose by any other name would smell as sweet" vowed Shakespeare's Juliet. But sometimes, it can also wind up as just one of the bunch.

In January 2013, State of the Media released the names of America's chief newspaper publishers for the previous year calculated by their combined weekday circulations (WC). The top 25, along with the name of their largest journal, follow:

1. Gannett, McLean, Virginia—4,859,360 WC, 80 dailies, *USA Today* (largest)
2. MediaNews Group, Denver, Colorado—3,098,580 WC, 63 dailies, *San Jose Mercury News*

3. News Corporation, New York, New York—2,618,850 WC, 2 dailies, *The Wall Street Journal*

4. McClatchy Company, Sacramento, California—2,100,590 WC, 30 dailies, *Miami Herald*

5. Advance Publications, Inc., Staten Island, New York—1,448,610 WC, 19 dailies, *The [Cleveland] Plain Dealer*

6. Lee Enterprises, Davenport, Iowa—1,343,650 WC, 52 dailies, *St. Louis Post-Dispatch*

7. New York Times Company, New York, New York—1,312,560 WC, 4 dailies, *The New York Times*

8. Hearst Corporation, New York, New York—1,220,100 WC, 17 dailies, *The Houston Chronicle*

9. Tribune Company, Chicago, Illinois—1,216,720 WC, 9 dailies, *Los Angeles Times*

10. Berkshire Hathaway, Omaha, Nebraska—882,347 WC, 27 dailies, *Omaha World-Herald*

11. GateHouse Media, Fairport, New York—865,615 WC, 90 dailies, *The [White Plains] Journal News*

12. Community Newspapers Holdings, Birmingham, Alabama—795,696 WC, 83 dailies, *The [North Andover, Mass.] Eagle-Tribune*

13. E. W. Scripps, Cincinnati, Ohio—716,669 WC, 17 dailies, *The [Memphis] Commercial Appeal*

14. A. H. Belo, Dallas, Texas—651,400 WC, 4 dailies, *The Dallas Morning News*

15. Halifax Media, Daytona Beach, Florida—609,055 WC, 23 dailies, *Sarasota Herald-Tribune*

16. Daily News Corporation, New York, New York—605,677 WC, 1 daily, *Daily News* [New York City]

17. Sun-Times Media Holdings, Chicago, Illinois—592,671 WC, 8 dailies, *Chicago Sun-Times*

18. Washington Post Company, Washington, D.C.—553,811 WC, 2 dailies, *The Washington Post*

19. Cox Media Group, Atlanta, Georgia—530,357 WC, 7 dailies, *The Atlanta Journal-Constitution*

20. Black Press, Ltd., Victoria, British Columbia—479,958 WC, 3 dailies, *The [San Francisco] Examiner*

14. Families in Distress

21. 2100 Trust LLC, New York, New York—435,618 WC, 7 dailies, *The Orange County* [Cal.] *Register*

22. Philadelphia Media Group, Philadelphia, Pennsylvania—435,291 WC, 2 dailies, *The Philadelphia Inquirer*

23. Alden Global Capital, New York, New York—433,133 WC, 20 dailies, *The Oakland Press* [Pontiac, Mich.]

24. Cablevision, Bethpage, New York—404,542 WC, 1 daily, *Newsday*, New York, New York

25. Anschutz Company, Denver, Colorado—393,244 WC, 2 dailies, *Washington* [D.C.] *Examiner*[27]

These statistics account for two out of five of the nation's dailies (573 of 1,380 papers, 41.5 percent).[28] Just 11 of the 25 American newspaper-publishing firms that reach the largest weekday circulations (above) own their biggest properties in the metropolitan districts in which they are headquartered. Meanwhile, two of the 25 owner-operators concentrate their focus on a single daily news journal.

Families in distress? Alas, almost the entire newspaper family is in distress. Encircled by grave issues that aren't about to dissipate anytime soon, a new breed of corporate executives has inherited the very troubles that flummoxed the previous owners, some of whom had demonstrated enduring linkages. After years of dedicated efforts without experiencing a lot of turnaround—and feeling their vulnerability in a depressed economic climate as they fought relentlessly against cuts that threatened to reduce the product, staff, and influence to which some dedicated their careers—they transferred titles of their prized possessions to new operators.

Assuming those publications with all their inherent ills, the successor custodians introduced yet another level of frustrations to the mix: by living great distances from the papers they bought (as so many do), they relied upon local overseers to steer their properties in ways that are often foreign to long-established practices of the past. And among the unanswered and urgent questions that remain is how they will confront the unremitting innovations that continue to be inspired by an increasing proliferation of newer technologies.

In the meantime the industry is closely watching a new breed of capitalists with deep pockets who are adding newspapers to their already-diversified portfolios. Is this a practical solution to some of the trade's perennial impasse? While ownership by billionaire corporate magnates isn't an altogether novel twist, the excitement it has engendered in the present day as a few pivotal dailies have gone that route is enough to extend hope that some saviors have joined the family. In a few cases, their buys have kept or returned a newspaper's control—for the foreseeable future at least—to the hands of one or two individuals, or a small handful. In some ways, it just may seem like the good old days are here again.

15

Falling from Grace to Disgrace

As this text has described on several occasions, some major shifting (and lifting) within the newsrooms of hundreds of American daily and weekly news journals has provoked some extraordinary consequences. One of the most immediately obvious in this period of aftermath may be seen in the staffing of the papers' nerve centers.

We have learned, for instance, that the newsrooms are now populated by conspicuously fewer editors and reporters and other writers than they were just a decade ago. Instead of using a paring knife to accomplish the job, it appears that several owner-publishers have taken an axe to trim the personnel tree. In any case, the figures who used to comprise the Fourth Estate in the majority of the nation's newspaper newsrooms have been significantly pruned back from their zeniths of only a few years back. What was at one time a vibrant faction of skilled professionals with enduring records of envied service—including the veterans as well as more recent additions who applied their creative skills to produce informative and absorbing papers, day in, day out—has been transformed into some barely recognizable remnants of a once-proud heritage.

The papers they represent may have been robust forces in their respective metropolitan centers back in the day. Maintaining a keen awareness of nearly every news generator within their potential reach, newspapers felt the pulse of the communities they represented. Alas, in many places this is no longer true. The losses of manpower (and womanpower) have left newspapers with fewer and fewer experienced, skilled journalists.

In many cities very few individuals who have been recognized for their sterling and sometimes award-winning achievements by their superiors and peers are still around. Instead the newsrooms are mainly comprised of a newer, younger crop of idealists now gathering, honing, and dispensing the details of what occurs in their communities. Also conspicuous by their absence is a delegation of long-standing, veritably priceless contacts who have traditionally linked those reporters with what is happening locally, out of the public eye. Unfortunately, the lines of communication don't necessarily extend from one occupational generation to another.

Whether the reductions in staff have been as universally drastic as that or merely professed as such, throughout the trade the faces that inhabit America's newspaper newsrooms are radically altered from only a few years ago. As many veteran journalists have departed, replacements not always given the latitudinal freedoms that their predecessors may have enjoyed are now occupying their desks. A few years ago a Pew Research Journalism Project started calling attention to the sizable transition of personnel passing through the revolving doors of urban newspapers throughout the nation:

> The culture of the daily newspaper newsroom is ... changing. New job demands are drawing a generation of young, versatile, tech-savvy, high-energy staff as financial pressures drive out higher-salaried veteran reporters and editors. Newsroom executives say the infusion of new blood has brought with it a new competitive energy, but they also cite the departure of veteran journalists, along with the talent, wisdom and institutional memory they hold as their single greatest loss. Clearly stretched to describe what is unfolding in their newsrooms, editors use words like, "exciting," "extraordinary," "nerve-wracking" and "tumultuous."
>
> ...The staff also is under greater pressure, has less institutional memory, less knowledge of the community, of how to gather news and the history of individual beats. There are fewer editors to catch mistakes.[1]

As if all of that isn't disconcerting enough to make the industry nervous, there still may be more dilemmas to be aware of. Some pundits are setting off alarms by hinting that the subordinates and possibly the successors to the assemblage currently filling the newsrooms of papers coast-to-coast may be even less well prepared for their tasks. From the standpoint of professional standards, the next generation of journalists could be lacking some of the basics that their ancestors exhibited. *The Mosaic Newspaper,* circulated by the San Jose Urban Journalism Workshop, speculated: "Newspaper journalism as a career option ... looks bleak. High school newspapers, staffed by the journalists of tomorrow, suffer from a lack of trained teachers, funds and student interest."[2] Not a good omen; a foreboding prophecy perhaps.

Although much of the upheaval experienced in the newsrooms in recent years is directly tied to the personnel changes—putting new faces into many of those facilities and reducing the number of skilled veterans needed to perform the duties—at the same juncture there has been a commensurate reduction in other areas beyond human beings. The size of the newsprint edition itself (including the physical dimensions of the pages) is often less than it was. There's been an observable decline in the number of sheets carried in each issue, too. Pew researchers in 2008 discovered that by dissecting the classically "revised" daily newspaper:

> It has fewer pages ... , the paper stock is thinner, and the stories are shorter. There is less foreign and national news, less space devoted to science, the arts, features and a range of specialized subjects. Business coverage is either packaged in an increasingly thin stand-alone section or collapsed into another part of the paper. The crossword puzzle has shrunk, the TV listings and stock tables may have disappeared, but coverage of some local issues has strengthened and investigative reporting remains highly valued.[3]

Let's face it: By and large the content of the package has been rather callously subjected to the same reductive tidal wave that has influenced the newsroom's staffing. As a consequence many times the end product is hardly recognizable when compared with the equivalent journal bearing the same moniker in earlier times. Now a shadow of those models, today's paper in the majority of American cities simply cannot come off very favorably when placed alongside its former glories. It's particularly sad that the downsizing is so pervasive, touching almost every major U.S. market.

In some places the contemporary version is bereft of what was once considered not merely as adequate reporting but coverage that exhibited something of stimulating brilliance. Cut to the bone today, the stories that finally make it into many daily news journals are purely factual now, with little room for the fluff that characteristically added some sizzle and sparkle to the basic content. A wordsmith only a few years ago had opportunities to exhibit whatever creative talents he possessed with the hope of attracting and engaging readers substantially beyond the cut-and-dried copy. While not all of this has completely disappeared, much has been eliminated to suit a modern audience's dwindling attention span.

At the same time, we know that less copy nets less space, which translates into fewer pages that finally can be reflected in hefty cost savings for a newsprint publication. It's a technique that many publishers across the country have embraced unreservedly. Devoid of some of the enticements of extraneous matters, the stories often can be quite bland in their bare-bones states. This is just another symptom of the cost-cutting binge that has swept through most U.S. newspaper newsrooms in today's environment. It's probably not going away, almost certainly not for newsprint editions.

Longtime media executive Alan Mutter lamented over what has become of America's "great newspapers" in a discourse dispatched by the Center for American Progress. That's an online blog that seeks to offer "progressive ideas for a strong, just, and free America." Those newspapers, said Mutter, have "staffs that range from 50 percent to 70 percent of what they were just a few years ago." On the cutbacks that have become commonplace at today's journals, he warned: "Newspapers are not investing in developing the products and services that would enable them to compete with the growing number of digital competitors lusting after local advertising dollars. The result is further deterioration in the value of these properties, even beyond the absolutely alarming deterioration we have already seen."[4]

In 2008, American daily newspapers shed 5,900 newsroom jobs, reducing the employment of journalists by 11.3 percent to the levels of the early 1980s, the American Society of News Editors (ASNE) reported.[5] By the start of 2010, some 22 percent of U.S. dailies' newsroom jobs (12,900 positions) had vanished since the industry's newsroom occupational peak experienced in 2001, when 56,900 posts established an all-time high. "Disproportionately, the older, the more experienced (and most highly paid) staff is targeted for buyouts and layoffs," an analyst correctly surmised.[6]

In 2012, ASNE announced that the trend toward trimming the staff was still flourishing even at reduced levels. A decline of 6.4 percent of full-time professional editorial jobs at U.S. news journals in that year witnessed the deletion of 2,600 more individuals from the payrolls. "That leaves the industry at 38,000 full-time professional editorial employees and is the first time that figure has been below 40,000 since the census began in 1978," according to the Pew Research Center.[7] Thus in the first 11 years of the current millennium (2001–2012), U.S. newspaper newsrooms lost 18,900 reportorial and editorial posts (56,900 minus 38,000, about 33 percent). That period of time has been anything but their finest hour.

"In addition to the [dwindling] number of reporters and copy editors," writes Philip Meyer in his little book *The Vanishing Newspaper,* "the competence of those people is bound to make a difference." How solid are the replacements? How much experience do they have? How reliable is their reporting? How are they at self-starting? How knowledgeable? How determined? How extensive is their contact network? "A newspaper that is understaffed," Meyer indicates, will be "more susceptible" to making errors "and the relative pain that different kinds of errors cause."[8]

Certainly this is so when compared with those publications employing a sufficient quota of proficient journalists who are familiar with their surroundings and its history and who have wide-ranging local links for ferreting out reliable details. Competency is yet another dimension of the staffing issue that publishers need to be cognizant of as long-tested journalists go out the door the last time. Meyer's own research and conclusions offer a fascinating study of how accuracy in reporting is quite often significantly improved when the staffing number and proficiency levels are boosted.[9]

In legions of places the shortcuts that publishers have taken have left their patrons unambiguously shortchanged. Media industry analyst Ken Doctor came up with a formula for predicting about how many newspaper stories in the nation that could be projected for publication are simply not being pursued. This includes those never written and therefore never read. His system is derived by the deletion of professional writing positions accompanied by the diminished print space as well as a perceived lack of editorial commitment for providing sufficient local coverage.

Based solely on the cutbacks of recent years in the writing staff at daily newspapers across the nation, Doctor ascertained that no fewer than 828,000 creditable stories per year are currently missing in action.[10] It's a sad state of affairs. The only unequivocal winners are the newspaper owners plus the upper management levels and the investors who perhaps should be sporting badges of shame. Some of these have tarnished the tradition and public perception of a formerly highly respectable occupation.

The fall from grace to disgrace has had profound implications for the newsrooms where most of the copy is originating. Doubtlessly the inception of the Internet has figured prominently in what has transpired in the newsprint newsrooms of America. It's possible that the Internet may also be cited as a principal catalyst in triggering the prevailing attitude in some quarters of "less product—more profit."

Several times I have noted that the replacement of costly production and distribution systems with newer online technologies has allowed the publishing trade to bank outsized bundles of cash. Could it be that the resulting bounty has contributed in mounting even greater stimulation for amplifying the profitability factor? It might be accomplished through still greater retrenchment perhaps. Although such a connection might be rather simple to demonstrate, almost invariably wherever it has been introduced has been at the peril of the news product, the staff, and ultimately the readership audience. Unwavering determination to cut costs at all costs may be paying off for owners and investors, but at what cost to the people for whom the entire operation is ostensibly in business to placate?

A great many of the traditional newspaper journalists of America whose permanent source of livelihood has been bound up in the newsprint model have viewed the shift from paper to pixels in one of two ways. According to the *Los Angeles Times'* Leah Gentry, those practitioners believed that the popularity of the Internet might be contemplated "as either the downfall of the free press or the heaven-sent salvation of a dying medium."[11] But which one, if either, will prevail? And which one is to have the most pronounced effects on the journalists' faltering careers, in which so many of their jobs still seem to be hanging in the balance?

How will the newsrooms cope in this environment should the current philosophy persist in the future, particularly if newspapers move toward greater or possibly total digital status? No one can answer for sure. While awaiting the outcome, nevertheless, thousands of accredited journalists with durable tenures are vacating the premises. As these

15. Falling from Grace to Disgrace

reporters and editors turn their backs on their profession, by choice or for other reasons, millions of news readers in cities large and small are being disenfranchised—denied all the news that's fit to print.

It's a circumstance in which there are few winners and a profusion of losers.

16

Connecting in a Multimedia Epoch

Up until now our attention has been riveted almost exclusively to the news journals circulated in diverse platforms on daily, weekly, or still other mixed-calendar timetables. Of course all of us realize that the momentum of the digital innovation embraces much more than solitary disciplines operating independently of one another. The next two chapters purport to shift my examination from focusing almost altogether on news journals. Now I will include some additional media that also have been aggressively predisposed by cyberspace's advancing intrusion into larger and larger dominions of our lives. Freed of whatever shackles had been imposed by analog systems, complete with their peculiarities and limitations, print and broadcast media are thriving in an age in which their mutual expressions have become at times effectively seamless. To many users of newer technologies they have become more satisfying, too.

As a result of this leap into a multimedia phase, one intellect, academician John Pavlik, asserted: "All modalities of human communication are available for telling stories in the most compelling, interactive, on-demand, and customized fashion."[1] Noting the constraints of newsroom traditions, training, and economics that bear on the outcome of those coordinated efforts, nevertheless Pavlik ascertained that the news product can be enhanced by the technology factor that is bringing those pursuits together.

Communications in contemporary times come with a factor not witnessed by previous generations as obviously as it can be now: what occurs in one order frequently and appreciably impacts the others. The escalating interconnectedness creates a symbiosis never previously beheld to the extent we are experiencing such fusions today. Particularly

16. Connecting in a Multimedia Epoch

is this true with the unparalleled qualities and opportunities that arise out of the phenomenon of the Internet. It seems only natural nowadays that what is transpiring over here often has some peculiar bearing on what is developing over there.

This is a far cry from the early perception of multimedia's exploitation by the unassailable "father of broadcast journalism," Edward R. Murrow (1908–1965). During the incubatory days of TV news, that eminent reporter expressed the very antithesis of what he himself would eventually come to embrace. In a piece written for *The New York Times* in February 1949, which was never published, incidentally, Murrow disclosed: "I cannot see that television news will become more than a supplement to the daily newspaper." (*Times* broadcasting critic Jack Gould told Murrow the paper could not use the article without some extra detail, which wasn't furnished.)[2] Murrow would soon preside over a couple of early video's most riveting and provocative news features—*See It Now* and *Person to Person*. And it wouldn't be long before the sage of electronic journalists acknowledged that there was room for a surfeit of media to disseminate their wares on a fairly uniform plain in propagating current events, even if he did so somewhat halfheartedly.

Gathering manifold media under a single corporate umbrella is nothing new to us in the present age, of course. Yet there is nevertheless mounting evidence that the traditional lines that have distinguished the disparate modes of communications from one another have grown hazy over the passing years. For instance, audiences today habitually receive the output of countless originators on one and the same platform. This unification of their multifaceted expressions has become an absolutely unequivocal media trademark in our time.

What's a good interpretation or characterization of *multimedia* anyway? A contemporary analyst of the trade, Ken Doctor, offered this interpretation:

> It's a media circus centered on multiplatform (print, TV, radio, Web) and cross promotion. It's an endless 24/7 game that is always being played or planned. The currency: building the brand awareness, bringing more people—audience—to your shop rather than the other guy's. The more audience, the more advertising you can sell, and that pays the bills.
>
> The Internet has proven to be the great meeting ground for … big news companies.[3]

Newspapers in Transition

In the opening years of the present millennium a couple of eyewitnesses to the powerful adaptations occurring among the nation's divergent communications systems expressed their views from a nifty vantage point in the nation's capital. Leonard Downie, Jr. and Robert Kaiser, whose professional lives interlocked at *The Washington Post* as they rose through the ranks from reporters to executives, proclaimed quite early: "The greatest potential of the Internet may be its capacity to combine many of the advantages of television, radio and newspapers in ways that *could* make it much more powerful than all three."[4]

The presumption of the integrated communications has been, of course, a genuine reality for several years. Those visionaries were plainly on to something at the time they advocated it, however. In a discourse on the shift to unification of the trade's inducements the pair of scribes contributed a few opinions that allow for some deeper insights into an innovative development that has taken the media by storm in plenty of localities in the intervening time:

> This is a time of experimentation for all news media as they try to adapt to revolutionary new technology. Newspapers, magazines and television networks and stations repackage their news daily on their Internet sites. Some newspapers and newsmagazines cooperate on news coverage with television networks, and put some of their reporters and editors on network news shows to talk about their stories.... These arrangements have given new exposure on television to print reporters, their publications and their Web sites.
>
> Some newspapers and local television stations are working together on news stories.... Many newspapers have put video cameras and fully equipped television studios into their newsrooms to make it easier for their reporters to appear on television or to tape video reports for the newspapers' Web sites.
>
> Collaborations like these exemplify an industry catchword, *synergy* that implies the combining of old and new media resources and technologies to create something bigger and better and more profitable than the component parts....
>
> Reporters at large newspapers with active Internet news sites and radio and television relationships can produce news for four different media in the same day...
>
> ...
>
> With a few exceptions, attempts at synergy have produced relatively little additional original or improved journalism or new revenue. They mostly have "repurposed" (another news term) journalism already being produced by one news medium for use by another. In practice, this usually has meant

repackaging newspaper journalism on television and the Internet, because newspapers continue to have ... the largest and most talented news-gathering staffs.[5]

The powerful stimulus that has taken place in multiple media has helped us to view communications truly as a cohesive endeavor. This is in opposition to one that is distracted and possibly fractured by the spirited and sometimes combative rivalries that frequently prevailed in times past. An accommodation mixing flexibility, stamina, and resiliency may yet win the day. Such cooperative efforts likely will succeed as whatever gaps separating the various media continue to narrow. The alliance of forces of varying persuasions is of benefit to the clients (or, in fact, the general public) of sometimes vastly differing persuasions. And doubtlessly, that cohesiveness can be a good thing.

A historian recounted the inimitable "days of yesteryear" when the various media competed not only with one another but also with themselves. Turning back the clock a half century, writer James O'Shea reminds us that Americans then had, for example, a trio of selections for news on evening network television—CBS' Walter Cronkite, NBC's Chet Huntley and David Brinkley, and ABC's Frank Reynolds. But once cable television emerged a striking change occurred in how some of those newly minted video addicts spent their time in front of the tube: "Suddenly, viewers could watch *I Love Lucy* reruns instead of tuning in to Cronkite," said O'Shea.

As cable subscribers soared, newspaper circulation declined. From a 1980s high, within three decades the network news audiences shrank by half of those earlier crests. O'Shea continued: "News literacy declined sharply among less educated Americans as they opted for the *I Love Lucy* reruns, while the educated class watched even more news as cable news shows proliferated."[6] It was a leading example of how a derivative (cable) of a medium (TV) that hadn't impacted very many citizens only a few years before was now subtracting not only from the original supplier but from another provider as well. In this case both broadcast television and news journals were harshly affected by the onset of cable television.

There are many other examples that could be given of the dogfights that the sundry media engaged in prior to the emergence of the World Wide Web.

In its transformative leap from paper to pixel, meanwhile, the magazine sector of print media merits pronounced scrutiny for the absolutely distinctive role it fills within the communications panorama. Sometimes considered the reverse side of the coin by which newspapers maintain their perceived sovereignty, magazines are often inadvertently overlooked in the pundits' haste to credit the Fourth Estate (democracy's watchdog journalists who ferret out the details that inform constituencies about how their governments are faring). Nevertheless, these often glossy, high-resolution, image-filled slicks serve their readers by providing educational and entertaining coverage of multidimensional topics. The explorative journey of the territory occupied by the magazines—revealing how they are responding in an era that is gaining momentum almost weekly in the shift from hard copies to electronic incarnations—will be addressed more comprehensively in the succeeding chapter.

On March 13, 1938, Ed Murrow and some of his radio cohorts introduced a wholly innovative programming device that is still being pursued by the *CBS World News Roundup* in contemporary America. Until its inception, a single reader usually sat ensconced before a microphone in a small studio in New York. Listeners were presented with the current headline-making "news of the world" emanating from that rather nondescript and insignificant venue. It wasn't very impressive, but it was a start.

The hypothesis employed by Murrow and company nevertheless engaged a deputation of reputable correspondents (often with newspaper training) stationed in a handful of far-flung locales around the globe. Each of the broadcast journalists added pertinent details to a collaborative effort with on-the-scene reporting of world affairs in solo newscasts. Their model has been preserved for generations and has even more relevance today in both audio and visual embodiments on the ether. "The *Roundup* format of an anchor calling upon correspondents in the field to report and analyze the news is a legacy felt during every news program today," confirms *USA Today*'s Michael Antonoff. "Except for shorter segments and a faster pace, the program has pretty much maintained the same format over the years."[7]

Murrow and his sidekicks instituted the diversified electronic method of gathering and disseminating the news while unknowingly setting the stage for still greater applications ahead. From little acorns mighty oaks do grow, however. Although the pioneers' experiences were, in a sense, a far cry from the realities associated with the digital technologies of the present, their works contributed significantly to the mixture that was to bubble over into proliferating facets of radio news coverage followed by television, satellite, cable, and finally the Internet. There it was to reach a pinnacle (so far) with the advancements of social media and other cybersonic concoctions. Making use of the World Wide Web, news programmers began to transmit the collective input of multiple users who became something akin to "civilian reporters," adapters, and reactors to the current events of history.

At this writing the *CBS World News Roundup* that celebrated its 75th anniversary on radio in 2013 is still rolling along every single day. Only now many listeners who tune in to its pithy presentations do so by applying a wide variety of devices, gadgets, gizmos, tools, apparatus, doodads, and doohickeys that would bewilder the imagination of—and be totally unrecognizable to—the venerated Murrow and his practiced contingent, were they to suddenly reappear on the scene.

It's not your father's radio anymore, for it's not the crystal sets, floor consoles, table models, and portable transistors that were standard issue long ago. Back then those appliances engaged millions of Americans who were largely dependent upon them for news, information, and amusement beyond their own homes. Radio offered people something that initially punctured the atmosphere as a novelty but later evolved into a resource that transformed, connected, and cemented a whole country. Virtually everybody was given the power to tune in to the same substance at the very same moment—the first time they had ever been able to do that. For a few decades anyway, radio was our sole instant unifying communications system. And it was to prompt advancements into further electronic explorations that rendered the multiplicity of expansive media available today.

Perhaps surprisingly to many, following a survey of competitive news sources that was conducted in 2012 by Fairleigh Dickinson University (FDU) of New Jersey, a coast-to-coast radio hookup had produced the "most informed" American citizens.[8] This presumably supersedes *The New York Times, USA Today, The Wall Street Journal,* plus all other TV and radio broadcasts and the Web as originating sources. For anyone who isn't a regular in the aural-only audience the results of that study may be astonishing. According to FDU's research, the commercial-free National Public Radio (NPR) system is the country's leading informant, topping all other models and methods of news dissemination to the nation's people. The Web, of course, is a crucial aid in the spread of NPR's programming.

Television, meanwhile, is applying an expansive dimension of platforms, too. Nowadays video is readily seen well beyond the confines of the flat screen on the wall, or the portable box on the bureau dresser, kitchen counter or table, or the stationary console model occupying a prominent spot on the family-room floor. The modern replica may have been launched by a leap to PCs and laptops, but the contemporary access has been enlarged to reach a plethora of gadgets and gizmos that have reduced the proverbial "small screen" to mere "pocket size" in some cases. The Diffusion Group is projecting that by 2020 nearly half (49 percent) of this country's TV viewers will be nursing their watching habits on PCs, tablets, smartphones, smart TVs, and streaming devices of manifold types.[9]

Making television transportable has been akin to radio's similarly phenomenal leap in the 1950s from wire-tethered boxes to unencumbered portable transistors. Television is today a mobile form of communications, turning heads just the way its broadcast predecessor did six decades ago in the transition to those transistors. Parenthetically, at the same time 32 million American domiciles had been equipped by 2013 with an ability to secure video over TV sets by using Internet applications. This observation by Forrester Research signifies a rapidly escalating trend in the interactivity linking the various systems.[10]

Nonetheless, even TV's relevance may be perishing in the wake of increasing technological developments, so some media critics hint. Those pundits underscore the fact that viewers are distancing themselves from their stationary sets. In a phenomenon known as "cord cutting," growing numbers of Americans have unplugged from giant cable operators to watch television over the Internet. It's much the same as the preceding transition from telephone lines to cell phones. As patrons kick their landlines out, they cozy up to cell phones to establish tighter loyalties by relying on them as their sole telephone gear. With television, viewers are subsequently obtaining what they want online and without spending a fortune to do it every month—sometimes costing them nothing extra in fact. The big losers here, temporarily at least, appear to be the cable and satellite operators.

"It signals the biggest change in media consumption since the Internet began killing newspapers over a decade ago," said *Time* analyst Rana Foroohar. "Television is now being disintermediated by the Web, just as print was. The transition has taken longer; television was starting from a bigger, richer base. But now that the technology is maturing, the shift will speed up."[11]

To say that the news won't be hand-delivered in the future (the key idiom here is *hand-delivered*)—at least on television—would be an altogether inappropriate conjecture. Many Americans are still receiving the news in their hands today, even as the newsprint journals fold, or are reduced in size and delivery, or diminish in relevance. And as the shift to screens becomes pervasively dominant on the nation's horizon, more and more news junkies no longer will traipse to the front porch, or the driveway, or the box to retrieve their news. They'll be applying an old but clever adage instead: "Let your fingers do the walking." It seems that digital can have more than one interpretation.

17

Digital Mags: Feel the Magic?

John Paul Titlow is a Philadelphia technology journalist whose occasional treatises are engaged in digital music, television's future, the trends in emerging media, the iOS mobile operating system, and copyright disagreements. He's also a journalism instructor at his alma mater, Temple University. On January 24, 2013, Titlow affirmed to fanciers of the Internet's *readwrite* blog, "On the whole, digital magazines have a long way to go."

He admonished: "As magazines make the transition from print to pixels, some publishers are using the move as an opportunity to jack up their prices for second-rate products." In some cases, rates for digital magazines are increasing beyond what they were for print copies, Titlow warily noted. "And that's for tablet versions that are too often crappy afterthoughts," he elucidated still more:

> There are some problems with driving up prices too much, though.
>
> For one, everyone knows it's cheaper to distribute content digitally than to print it and mail it. Asking buyers to pay more for something that costs you less to deliver is the kind of tactic that makes many subscribers feel exploited. It's a head-scratcher, if not a subscription-canceler. Sure, magazine makers may still be coping with meaty legacy cost structures. But that's not our problem, is it?
>
> There's also much more competition. Long gone are the days when magazines competed only with each other. Today, the entire Internet churns out content at a volume too great for any one human to keep up with—and it's all instantly available at any time....
>
> Still, some magazines have done pretty well with their digital editions, especially when they bundle them with print. In the United States, tablet publications are the second highest-grossing category of apps on iOS.... Time and Condé Nast are selling the most digital mags, with news and women's interest magazines dominating those sales.

17. Digital Mags: Feel the Magic?

Half of *Wired's* revenue now comes from digital, which is a rare but promising milestone for a legacy publisher.

On the other hand, Titlow reminds his audience that readers can arrive at a point at which the digital product is simply no longer worth its asking price. Instead of raising rates to help them recover from dwindling circulations, he's persuaded that "folks who want to remain in the publishing business need to figure out a hybrid model that works."

Titlow also warned: "The business model isn't the only issue here. Just as important is the consensus that most digital magazines just aren't very good." Too often, he declared, "subscribing to a magazine on your tablet means downloading a bloated, glorified PDF that hardly delivers the potentially magical experience the form factor allows."[1]

The *magical experience* the form factor allows.

Have you felt the rush gained by reading your favorite glossy-print periodical on a tablet or other mobile device, or even on a laptop or PC?[2] Millions have sampled that innovation already and some are singing its praises as members of the choir. Their numbers are relatively small thus far (in mid-2013). Especially is this true when their figures are compared with those of their rag-based ancestry. Yet, just as is the case for newspapers, a tendency for magazines to become more and more accommodating of pixels is predictable.

For some foremost icons of the trade that have shifted in that direction already—and have wholeheartedly embraced the digital experience (the most notable example may be *Newsweek*, the first national news magazine to go digital-only[3])—there can be little thought of turning back. With a trend that is quite clearly here to stay and an army of zealous stalwarts marching together in lockstep, unfurling the anointed innovation's banner as they strut, they make an impressive sight. The transfer from coated stock to electronic embodiment is an application whose time is approaching so rapidly that in at least some quarters it is already here.

Nevertheless, writer-designer-publisher Craig Mod, with provocative thought pieces turning up in venerated forums such as NYTimes.com, *New Scientist, Contents Magazine,* and *Codex Journal of Typography,* lamented over an element of the transition from paper to pixel that seems at least to him to be foreboding. Speaking for a specific sector of the digital era's magazine readership, he regrets a phase of the experience that is carrying readers into a never-never land without any of the accustomed or traditional corporeal limitations we've always taken for granted:

> Forget everything we know and love about physical magazines. Forget their length. Forget their size. Forget their weekly or monthly publishing schedule. Forget all these qualities except for one: What it's like to come to an end, and to take a deep breath.
> Like *Newsweek,* almost all magazines will eventually go purely electronic. This shouldn't surprise anyone. Already, nearly 40 percent of tablet owners read digital newspapers or magazines, with nearly 10 percent doing so daily. Still, as I watch this shift, I can't help but feel a twinge of nostalgia. Not for the paper, but for the boundaries.
> I miss the edges—physical and psychological. I miss the start of reading a print magazine, but mostly, I miss the finish. I miss the satisfaction of putting the bundle down, knowing that I have gotten through it all. Nothing left. On to the next thing.
> ...
> While a stack of printed back issues of National Geographic may seem intimidating, it is not unapproachable. The magazines may be dense, but you know where you stand as you read them. But what about staring at an empty search box leading into the deep archive of nationalgeographic.com?
> Petrifying. Boundless. Like standing on the edge of a giant reservoir in the dead of the night, looking down into its infinite blackness. Link after related link keeps pushing you along....
> Magazine websites, like the World Wide Web itself, open one up to continuous exploration through links and related content. There's beauty in that, if one is up for total immersion. But it's easier to become overwhelmed, or lost.
> ...
> As more of our content consumption shifts digital, the onus lies on tablet and smartphone applications to find a way to create cleaner and more bite-sized forms of boundaries in a medium that doesn't want to be contained.
> ...We're losing the paper, the touch and the romanticism of the printed object. But hopefully, we'll find a way to create new edges.[4]

Blogger Susan Currie Sivek (sivekmedia.com), magazine correspondent for *MediaShift* and assistant professor of mass communication at McMinnville, Oregon's Linfield College, raises still another concern about the conversion from paper to pixel. While acquiring a tablet may be a relatively easy exercise for many patrons, she's convinced that pursuing the actual ability to transfer a print subscription to one that's digital can furnish the real rub. It often leaves its victims in frustration and

17. Digital Mags: Feel the Magic?

angst, Sivek hints. It's a dilemma you may not have considered before being there and doing that:

> Buying that new iPad, Kindle or Nook ... is just the first step in becoming a digital magazine reader. While shopping for books and movies is a fairly straightforward process, getting your favorite magazines onto your new e-mailing device can be trickier.
>
> ...
>
> It's helpful to know when your print magazine subscriptions expire if you really want to switch fully to digital-only subscriptions. If you have only one or two print issues left, you might want to wait until the print subscription ends to sign up for a new digital-only subscription.... The reason ... is that the "midstream" print-to-digital subscription switch is challenging for publishers right now. Some magazines can immediately convert your subscription to digital and stop your print issues from arriving in the mail; some can't.
>
> ...
>
> For now, don't count on being able to immediately go all-digital for your existing magazine subscriptions. Depending on the magazine's policies, you may be better off waiting until the end of an existing print subscription, or may have to continue the print subscription to get digital access.[5]

Sivek has highlighted an aspect of a complex issue that most of us probably never really considered. As time elapses, whatever stumbling blocks in making the conversions may exist, we can have little doubt that skilled intellects will find one or more satisfying methods around them. By the time you read this, of course, such matters could be non-issues already. In and of itself, this one is not an earth-shattering contemplation. But it testifies to the growing evolution of digital's machinations and the baggage that surfaces with it. The industry must, can, and will figure out ways to accomplish what appear to outsiders to be relatively simple solutions to complicated tasks. This case implies that solving problems is a constant by-product of expanding innovative technologies.

Leaving that topic, the testimonial of magazine editor Stephen Shepard will be illuminating for some. During the early applications of digital technologies with a weekly periodical, he discovered a few overtly paradoxical differences:

> The rise of the World Wide Web ... posed colossal challenges for the news media. As did everyone else, we saw opportunity. Delivering the magazine via the Internet would slash our biggest expenses—printing, paper, and postage—the so-called three Ps of magazine publishing. Readers would ben-

efit from instant delivery, timely updates, and the opportunity to participate in two-way conversations.... And advertisers could target their messages to specific groups of readers.

In 1994, we jumped into these uncharted waters by signing a deal with AOL to publish *BusinessWeek Online*. We dedicated a few staffers ... to ... "putting it up" every week, and we soon began updating the stories and adding new pieces done by the existing editorial staff....

As the web caught on ... we switched to our own Internet edition. Soon, about 1.1 million people had registered to receive *BusinessWeek Online*, and 70 percent of them were not subscribers to the print edition. Why were they coming to a site called *BusinessWeek* if they weren't coming to a magazine called *Business Week*? It turned out that most ... were surfers—usually people directed to us by search engines to read a particular story. They came, they read, they moved on....

The disadvantages were now obvious. There was no apparent way to make much money.... We didn't charge readers for the magazine online, following the conventional wisdom of the time....

...But we were in the game, gaining experience and learning as we went.[6]

Other early adopters were encountering similar revelations that automatically coincided with the advancements promulgated by cyberspace.

Having introduced the topics of both magazines and multiplatforms, let us concentrate on these enlightening and entertaining periodicals further, perhaps discerning a more comprehensive assessment of the territory. As a principal player in print media—sometimes considered the reverse side of the coin to newspapers—magazines are sometimes inadvertently overlooked in the industry's haste to credit the Fourth Estate (again, democracy's watchdog journalists who ferret out the details of informing constituencies how their governments operate). Frequently left in the dust, these often glossy, high-resolution image-illustrated slicks nevertheless fill strategic functions in keeping their readers aware. They cover a wide assortment of subjects extending into the most infinitesimally narrowly defined sectors. If there's an interest, there's often a periodical.

Long before there was a Web with a multiplicity of specialized attractions there were magazines appealing to the curiosities of readers in incalculable persuasions. Although their circulation—certainly of their paper-and-ink editions—may have diminished somewhat since the inception of the Internet, magazines and similar periodicals still

17. Digital Mags: Feel the Magic?

supply an insuperable source to their clientele. For the foreseeable future many of the most popular of their number will persist.

A grand total of 406 consumer magazines in the United States were measured by the Alliance for Audited Media (AAM)—formerly known as the Audit Bureau of Circulations—in 2012. Of that aggregate 91 percent of their circulation consisted of paid subscriptions.[7] (The remainder was presumably provided by single-copy sales through retail vendors.) Late that year the AAM named the following publications as the leaders of the national pack in circulation (with their publishers in parentheses). The top 25 are:

1. *AARP The Magazine*—22,721,661 (AARP)
2. *AARP Bulletin*—22,403,427 (AARP)
3. *Game Informer*—7,864,326 (GameStop)
4. *Better Homes & Gardens*—7,621,456 (Meredith)
5. *Reader's Digest*—5,527,183 (Reader's Digest Association)
6. *Good Housekeeping*—4,354,740 (Hearst)
7. *Family Circle*—4,143,942 (Meredith)
8. *National Geographic*—4,125,152 (National Geographic Society)
9. *People*—3,637,633 (Time Warner)
10. *Woman's Day*—3,374,479 (Hearst)
11. *Time*—3,281,175 (Time Warner)
12. *Taste of Home*—3,268,549 (Reader's Digest Association)
13. *Ladies' Home Journal*—3,230,450 (Meredith)
14. *Sports Illustrated*—3,174,888 (Time Warner)
15. *Cosmopolitan*—3,023,884 (Hearst)
16. *Prevention*—2,921,618 (Rodale)
17. *Southern Living*—2,867,235 (Time Warner)
18. *Maxim*—2,543,563 (Alpha Media Group)
19. *AAA Living*—2,455,280 (American Automobile Association)
20. *O, The Oprah Magazine*—2,439,747 (Hearst)
21. *Glamour*—2,324,170 (Advance Publications)
22. *The American Legion Magazine*—2,268,015 (American Legion)
23. *Parenting*—2,232,707 (Bonnier)
24. *Redbook*—2,214,603 (Hearst)
25. *ESPN The Magazine*—2,142,937 (ESPN)

In the Alliance for Audited Media tabulation for late 2012, of the magazines included in a top 100 ranking by circulation seven publishers accounted for three or more entries within that coveted group, in this order: Time Warner, 17; Hearst, 14; Advance Publications, 12; Meredith, 12; Reader's Digest Association, 6; Bonnier, 3; and Rodale, 3. The remainder earned dual or single spots. Several of the enterprises represented in the top 100 registered by the AAM are linked with other media, including newspapers, broadcast and cable television, radio, and the Web.

In early March 2013, Time Warner acknowledged that its magazine unit—then operating as a subsidiary under the name Time Inc.—had become more of a drag on its bottom line than it wished to feed.[8] Time's first-quarter earnings that year fell 5 percent (to $737 million) with circulation revenue dipping 11 percent in the same period. Time Inc. had begun 2013 by terminating 6 percent of its global staff, some 500 employees.[9] Thus that portion of the "awesome giant" (according to the *Los Angeles Times*) that was derived in 1990 by pooling Time's powerful portfolio of slicks with the entertainment colossus Warner Communications had lost its gloss by 2013.[10] Time Warner said it planned to spin off the periodicals to allow the multinational to focus on more profitable film and TV ventures.

In the wake of that action one mystic, *USA Today*'s Rem Rieder, expressed a detectable trace of disappointment: "The golden era of soaring profits that came to a halt when the recession arrived in 2008 isn't coming back," said he. "And while the advent of the tablet seems to offer promise for magazines, progress has been slow. But many magazines still make money. Nearly 200 titles [were] launched last year," mused Rieder.

The University of Mississippi's Samir Husni, nicknamed Mr. Magazine by cohorts and founder-director of that institute's Magazine Innovation Center, expressed still deeper regrets in Time Warner's decision. He termed it "a consequence of having business people with no regard for magazines running a company that was launched by a visionary journalist." The reference was to pioneer publisher Henry Luce (1898–1967), who helped in launching *Time* in 1923, establishing a peerless model for today's newsmagazines.

Rieder noted that Time Warner already had spun off AOL, Time Warner Cable, and Warner Music into stand-alone businesses in order to concentrate on more lucrative prizes in its portfolio. In addition, he named a few more of the trade's corporate giants that were downsizing to improve their bottom lines, suggesting that less sometimes supplies more, at least in principal:

> All that spinning reflects a major shift in the media business. No longer does bigger seem better. Companies are focusing on what's most profitable and what they do best. News Corp. is creating a separate company for its newspapers, which are far less lucrative than its film and TV holdings. The New York Times Co. has shed (or is trying to shed) virtually all of its other holdings to concentrate on the core product.[11]

In the modern era some of the onetime goliaths of the industry with pervasive offshoots extending to a multiplicity of media have refocused their operations on segments that furnish the largest financial gain. In some quarters magazines aren't supplying their keep and are being abandoned by their keepers. Presiding over a collection in the Mississippi magazine repository that exceeds 28,000 first editions, Samir Husni expressed his strong dismay upon learning of Time Warner's intents.

He feared the spin-off would induce a breakup of an impressive array of periodicals as a unit (including *Entertainment Weekly, Essence, Fortune, Golf Magazine, Health, Money, People, Southern Living, Sports Illustrated, Time,* and more). That, said Husni, could result in "vultures from all over the place that will pick off the magazines piece by piece."[12] (At press time, final decisions were hanging in the balance.)

One of the precarious uncertainties impinging upon the bottom lines of whatever is being delivered by the U.S. Postal Service is the rising costs linked to mailing. Coupled with this is a sender's (in this specific case, magazine publisher's) inability to do very much about it, particularly with a paper-and-ink construct. Of course this expenditure is greatly diminished and actually may be eliminated in point of purchase sales at newsstands and retail outlets. But at least until contemporary times, to reach most subscribers magazines had to charge subscribers enough to foot the bill for delivery to individual addresses. At times that has become an economic behemoth sapping dwindling revenues generated mostly by advertising and circulation.

One big thing worth noting that remains in magazines' favor, however, actually pertains to their distribution expense. Over the long run, it's almost always less costly to deliver something to a physical address weekly or monthly as opposed to daily. It's a formula—as we've already seen—that even some of the major newspaper chains have begun to emulate.

When the Postal Service announced in early February 2013 that it would eliminate Saturday mail deliveries later that year (an order it would later rescind), the magazine-publishing coterie was among the first to rise up in protest. Steven Kotok, president of *The Week,* proclaimed that his periodical was explicitly designed to be "a weekend read" reflecting a leisurely lifestyle between workweeks for many subscribers. Delivered to the bulk of its circulation on Saturday, *The Week* could lose its momentum, Kotok said, if its arrival in homes was delayed.[13]

The official announcement of the cutback prompted newspaper wordsmith Rick Hampson to wax both nostalgically and realistically as he mused over the revolutionary changes the decision would bring to the industry:

> The news … that Saturday mail delivery will end … revealed a generation gap between those of a certain age—some of whom can even recall twice-daily delivery—and those who read any mail worth reading on their phone….
>
> …
>
> It's hard to exaggerate how irrelevant the mail—on Saturday or any other day—is to the life of many people younger than 40….
>
> …
>
> To older generations, the mail means something else, and the end of Saturday delivery is one of many bewildering and disturbing cultural changes afoot….
>
> …
>
> For every hipster with an e-mail app on his smartphone striding through Brooklyn with the future on his side, there's a grandmother out in the suburbs sitting in the front room, looking out the window, waiting for her letter carrier….
>
> …
>
> …Once there was nothing anywhere like the U.S. Mail.
>
> It helped pioneer long-distance stagecoach, rail and air travel. Its couriers were stayed by "neither snow nor rain nor heat nor gloom of night"—words borrowed from Herodotus and chiseled in stone over the great colonnade of the Farley Post Office in New York City.
>
> The Postal Service still delivers 40 percent of the world's mail, and is the physical representation of federal authority from Post Office Square in Boston to the end of the long, bumpy road to the Maui village of Hana.

17. Digital Mags: Feel the Magic?

...
> Now, the end of Saturday delivery may be the greatest single retreat yet from the level of postal service to which generations of Americans became accustomed.[14]

Despite earlier disclosures by the Postal Service that it intended to end Saturday deliveries, the declaration that it was truly going to do so seemed to catch many of their fellow men and women by surprise. Although a subsequent communication proclaimed that the start date had been delayed, nonetheless its impending implementation sent shockwaves throughout the country. Mass volume mailers, including magazine publishers, scrambled to assess long-term financial effects of that decision:

> Like the Postal Service, the industries that rely on traditional mail delivery—newspaper publishers, ad mailers, bill-payment processors—have made digital investments.
>
> But the steady revenue streams that come from the print mail model have been difficult to abandon even as they shrink each year. And the cutback in mail delivery is another stark reminder that the digital transformation continues unabated and that difficult choices lie ahead for the slowly dwindling number of companies that rely on physical delivery of products.[15]

Outspoken reactions to USPS' decision also surfaced from the National Newspaper Association representing small community news journals that either publish Saturday editions or mail ad packets on that day. They would have to find other delivery contractors—probably a difficult task in smaller towns—or upset advertisers by ending Saturday editions that typically snag higher ad rates, according to Max Heath, head of the association's postal committee. This is particularly hard for undersized newspaper publishers, Heath said, for many have returned to mail in recent years due to higher gasoline rates driving up the cost of home delivery contractors: "Some will move to home delivery even if they don't want to."[16]

While that may work for some newspapers, it doesn't solve the dilemma faced by many magazine publishers, should the USPS declaration go into effect. (As this is written it has not.) The action reflects a commercial enterprise in a state of flux, surrounded by pressures that persist in squeezing the bottom line.

All of the aforementioned notwithstanding, "the most expensive single thing" in producing a magazine such as *Time,* affirmed its managing editor, Richard Stengel, is "to chop down trees and put ink on paper and then put it on a truck and deliver it to your house." Yet publishers retain their "anchor product" to create a halo-effect "for the rest of the brand," according to *Advertising Age*'s digital editor, Michael Learmonth. He adds: "Print will no longer be the main profit driver of anybody's media empire, but it can remain a pretty prestigious calling card."[17]

For *Newsweek* to survive with a digital, subscription-based version only, Learmonth noted, content will have to be "good enough" that news junkies will select it over a profuse range of readily accessible content they can find for free. "It is very tough to compete with 'free' if your product is not significantly better," said he, "and your audience decides on what's better."

So drop the paper manifestation altogether? It doesn't sound like it, at least not immediately so, and certainly not for *Time* anyway. In Stengel's estimate, his company's namesake publication is "the centerpiece of the brand" currently available on "every platform." For now, at least, the multiplicity of formats seems to be working favorably.

The defining subscription sales for newsmagazines are still derived from their print embodiments. Only a diminutive fraction of their circulation totals are generated by digital replicas. Digital replicas—essentially reproducing the editorial and advertising content of the print edition—account for only 1.7 percent of all magazines' circulation, according to Hearst's Condé Nast unit. That's up from less than one percent in a year.[18] In the second half of 2012, that source identified the top 15 U.S. magazines with digital replicas by their circulation sales figures (with publishers' names in parentheses) as follows:

1. *Game Informer Magazine—1,218,634* (GameStop)
2. *Maxim—284,824* (Alpha Media Group)
3. *Cosmopolitan—185,673* (Hearst)
4. *Poder Hispanic—170,868* (Televisa Publishing)
5. *National Geographic—134,656* (National Geographic)
6. *Popular Science—93,037* (Bonnier)
7. *O, The Oprah Magazine—81,259* (Hearst)
8. *ESPN The Magazine—76,600* (ESPN)
9. *Nylon—75,600* (Jaclynn B. Jarrett)
10. *Parenting—74,790* (Bonnier)

11. *Wired—68,776* (Condé Nast)
12. *GQ—60,031* (Condé Nast)
13. *Men's Health—59,536* (Rodale)
14. *Women's Health—51,403* (Rodale)
15. *Electronic House—50,098* (EH Publishing)

The State of the News Media 2013 offered fresh information on the march to digital incarnations by the half-dozen U.S. newsmagazines. The examples were analyzed in 2012 by the Pew Research Center and reported on the Web.[19] *Time* and *Newsweek* were the perennial leaders of the breed, followed by a quartet of lesser niche periodicals—*The Economist, The Atlantic, The Week,* and *The New Yorker.*

While magazines overall were experiencing an 8.2 percent shrinkage in advertising billings over a year earlier, newsmagazines as a group fell strikingly on harder times. They lost about a quarter more advertising pages than the full category's shortfall compared with 2011, incurring a drop of 10.4 percent in ad revenues. And on the newsstands, their single-issue hard-copy sales were in even bigger trouble: for all consumer magazines bought at those venues, there was a slide of 8.2 percent in the year. The notch occupied by those same six newsmags, however, nearly doubled in contraction, reduced by 16 percent. Times were tough all over and this veritably underscored that people were finding other preferences for spending their time and money.

With *Newsweek*'s transition to an all-digital format at the start of 2013, *Time* persisted as the solitary survivor of newsmagazines with print editions that still appealed to a mass-market general interest readership. Of the half-dozen newsmags meanwhile, *Time* alone saw all three of Pew's audience measures (newsstand sales, subscriptions, and total circulation) decline in 2012. Its ad page billings for the year fell 12.2 percent.

Assessing the newsmagazine category from a yet wider perspective, the *State of the News Media 2013* annual report provided these additional insights:

> All of the publishers say that large numbers of their print subscribers now access mobile versions for at least some of their magazine reading. A slow transition is under way. At *The New Yorker,* for example, some 330,000 people have authenticated its iPad app, the vast majority of who are print subscribers who have paid an additional $10 to gain digital access as well. "People love

all access," said *New Yorker* publisher Lisa Hughes...."They want to be able to read on their tablets while they're traveling, or on their phones on the subway—and they're willing to pay for it."

...

News magazines have been particularly hard hit by the enormous rise in competition from Google, Yahoo, Facebook and other websites, says Ken Doctor, a former Knight-Ridder executive.... "News magazines were once a great place to reach an educated, upscale slice of the audience, but with all the digital targeting available through other sites today, advertisers don't need a magazine brand to do that anymore," he said....

...

With 31 percent of American adults owning a tablet and 45 percent owning a smartphone, news publishers focused even more in 2012 on mobile, where they are also counting on tablet apps to help convert nonpaying website readers into paying digital subscribers.

For now at least, magazine reading is a relatively small part of how people use these devices. Some 11 percent of smartphone owners read magazines on their phones weekly, as do 22 percent of tablet owners, according to Pew Research Center data from the fall of 2012. But news in general ranks near the top of their mobile activity, with 64 percent getting news on their tablet at least weekly, and 62 percent on their smartphones.

Even more promising for magazines is the type of reading and news consumption that is occurring. Fully 78 percent of tablet news users read in-depth articles at least sometimes on their device. Moreover, most of those consumers, 61 percent, said they read two to three articles in a sitting, while 17 percent read four or more. A vast majority, 72 percent, said they often read in-depth articles they did not set out to read, or what is known in the media as serendipity.

It is still early and it remains far from clear if mobile can ultimately provide the revenues needed to revive the industry. But news publishers, hopeful that it will provide a lifeline, intensified their efforts to develop tablet and smartphone offerings for readers and advertisers alike.

...

Digital is still far from balancing out the broader slide in print revenues. VSS [Veronis Suhler Stevenson investment firm] estimates that overall revenue for consumer magazines fell 2.7 percent, to $19.82 billion, in 2012, due to declining print advertising and circulation.

And, even after four years of double-digit growth, digital spending will still bring in a relatively small share of the consumer magazine revenue: VSS projects it will tally just 14.5 percent of total revenue by 2016, compared to 6.6 percent in 2012.[20]

In a more recent report of magazine subscription and newsstand sales at mid-year 2013, the Alliance for Audited Media (AAM) noted

17. Digital Mags: Feel the Magic?

that while paid and verified subscriptions declined by 1 percent in the first half of the year, newsstand sales, often an indicator of a magazine's appeal, had plunged a more substantial 10 percent.[21] And celebrity and women's titles were among the hardest hit in six months. *O, The Oprah Magazine*, fell 22.7 percent; *Cosmopolitan*, 23.9 percent; and *Glamour*, 28.8 percent.

Steven Cohn, editor of the *Media Industry Newsletter*, declared: "I'm not sure whatever they can do can make a difference. It's very newsstand-dependent." But Hearst Magazines, the owner of *Cosmopolitan* and *O, The Oprah Magazine*, observed that both of those periodicals had significantly increased in digital subscriptions. The former grew by 33 percent in the period while the latter rose 22 percent.

Digital editions are nonetheless "relatively small to the mix," Cohn rationalized. "I would expect these numbers to grow rather steadily. It's like everything else. You have to walk before you run. Things will accelerate."[22] Meanwhile the AAM said that with 10.2 million subscribers in mid-2013 ordering digital replica editions of their favorite magazines, that segment of circulation had already reached 3.3 percent of the total and was trending upward.

While the explosion of hard-copy matter on handheld devices, PCs, and laptops continues to surge, popular consumer print magazines, as a genre—for the foreseeable future, at least—is hardly going away. In October 2012, the Alliance for Audited Media discovered that just 5 percent of U.S. magazine publishers intended to offer their readers a digital-only subscription. And unlike *Newsweek*, just 3 percent anticipated that their publications would be, by 2017, transported to digital-only status. That leaves a whole lot of latitude for the still widely acclaimed slick magazines in all their traditional glory to remain with us.

The findings don't indicate that the hybrid format will not be in existence or that it won't proliferate, either. That trend may become the magazine's most acceptable and a new-norm solution to the persistent quandary faced by the trade: rising costs and dwindling advertising pages and falling circulations in a world in which the problem is exacerbated by increased competition for readers' attention and time, now running rampant—not only on the Web but elsewhere as well.

In that regard—despite revelations of magical technologies that rivet our attention as they continue to startle and stun—the collective consumer magazines' print editions aimed at an expectant clientele might not be in danger of running their course in the at least short-term foreseeable future. While a whole lot else may be moving to the Internet, it looks as if the U.S. postal carriers may still have something to put in the box, no matter how many or how few days their service persists.

18

The Future of the Form

In an era in which many Americans remained apprehensive about providing their credit card numbers to the purveyors from whom they sought to purchase goods and services on the Internet, information gleaned from an inquiry in the late 20th century was definitely illuminating and to some extent astonishing at the same time.[1] Among respondents who had made peace with the proliferation of online sites back in the 1990s, four out of five also embraced the notion of receiving some of their news via established Web-based sources. In providing their answers to the survey, that 80 percent's responses may appear to be somewhat surprising for that point in time in the nation's history: The faction plainly *trusted* the *authenticity* of what they were reading online *as much as they did* the printed word and the then-current cable TV news services. And (get this), some seven percent of that bloc believed that the generators of online news were actually *more reliable* than their conventional equivalents. Think newsprint journals, magazines, broadcasters, et cetera.[2] Are you keeping in mind that this research was conducted well over a decade and a half ago?

Can you (pardon the pun) *believe* it?

In an age in which a prominent journalism academician dismissed the news on the Internet as little more than a "novelty," this somewhat defining moment was quite obviously a fairly early gauge that was pointing the country to the future of communications.[3] Out of it was a clue that powerfully hinted how pervasively cyberspace was going to alter the nation's informational terrain within an exceedingly short time—not so long after Americans began realizing just how immense the territory was that its possibilities encompassed.

One informant, writing a dozen or so years afterward, correctly observed that not only had many of the nation's denizens become regular customers of cyberspace usage, but also in the intervening time legions had altered their methods of capturing online material:

> When we began reading news on the Internet in the midnineties, we were tethered to large, bulky desktop computers. We went to the only available digital reading source. Now we can take all manner of reading sources with us. First, the portable laptop joined the desktop. Now ... we've got iPhones, Kindles, Sony Readers, and this year [2010] a slew of new more-paperlike screens....
>
> Compare that to the desktops and laptops; those were machines—"computers"—aimed at helping us produce things. So, long way around, we're moving back to products, like newspapers, that are about us as consumers.[4]

In the spring of 2013, *USA Today* acknowledged that a glut of tablet shipments was on its way to America's consumer showrooms that would exceed laptop computers that year as the buying public's preferences discernibly shifted.[5] Tablet deliveries of 229.3 million units were projected globally by the research firm IDC. This accounted for an increase of nearly 85 million units in a single year. Still more stunning was IDC's forecast that tablets would outperform sales of the combined PC-laptop market altogether by 2015.

Devices with screens that are dimensionally below eight inches in size are swelling the demand for tablets, according to *USA Today*. Although screens between 8 and 11 inches grabbed 73 percent of the market share as recently as 2011, IDC expected a slump to 37 percent for gadgets in that range by 2017. In the meantime the firm predicted that appliances with screens below eight inches would continue to witness soaring market share, up from 27 percent in 2011 to 57 percent in 2017.

Falling retail prices are escalating the trend, the published report said. In 2013, IDC compared the typical cost of a PC at $635 with a tablet at $381, noting that fees for tablets were dropping steadily, about $42 (10 percent) under the previous year. Charles King, principal analyst at market researcher Pund-IT, commented: "The PC is the equivalent of the land-line phone. What do you need it for?"

If we take all we have heard and read and believe about the industry's consumer products as a whole, doesn't it stand to reason, with reports affirming matters like this, that—in the not too distant future, if not already—many of us will be carrying around our daily and weekly newspapers with us? (Many are already.) Isn't this fairly corroborating evidence that the idea of reading the electronic newspaper in one hand or balanced on our knees or on screens at our desks will be getting the majority's nod within the lifetime of most living Americans? (It's happening now.)

The manifestation of the electronic newspaper may be with us in purses, pockets, portfolios, attachés, and whatever else we tote in our hands until something else intervenes on the ever-evolving innovative horizon. If that presumption is valid, how we read the newspaper in the future certainly will be isolated from how most of us were reading it at the turn of the current century.

Imagine entering a waiting area at an airport or medical lounge in which many of the adults who are interested in keeping up with what's going on in the world are perusing the very latest news on an eight-inch or still much smaller screen. Can you envision it? Surely so; most such common waiting quarters right now include some individuals who are reading *something* by Kindle or Nook or iPad or iPhone or on another innovative gizmo's platform.

While most may not yet be reading the daily newspaper, before this decade reaches its conclusion the majority of newspaper readers could be receiving their daily dosage digitally as the comfort, feel, and habit of the newsprint model fades, possibly becoming even somewhat quaint as distance grows from it. (And maybe extinct? That's hardly likely, but almost certainly the paper-and-ink edition will no longer be a force occupying the commanding proportions that it has always held in the past.)

E-readers, one of the more popular processes for obtaining current newspaper replicas, persist in gaining ground among an ever-increasing segment of the reading audience who have wholly embraced wireless innovations. Late in 2013, a limited inquiry into existing practices in the field provided some intriguing revelations. The intent of the investigation was to compare the fees of a single leading application—in this demonstration, Kindle—with those of a handful of U.S. news journals in large, medium, and small metropolitan markets. Figures from the dozen individual publications compared, taken at random, included actual or approximate local print delivery charges for seven days weekly that also provided digital access. Calculations were based on ongoing subscriptions then in effect beyond whatever introductory discount enticements or easy-pay plans might be in place. Rates are monthly and reflect the following results:

The Arizona Republic—e-reader, $9.99; print + digital, $26.50
The Atlanta Journal-Constitution—e-reader, $9.99; print + digital, $25.18
Austin American-Statesman—e-reader, $9.99; print + digital, $27.95
The Charlotte Observer—e-reader, $6.99; print + digital, $16.12
Chicago Tribune—e-reader, $9.99; print + digital, $24.92
Los Angeles Times—e-reader, $9.99; print + digital, $21.62
The New York Times—e-reader, $19.99; print + digital, $55.03
The Oklahoman—e-reader, $5.99; print + digital, $12
The Philadelphia Inquirer—e-reader, $9.99; print + digital, $30.33
The Post and Courier (Charleston, S.C.)—e-reader, $8.99; print + digital, $20.25
St. Louis Post-Dispatch—e-reader, $6.99; print + digital, $15.12
Tampa Bay Times—e-reader, $9.49; print + digital, $16.25

From a purely economical standpoint, it's obvious that the digital-only model offers the best deals for a purchaser's pocketbook. However, as more and more journals shift to fewer print days as is anticipated of course, the costs for delivery with full digital access are expected to diminish. None of the papers in the sample were currently printed fewer than seven days per week when the analysis was completed.

A number of assessments issued by some keen observers who are on top of what's transpiring in the trade tend to underscore the possibility that an enveloping transfer from paper to pixel is imminent. This will occur in practical experience as well as in acceptance by the mainstream public within a short while. In a piece issued under the auspices of Harvard University's Nieman Journalism Lab, veteran New England newspaper publisher Martin C. Langeveld predicted what seems so be consistent in the minds of a growing contingent of his contemporaries:

- Because of the rapid adoption curve of tablets and the convenience of news consumption on them, *the business model for seven-day printed newspapers in most markets is toast.* We'll start to see frequency reductions to two or three days a week at an accelerated pace. By the end of 2015, fewer than half of the current dailies will still be printed every day.

18. The Future of the Form

- While we're still seeing more papers hopping on the paywall bandwagon there will be a growing realization that simple paywalls that just provide access to the content of a single newspaper are not the answer. So *paywalls will begin to morph into membership models,* where subscribers get access not only to content but to a range of services and benefits.
- As part of membership thinking, newspapers will finally start adopting the "jobs to be done" thinking advocated in the American Press Institute's Newspaper Next project (2005–08)—the idea that *the resources of the news organization can address a wide variety of problems that readers and advertisers need solutions to.*
- Membership thinking will also encourage the idea of paid (or unpaid) access to content from a network or cooperative of news organizations—sort of *an E-ZPass approach,* in which your paid digital subscription at a local news site might also provide you with access to regional and national news sources along with topical news from sites that specialize in business, finance, travel, sports, food, design, or whatever suits your fancy.[6]

Langeveld, who has owned newspapers for three decades in Massachusetts and Vermont, supplied some additional commentary that seems relevant and pertinent to the matters presented here. Said he:

> I've been suggesting since 2008 that to transition from a print-centric business model to a digital-centric one, newspapers need to go through an essential and strategic transition: cut print publication from six or seven days a week to two or three days. And when they do this, the printed product should be understood as a niche byproduct of a news organization that understands itself as being above all a digital-first enterprise.[7]

Noting the fact that the industry experienced 25 consecutive months of advertising declines and that currently "only 23 percent of U.S. adults read a printed newspaper," Langeveld offers a few more astute observations: "The industry has reacted with multiple rounds of cost-cutting, managing to preserve a semblance of its high historic profit margins in the process—and thus further postponing the day of reckoning."[8] But that house of cards has begun to fall, Langeveld claims.

He cites the steps taken by Advance Publications, Inc. (API)—introduced in chapter 7—as a pacesetting ideal for the industry. "Despite the continuation of healthy profit margins," Langeveld continues, "I'm convinced that moves of this type are being contemplated in every newspaper company's executive suite, and that the prime mover in these discussions is the seismic shift in readership habits brought about by tablets." He goes on: "Publishers are doing their best to hide the fact, but the zooming tablet trends are clobbering what's left of printed newspaper subscription and single-copy sales levels."

Recalling sharply declining circulation figures for the nation's top 25 dailies in 2011 and 2012 (highlighted earlier in this text), the publisher argues: "Numbers like these are not the hallmark of a sustainable business model." Once again Langeveld points to the trailblazing position of recent years pursued by API. "The rest of the industry is trying to figure out when, not if, they should follow suit. As noted, count on a lot of conversions during 2013 and an avalanche during 2014 and 2015," he posited.

There you have it in black and white. There's no mistaking the tone of this message. In that longtime publisher's opinion, it's already a done deal. So if we can accept that notion as the wave of the future, what is our newspaper going to look like by, let's say, 2020? It's not very far off, and it appears that many Americans will be accustomed to something categorically different from what they hold in their hands to peruse today. Here are some possible parameters:

- It will arrive not on the driveway or in the same box that the U.S. Postal Service uses but in another kind of mailbox altogether.
- While it can still be read in one's hands, it will appear on an electronic screen of some type, which may be battery operated or connected to an electrical outlet or powered by yet another source.
- It will draw upon a multiplicity of human senses. Beyond the eye it will have implications for the ear, touch, and—who knows now?—perhaps the senses of smell and taste ultimately as well.
- You won't have to wait any longer for the news at a specified time period such as breakfast or noon or the late afternoon, early evening or late night hours. The current events will be just that—in in your electronic mailbox every hour of the day, updated regularly as the hours advance.
- Along with the major stories, you'll be getting an abundance of what newspapers have traditionally referred to as "sidebars." But now

18. The Future of the Form

those "adjacencies" will be offered in literal profusion—e.g., tables, graphs, charts, illustrations, photos, linked stories, references, biographies, history, projections, comparisons, recipes, scores, music, speeches, events, interviews, related history, and what have you.
- There'll be no more missed papers, none thrown in the rain or mud or bushes; no delivery person at whose mercy you are helplessly dependent for your paper's arrival; and nobody to inform that you want your paper held "while I'm away."
- You won't be deprived of what you threw out in the trash today and would like to retrieve. After reading today's edition for a stash of yesterday's news, you should be able to add it to an archive of previous editions. It won't go away until you are ready to dispatch it, however—it will be available at your fingertips, needing but a flick of the wrist to access.

If all of this comes to pass as seems to be ordained, we will witness the largest single transformation in the history of print journalism during our life spans. In fact, these implications will be exceeded throughout history by just Johannes Gutenberg's invention of the printing press in the mid–15th century. The conversion from paper to pixel surpasses all other changes in print journalism in nearly 600 years.

The digital transmission of the printed word is still in its infancy of course. The discoveries that await future technological wizards, now beyond the comprehension of most of us, still convince us that none of this is most likely a done deal. If you don't believe it, think where we were only a couple of decades back. We've come light-years in the intervening time. And as new revelations unwind we'll realize again that there are yet even better ways of communicating the news than we have ever dreamed possible. Its dissemination will be timely, rapid, economical, comprehensive, and tailored to our specific expectations and needs. And just as we have today, people will embrace the newer processes that arrive to convey information in excitingly fresh encounters.

In the meantime—observing from our strategic contemporary vantage point—the communications secrets that are awaiting detection just over the blue horizon are prompting many forward thinkers to salivate. What a moment to be an observer of such absorbing developments—and to be a beneficiary as well!

Epilogue: Gimme Five

If you've read this far then you've been exposed to a whole lot of the impending plight and foreboding circumstances that threaten America's daily newspapers at this interval in history. You've discovered that, for instance, the industry is nearly weighted down by financial troubles of enormous proportions that continue to proliferate as time elapses. Very likely you had some notion of that calamitous adversity even before you picked up this tome. You've also found that more revenue could fix a whole lot of those issues if it were only there. But you probably knew that, too.

Newspaper publishers are groping for answers to the perplexing questions they face. Advertisers and readers are bailing out on them. Rival newspapers, which may be more deeply entrenched in the same market than they, and burgeoning online upstarts, plus a few "national" newspapers, are confronting them with stiff competition. Escalating expenses for overhead and rising personnel costs—often for remaining demoralized occupants of once-robust newsrooms—are exceedingly depressing. The transfer from paper to pixel requires not only the conversion of skilled staff who were trained in another medium but the added investment in capital for the changeover.

From many vantage points these are perilous times for newspaper owners. If they aren't able to do this right the entire operation could go down the drain. Let there be no mistake about it: A significant infusion of cash could go a long way in blunting their frustrations. Sufficient resources for the majority are nonetheless meager or almost nil. That circumstance is pushing some well-intentioned publishers to the wall.

All of it has induced some highly innovative thinking about introducing new methods of doing more with less. As owners seek to stem the tide of their faltering enterprises they are exploring creative new ways of attracting previously untapped funds to their operations. Over the past decade massive layoffs and other retrenchments have seen the product shrink to minimal dimensions while the geographical turf that the papers cover as well as the terrain of their home delivery has been slashed. As they achieve some cost savings through these enactments, they increase their costs through a reduction in image, patronage, and the number of commercial underwriters that used to rely on a newspaper's sweeping outreach to connect with their potential clients.

Despite all of these dire consequences, not many news journals have yet run up the white flag to surrender. But it could well happen and possibly soon. Thus far, so it seems, there's still enough entrepreneurial spirit prevailing among the powers-that-be to press onward. In the bleakest of scenarios that U.S. newspapers have ever faced, publishers continue to attempt to overcome the curves that fate has tossed their way.

While the jury is still out on where all of this will lead, if the author could be permitted to put on the hat of a clairvoyant momentarily—perhaps as a mystic possessing a somewhat cloudy glass ball—I'd submit a few impressions to you about that precarious-sounding future. This comes after a lifetime of professional journalistic activity and a recent year devoted to data sources tailored to the history and status of the contemporary U.S. daily and weekly newspapers. A blueprint for the near future offered to you, readers, during the second decade of the 21st century comprises a few personal reflections, assessments, and projections:

1. *We may have it both ways, but for only so long.* Although virtually all U.S. dailies and weeklies now furnish paper and pixel editions, the time will come when the financial pressures prompt a majority of U.S. news journals to permanently opt for electronic incarnations. This will increasingly occur over the next decade as a rising crescendo of readers embrace the concept.

2. *Never think you've seen it all.* Until most papers drop their newsprint editions, owners will apply extraordinary measures to reduce costs. So far we may have missed only *some* of the staffers, stories, sections, page size and number, and days on which a newsprint version

arrives; invariably more cuts *can* occur. Ultimately we may need a magnifying glass to see the leaflet that was once a thick paper. Look for cuts in markets with absentee ownership first and foremost—where community ties encompass only a plant located there.

3. *Consolidation is here to stay; get used to it.* Not only are conglomerates buying more newspapers for portfolios already bulging, but also media companies will flourish. They'll stash diverse communication systems under unified corporate umbrellas. Paper-and-pixel journals will exist among the mix.

4. *Ambidextrous journalists prevail.* Writing for newsprint may be out of style, but scribes are in demand for online gigs (reporting for eminent news sites, aggregators, blogs, and software developers). Calls for wordsmiths rise as media conglomerates rearrange duties to secure myriad communications quests—Web, broadcast, film, newspaper, et cetera. Journalists savvy in keyboards and cameras are indispensable. Live interviews become a natural phenomenon. Those proficient in digital innovations are at the forefront of what's happening.

5. *We'll get with the program.* Although there will be weeping and wailing and gnashing of teeth as newsprint sputters and dies, we'll get used to it and survive. Think of radio in 1960: only our youngest citizens hadn't heard a profusion of aural programming all their lives before it was swept away. Suddenly television was our prime in-home entertainment. While many looked back, most didn't. So it will be when the newsprint edition is a goner.

6. *Publishers will be wearing smiles.* Profitability isn't a thing of the past. After newspapers move beyond the appurtenances of buying presses and repairing them, newsprint and ink, printing, warehousing, delivery trucks, and people to make it all happen, including carriers and vendors, and systems and journalists are converted to electronics, owners/investors will be substantially rewarded for their patience, whistling "Happy Days Are Here Again."

7. *Newspapers will continue doing what they do best.* Despite the fact they work in a new venue, newspapers will remain distinctive. Nobody ever ferreted out the corruption at City Hall, reported Mrs. Field's fourth grade community center restoration project, or found an impoverished family sharing scanty resources with a clan whose home burned like the local paper covered those stories. That won't change. The people and

events nearby are the heart and soul of the dailies and weeklies, a trait that readers have relied on forever.

There are more trends that are imminent. You may think of some. These are a few of the imponderables that seem to characterize the industry in America for the next decade. A reality check in the mid-2020s could produce some altogether different conclusions, of course.

Let me leave you with a methodical analysis supplied by a highly venerated wellspring of information, CBS News. While this essay was originally aired in 2009, admittedly dating it to an extent, its basic premise is essentially as worthy today as it was back then. Its discernment and implications for the trade appear to be as valid now as they were at that time. The theme of this short discourse is the decline of the daily newspaper. Its author remains incognito.

> There's been lots of blog talk about the decline of newspapers…. A lot of it focuses on the fact that although the raw number of news outlets has decreased, in practical terms we all have access to far more news than we used to. And that's true for now. But here's the problem:
>
> Serious, daily, national reporting is overwhelmingly the preserve of a tiny handful of big-city newspapers with large staffs and worldwide bureaus. Of these, *The Los Angeles Times* is under pressure to downsize by its parent company, as is *The Washington Post*. Knight Ridder was recently purchased by McClatchy.[1] And every big-metro daily in the country … is under relentless pressure from deteriorating circulation, poor demographics, loss of classified ad revenue to the Internet, and the decline of urban department stores—storms that private owners might have weathered but institutional investors have no stomach for.
>
> When these dailies succumb, there's really nothing to replace them. Television news does very little in-depth daily reporting, most radio is hopeless, and blogs simply don't have the resources. Magazines do some good work but come out only weekly or monthly. So while the raw numbers of media consolidation may be the most dramatic symptom of the problem, it's the small number of national dailies at the core of today's MSM [mainstream media] that ought to be the biggest cause for concern.
>
> …Upwards of two-thirds of serious, daily reporting on national and international topics in the U.S. press comes from five sources: *The Los Angeles Times, The New York Times, The Washington Post, Wall Street Journal,* and McClatchy. If *The Denver Post* dies, that's bad for Denver, but what happens when the Big Five die? There's really nothing to replace them.
>
> Now, sure, there are other sources of information. I can read the *Guardian* and the *Financial Times* [UK papers] anytime I want. There's plenty of good reporting in weekly and monthly magazines. Wire services and TV can pro-

vide basic coverage of press conferences and congressional hearings. It's not as if we'll be bereft of news.

But when it comes to daily reporting from Iraq; when it comes to uncovering things like the NSA's warrantless wiretapping program or the identity of Curveball; when it comes to serious investigations of federal corruption or corporate malfeasance—well, most of that is done by the Big Five. Not all of it. But most of it. And I'm not quite sure who's up to the task of doing the kind of very costly reporting that this stuff requires if these big dailies either go away or shrivel into mere local outlets.[2]

The introspective proffers five sources that the newspaper industry has depended upon for more than a few decades. If any one of them was to become extinct the nation would fall under a curse that would severely handicap it in obtaining the global and domestic reportage that we have relied upon—dispatched to us in a timely, comprehensive manner that is unequalled by any other source. The capabilities of others to consistently step up to the plate have never been demonstrated. Let us celebrate these five resources for all that they deliver.

These are historically changing times in the life of U.S. newspapers. "Old things are passed away; ... all things are become new"— so an idiom in the Good News waxes eloquently.[3] The looming transfer from paper to pixel is very real. Within a brief interlude you may look for it to effectively convert what we have accepted all of our lives into a form that is radically transposed from that. The oft-repeated saw that "there's nothing as old as yesterday's newspaper" will ultimately be relevant in more than one way.[4] And as the old passes from the scene, its replacement will offer a fresh, modern, presumptively invigorating approach to finding out what we really need and want to know.

Put another way, *there's nothing as new as today's newspaper.* You may be certain that the publishers are banking on it.

Expectantly so.

Appendix

Highlights of American Newspaper History

1690

- Boston's Benjamin Harris launches the first locally produced newspaper in the New World, *Publick Occurrences, Both Forreign and Domestick*. One issue is enough to disturb his English superiors, who shut his press down.

1704

- Postmaster John Campbell inaugurates the second local newspaper in the New World. His *Boston News-Letter*, sans controversial topics, is successful. It persists for 72 years, until the United States declares itself independent of its Mother Country (1776).

1844

- Samuel F. B. Morse's invention of the telegraph makes a new dimension in reporting possible. Newspapers gain accurate reflections from across vast stretches of terrain without an eyewitness writing the details on paper.

1846

- Newspapers across the country band together to form the Associated Press to feed news from bureaus to one another by capitalizing on the telegraph's capabilities.

1920

- Commercial radio is christened, the first unifying mass communications method. In time it will be capable of reaching the whole nation simultaneously with news and amusement and to challenge newspapers for content and advertising.

1941

- For the next four years U.S. newspapers will be superseded by the nation's four transcontinental radio chains as they transmit wartime coverage from overseas battlefields to listeners' homes often as it occurs. It's a new exercise in reaching masses.

1960

- U.S. newspapers reach their zenith in the early 1960s in circulation, advertising revenues, and pervasive popularity, although a downward spiral from which they never recover isn't long in coming.

1963

- Television news comes to the forefront of the public's conscious in four days of intensive viewing at the death of President John F. Kennedy. The event elevates television to a new level of respect; thereafter the nation turns to television for breaking news of great import.

1964

- Eighty-one percent of U.S. adults are recurring newspaper readers, say Leonard Downie, Jr. and Robert Kaiser, *Washington Post* veteran journalists launching tenures this year.

1969

- The U.S. Defense Department inaugurates plans for a computer network that is to evolve into the Internet. It will profoundly affect U.S. newspapers in the 1990s.

1980

- Astute media analyst Anthony Smith champions the computer as the ultimate storage and retrieval system, giving readers exactly what they want, at a time most people have yet to hear of the Internet. He advocates new ways to collect, store, and circulate newspaper copy, well ahead of most of his peers.

1982

- The first online venture of a newspaper, StarText, a dial-in bulletin board service, is introduced by the *Fort Worth Star-Telegram*.

1983

- The Internet is launched.

1995

- *USA Today* starts an online version through CompuServe, initially with a fee but later free. Before the year ends 700 U.S. newspapers are online, up 600 in a year.

1996

- Eleven percent of U.S. homes are equipped with Internet connections by April.
- *The New York Times* and *The Wall Street Journal* are two of more than 1,600 U.S. newspapers with digital editions by year's end. The *Times* and *Journal* launch sans fees, but the *Journal* adds it within five months; the *Times* postpones it for a while.
- The Telecommunications Act of 1996 lifts tight limits on media ownership to let behemoths flourish. A handful controls powerful segments of the nation's airwaves and daily papers, pushing out small family-run enterprises that were typical for a long time.
- Craigslist debuts on the Web.

It's soon taking billions of dollars annually out of U.S. newspaper coffers that had underwritten classified advertising for decades.

1998

- Even before the turn of the 21st century Christopher Harper, veteran TV, magazine, and wire journalist, labels those forms of news transmission passé while forecasting that "digital journalism is the way it will be."
- Advertisers fill U.S. newspapers' coffers to the tune of $44 billion this year, $18 billion of it from classifieds. Courted by Wall Street, papers post profits of 20 percent or higher. Let the good times roll!

2000

- Half of American homes are Internet equipped by June.
- U.S. newspaper advertising revenues peak at $49 billion. They won't have long to celebrate: Within a decade that source will plunge to $25 billion.
- A Princeton Research Associates study finds that 89 percent of those retrieving news from digital sources are still doing so without having to pay anything for it. And 83 percent of those respondents say they'd be unwilling to pay for it if requested!

2001

- Harvard's Howard Gardner releases some conclusions after looking into newspapers as a vocation. He finds the troops in despair, claiming they can't "pursue the mission that inspired them to enter the field," for it simply doesn't exist anymore.
- Media analyst Ken Doctor will later observe that newspaper newsrooms have reached their peak this year, staffed by 56,400 journalists. A massive spiral downward begins now with 25 percent of these facing layoffs within five years.

2002

- In a new book journalists Leonard Downie, Jr. and Robert Kaiser cite newspapers as "the last real mass medium in America" in a day in which the Internet is flourishing.

2005

- News Corporation's chief guru Robert Murdoch tells the American Society of Newspaper Editors: "Many of us have been remarkably, unaccountably complacent ... quietly hoping that this thing called the digital revolution would just limp along."

2006

- After being flush with revenues, newspapers begin a dramatic drop from which they have never recovered. In the next three years revenues will plummet every quarter, with 2009 even worse than that interval.

2007

- Nineteen percent of the circulation of U.S. dailies is vested in just ten newspapers, reports the Project for Excellence in Journalism. At the same time these ten journals supply 29 percent of the traffic at newspaper Web sites.

2008

- Newsroom staffers take a colossal hit: 5,900 journalists' jobs vanish this year, a cutback of 11.3 percent of the editorial labor force. It's the biggest number of layoffs in the American Society of Newspaper Editors' 87-year history, when record keeping began. Only two-thirds of dailies reported, however, and no weeklies, so the total is actually far worse.
- A Pew study finds there are more Americans receiving their news online for free than there are paying for it as subscribers to newsprint editions.

2009

- U.S. newspaper revenues plunge 29 percent below their 2008 level—their largest reversal in a single year since the Great Depression at least 75 years earlier. Display advertising falls an unprecedented 29.7 percent in one year.
- As if the aforesaid isn't bad enough, 395 U.S. dailies report a loss of 7.1 percent of their circulation in the last six months. At that rate, industry pundits Robert McChesney and John Nichols calculate, nobody will be reading them in under eight years!
- In June, Moody's Investor Service states that pen-and-ink dailies are "no longer commercially sustainable." To remain solvent it urges the trade to hastily turn onto the cyberspace superhighway.
- *Time* magazine publishes a list of "the 10 most endangered newspapers in America" and cites reasons for their selection. In a foreboding piece some are predicted to fail in the near future. Almost five years hence, however, all ten will still be operational, although two will have reduced their home deliveries to three days weekly.
- The *Christian Science Monitor* is reduced from five days to one day weekly.
- Founded in 1863, the *Seattle Post-Intelligencer* banishes its newsprint edition altogether, moving to a digital format only.
- Denver's *Rocky Mountain News*, a financially failing daily dating to 1859 and unable to make it work any longer, folds its tent and shuts its doors altogether.
- The *Ann Arbor* [Mich.] *News* is the "guinea pig" for a new strategy of Advance Publications, Inc., to be pursued at many more of its 31 dailies. Delivery of the newsprint version is reduced to two or three days weekly while a daily digital model is accentuated.
- Giving content away online is

self-defeating, wails *Time* editor Walter Isaacson. It will lead to "a time when some major cities will no longer have a newspaper and when magazines and network-news operations will employ ... [only] a handful of reporters."

• "The paywall is history," writes outspoken media mogul Arianna Huffington in a piece appearing in the UK's *Guardian*. She says paying for Web news won't make it.

• Fitch Ratings says "all the two-newspaper markets will become one-newspaper markets, and ... one-newspaper markets [will] become no-newspaper markets."

• Princeton University colleagues interpret the cessation of *The Cincinnati Post* for residents, reporting disturbing trends: fewer vote in elections; number of candidates for local offices reduced; incumbents being able to remain in office longer. With fewer news stories, the researchers deduce, people don't care as much about their towns anymore.

2010

• We get our news throughout the day from many sources, pundits Bill Kovach and Tom Rosenstiel recognize in a new book. It's often a story at a time, as opposed to a package of stories supplied to earlier generations by a daily newspaper or TV newscast.

• Journalists Robert McChesney and John Nichols publish their views, predicting pending death for the newsprint edition followed by a fading of the digital form and that—if the latter survives—it will only appeal to tiny slices of niche-oriented markets.

• Pew Research Center discloses that 35 percent of U.S. citizens get their national and global current events from daily newspapers while 40 percent seek it on the Internet. It's the first time newspapers have lost this competition, but it won't be the last.

• The newsprint used by U.S. dailies has been trimmed by 40 percent in the last five years. It suggests that not only is advertising down, but also content has been severely cut.

• Harris Interactive reveals that an alarming 17 percent of U.S. 18-to-34-year-olds *never* read a newspaper. Another 60 percent in that range read one occasionally—"a few times a week or year." Just 23 percent of those cohorts read one "almost daily."

• Home delivery of combined dailies in Detroit are reduced to Thursday, Friday, and Sunday. "Skinny" editions are at newsstands daily, with an online edition also daily.

• "There is little reason to believe that paywalls could actually work with consumers" for the digital news they retrieve, state media analysts Robert McChesney and John Nichols. It would be taking the Internet "in the wrong direction," they say.

- One theorist applies a formula based on the cutbacks in U.S. newsrooms in recent years to project that 828,000 fewer stories are appearing in U.S. dailies annually.

2011

- Audit Bureau of Circulations says 44.4 million U.S. households receive a daily paper, 14.2 percent of the total households, nearly half of the 26.8 percent in 1984.
- At year's end a University of Southern California entity releases a projection that by 2016 just four U.S. dailies will still be publishing print editions: *The New York Times, USA Today, The Wall Street Journal,* and *The Washington Post.*
- Seventy-one U.S. dailies change hands in 11 separate transactions, the busiest exchange of ownership since 2007, the Poynter Institute announces.

2012

- In January, it's reported that 30 percent of U.S. adults own a tablet or e-reader.
- American newspapers exhibit entrepreneurial skills in creating new streams of revenue. This year they bring in nearly $6 billion by offering marketing advice and services to myriad clients; engage in e-commerce ventures; and host local events.
- Pew Research Center announces that for every dollar they earn digitally newspapers are losing $10 in print revenue. There's not much to cheer about.
- Just 29 percent of Americans now read a newspaper regularly, says one report.
- While 40 percent of the nation's residents are over age 45, that group nets 75 percent of the readership of U.S. newspapers, according to consultant Alan Mutter.
- All hell breaks loose in New Orleans when Advance Publications announces it is trimming the venerated *Times-Picayune* to home delivery three days weekly. The owner isn't prepared for the sustained rancor that follows but doesn't alter its plans. Similar cutbacks at its three key Alabama journals escape without extreme protests.
- In the wake of disastrous reaction to trimming New Orleans' *Times-Picayune* to three days weekly, *The Advocate* in nearby Baton Rouge sets up a shop in the Crescent City. It launches a local edition for home delivery seven days weekly.
- The Audit Bureau of Circulations reports that total circulation for *The New York Times* jumped an astonishing 73 percent in 12 months ending March 31. Most of it is attributed to charging patrons for unlimited access to its Web site and e-reader models, the antithesis of what many observers might anticipate.

2013

- One out of five Americans still has no Internet connection, reports

The New York Times. This is by choice (lack of interest or computer skills) or insufficient funds.

• In March, based on unique monthly visitors, the top five online news Web sites are, in order: Yahoo! News, CNN, MSNBC, Google News, and *The New York Times.* Just a trio of newspapers is in the top ten (including Washington and L.A. dailies).

• Pew Research reveals that the typical online news seeker gives about three minutes per day to reading news while the average newsprint reader takes 40 minutes.

• Media tech consultant Alan Mutter notes that today's newspaper readership includes 6 percent in their twenties, 16 percent in their forties, and 48 percent age 65 and up.

• Owners of Newark's *Star-Ledger* warn of a shutdown by year's end if unionized printers don't negotiate a new contract in good faith. Such drastic threats hint that publishers with their backs to the wall will do whatever it takes to remain solvent.

• Feeling the heat as the Baton Rouge *Advocate* starts a seven-day-a-week local edition in New Orleans, *Times-Picayune* owners Advance Publications—after cutting home delivery to three days weekly—adds a tabloid at newsstands on three other days.

• Advance's strategy of cutting seven-day dailies to two or three for home delivery persists as more in its portfolio follow suit: *The Patriot-News,* Harrisburg, Pennsylvania; *The Post-Standard,* Syracuse, New York; *The Plain Dealer,* Cleveland; *The Oregonian,* Portland.

• The Newspaper Association of America admits what a foolish thing it was for the papers with online editions to have overlooked charging for content for many years.

• By spring 33 percent of the United States' 380 dailies have instituted paywalls or have plans to do so for readers to access online news. A work in progress, more are expected to follow.

• Warren Buffett, one of the planet's wealthiest individuals, changes his mind, admits his mistake, and says he was out of line to think paywalls were a bad idea. He owns copious newspapers, most with Internet versions, and may be poised to buy more. He doesn't care about the money—wants to "protect the content" by not giving it away.

• In August the principal owner of the Boston Red Sox buys *The Boston Globe* from The New York Times Company. It's an omen of transitions out of the hands of journalists.

• Subsequently, venerated eight-decade overseers of *The Washington Post,* a paper dubbed "the nation's moral compass," reveal they will sell the celebrated property to an online retailer without journalistic experience. The staff and industry are stunned.

2015

- Ken Doctor cites a "Digital Dozen" of global firms at the forefront of every media facet by this year. "I think the winners will all be known to us as big news brands … with all forms of taking in the news—reading, viewing, and listening," he says.
- This year, says IDC, sales of tablets will pass sales of PCs and laptops combined.
- By year's end, a report issued under Harvard auspices projects, fewer than half of current U.S. dailies will still be issuing newsprint versions seven days weekly.

2017

- By this year, avow 38 U.S. news executives in a 2012 Pew inquiry, the mass of U.S. dailies still in newsprint will deliver only a few days weekly, maybe just Sunday.

Chapter Notes

Prologue

1. Anne D'Innocenzio, "Change Management: Cash Registers Fade," *The Courier-Journal*, Louisville, KY, March 23, 2013, p. B4.

2. Since about 1450 is one answer, when Johannes Gutenberg is credited with giving the world the printing press, although people had been communicating in writing for centuries before that (Jim Cox, *Radio Journalism in America: Telling the News in the Golden Age and Beyond* [Jefferson, NC: McFarland, 2013], p. 6).

3. As of late 2010, the U.S. Census Bureau acknowledged that almost 77 percent of U.S. households were computer equipped. A proliferation of myriad types of handheld computer devices is also prominent in undocumented domiciles (http://www.census.gov/hhes/computer/publications/2010.html, Table 1C).

4. William Henry Shakespeare, *Macbeth*, act V, scene 1.

5. Psalms 24:4, New International Version.

Chapter 1

1. Bulletin-style reports of current events were displayed in the Roman Empire in 59 BC The first handwritten newspaper is thought to have been circulated in Beijing, China, in A.D.748, while weekly handwritten news sheets were similarly issued in Venice in 1566 and dispatched as far away as London. Some claimants assert that a 1502 printed German newspaper was possibly "the prototype of the genus" and the first English-language news sheet arrived in 1513. Two ensuing weeklies from 1609, both German, are cited as the oldest surviving printed papers (Mitchell Stephens, "History of Newspapers," *Collier's Encyclopedia*, ca. 1992, www.nyu.edu/classes/stephens/Collier%27s%20page.htm; Jim Cox, *Sold on Radio: Advertisers in the Golden Age of Broadcasting* [Jefferson, NC: McFarland, 2008], pp. 9, 303.

2. Anthony Smith, *Goodbye, Gutenberg: The Newspaper Revolution of the 1980s* (New York: Oxford University Press, 1980), p. 321.

3. Philip Meyer, *The Vanishing Newspaper: Saving Journalism in the Information Age* (Columbia: University of Missouri Press, 2004), p. 202.

4. Eric Alterman, "Out of Print: The Death and Life of the American Newspaper," *The New Yorker*, March 31, 2008.

5. Ibid.

6. Stephen B. Shepard, *Deadlines and Disruption: My Turbulent Path from Print to Digital* (New York: McGraw-Hill, 2013), p. 299.

7. The Internet began as a U.S. Defense project in 1973. The Advanced Research Projects Agency (ARPA) believed a redundant, noncentralized global computer network could be vital in passing info in a nuclear disaster or other cataclysmic event. ARPA created "packet technology," sending data by breaking it into discreet packets addressed to a unique network machine. The common language in sending data packets on the Internet is dubbed a protocol. Different services have distinct languages or protocols. The Internet supports many pro-

tocols, of which the WWW is one (www.wisegeek.com/are-the-internet-and-the-world-wide-web-the-same-thing.htm).

8. By early 2012, three out of ten U.S. adults owned a tablet or e-reader (Lee Rainie, "Tablet and E-Book Readership Nearly Double Over Holiday Gift-Giving Period," January 23, 2012, www.pewinternet.org/Reports/2012/E-readers-and-tablets.aspx.)

9. www.naa.org/info/facts/18.html.

10. Ken Doctor, *Newsonomics: Twelve New Trends That Will Shape the News You Get* (New York: St. Martin's Press, 2010), p. 3.

11. Smith, p. 14.

12. Ibid.

13. Ibid., p. 73.

14. Doctor, pp. 24–25.

15. John V. Pavlik, *Journalism and New Media* (New York: Columbia University Press, 2001), pp. 167, 169.

16. Smith, pp. 14, 15.

17. Ibid., p. 319.

18. Shepard, p. 303.

19. Ibid.

20. Ibid., p. 304.

21. Ibid.

22. Robert W. McChesney and John Nichols, *The Death and Life of American Journalism: The Media Revolution That Will Begin the World Again* (Philadelphia: Nation Books, 2010), pp. 173, 172.

23. Clark Gilbert, "Newspapers and the Internet," *Nieman Reports* 56:2 (Summer 2002): 37.

24. Shepard, p. 263.

25. Meyer, p. 227.

26. Henry K. Lee, "Cronkite Pans TV News at Caen Lecture; He Says Internet Presents Society 'Frightful Danger,'" *San Francisco Chronicle*, November 13, 1996, sec. A.

27. Leonard Downie, Jr., and Robert G. Kaiser, *The News About the News: American Journalism in Peril* (New York: Alfred A. Knopf, 2002), p. 257.

28. Edward Wyatt, "Most of U.S. Is Wired, but Millions Aren't Plugged In," *New York Times*, August 19, 2013, pp. B1, B3.

29. Christopher Harper, *And That's the Way It Will Be: News and Information in a Digital World* (New York: New York University Press, 1998), p. 3.

Chapter 2

1. Bill Kovach and Tom Rosenstiel, *Blur: How to Know What's True in the Age of Information Overload* (New York: Bloomsbury USA, 2010), p. 13.

2. Anthony Smith, *Goodbye, Gutenberg: The Newspaper Revolution of the 1980s* (New York: Oxford University Press, 1980), p. 4.

3. Kovach and Rosenstiel, p. 13.

4. Ibid., p. 15.

5. www.phrases.org.uk/meanings/247100.html.

6. Smith, p. 9.

7. For more detail on the historic beginnings of newspapers, see Jim Cox, *Radio Journalism in America: Telling the News in the Golden Age and Beyond* (Jefferson, NC: McFarland, 2013), pp. 6–7.

8. Joseph E. Persico, *Edward R. Murrow: An American Original* (New York: Dell Publishing, 1988), p. 88. For the uninitiated, *antipodes* are "persons dwelling at opposite points on the globe" (Webster, 2001).

9. Persico, p. 90.

10. Michael Emery, Edwin Emery, and Nancy L. Roberts, *The Press and America: An Interpretive History of the Mass Media*, 9th ed. (Boston: Allyn and Bacon, 2000), p. 8.

11. Ibid., p. 19.

12. "Harris got into trouble with the local authorities ... because he printed the truth as he saw it" (ibid., p. 23).

13. Michael Stephens, *A History of News: From the Drum to the Satellite* (New York: Viking, 1998), p. 201; James Playsted Wood, *The Great Glut: Public Communication in the United States* (Nashville: Thomas Nelson, 1973), p. 21; John Clyde Oswald, *Printing in the Americas* (New York: Hacker Art Books, 1968), p. 9; Frank Luther Mott, *American Journalism: A History of Newspapers in the United States Through 250*

Notes—Chapter 3

Years, 1690-1940 (New York: Macmillan, 1941), pp. 11–14; Frederic Hudson, *Journalism in the United States, from 1690 to 1872* (New York: Harper & Brothers, 1873), pp. 52–58.

14. In the first Industrial Revolution, generally between 1760 and 1840, technological, socioeconomic and cultural shifts occurred in droves. Power-driven machinery replaced manual labor and animal-driven effort. Textile production was mechanized; iron-making skills advanced, netting cultivation of machinery; improved waterways and roads occurred; steam power and railroads were launched (Jim Cox, *Rails Across Dixie: A History of Passenger Trains in the American South* [Jefferson, NC: McFarland, 2011], p. 11).

15. www.invent.org/Hall_Of_Fame/106.html.

16. A concept suggested by Robert W. McChesney and John Nichols, *The Death and Life of American Journalism: The Media Revolution That Will Begin the World Again* (Philadelphia: Nation Books, 2010), p. 15.

17. Smith, p. 14.
18. Ibid., p. 15.
19. Ibid., p. 19.
20. Ibid., p. 23.
21. Adapted from W. Russell Neuman, *The Future of Mass Audience* (New York: Cambridge University Press, 1995).
22. Christopher Harper, *And That's the Way It Will Be: News and Information in a Digital World* (New York: New York University Press, 1998), p. 201ff.
23. Mark Fitzgerald, "Get Out of the Printing Business, Moody's Tells Newspapers," *Editor & Publisher*, June 4, 2009, www.editorandpublisher.com/eandp/news/article_display.jsp?vnu_content_id=1003980461.
24. www.youtube.com/watch?v=5WCTn4FljUQ.
25. Kovach and Rosenstiel, p. 24.

Chapter 3

1. Bill Kovach and Tom Rosenstiel, *Blur: How to Know What's True in the Age of Information Overload* (New York: Bloomsbury USA, 2010), p. 171.

2. Ibid.

3. Walter Isaacson, "How to Save Your Newspaper: It's Now or Never for America's Dailies," *Time*, February 5, 2009.

4. Robert W. McChesney and John Nichols, *The Death and Life of American Journalism: The Media Revolution That Will Begin the World Again* (Philadelphia: Nation Books, 2010), p. 11.

5. Ibid., pp. 172, 173.

6. James O'Shea, *The Deal from Hell: How Moguls and Wall Street Plundered Great American Newspapers* (New York: Public Affairs, 2011), pp. 3–4.

7. Erik Sass, "AP: Newspapers Cut Young Employees," MediaDailyNews, September 1, 2009, www.mediapost.com.

8. Newspaper Association of America, www.naa.org/TrendsandNumbers/Advertising-Expenditures.aspx.

9. McChesney and Nichols, pp. 12–13, 14.

10. Figures in this section are supplied by McChesney and Nichols, p. 18.

11. O'Shea, pp. 11–12.

12. Jeff Jarvis, "My Testimony to Sen. Kerry," *Buzz Machine*, April 21, 2009, http://www.buzzmachine.com/.

13. McChesney and Nichols, p. 31.

14. David Weaver et al., *The American Journalist in the 21st Century* (Mahwah, NJ: Lawrence Erlbaum Associates, 2007), p. 3.

15. McChesney and Nichols, p. 34. "We do not doubt that if we could have replaced all the corporate-media CEOs with different people, they would have pursued essentially the same approaches, with more or less the same consequences—and if they deviated from the course, they would have lost their jobs. The one thing we do know is that at the same time as they gutted newsrooms and dumbed down their own papers, the corporate-media CEOs were fattening their personal bank accounts big-time" (p. 38).

16. Howard Gardner, Mihaly Csikszentmihalyi, and William Damon, *Good Work: When Excellence and Ethics Meet* (New York: Basic Books, 2001), chap. 7.

17. Deborah Potter, "Pessimism Rules in TV Newsrooms," *Columbia Journalism Review*, November/December 2002, p. 90.
18. McChesney and Nichols, p. 51.
19. Alex S. Jones, *Losing the News: The Future of the News That Feeds Democracy* (New York: Oxford University Press, 2009), p. 4.
20. John Nichols, "Newspapers and After," *The Nation*, January 12, 2007.
21. Rem Rieder, "Extra, Extra: Newspapers Aren't Dead," *USA Today*, April 11, 2013, p. 6B.

Chapter 4

1. Anthony Smith, *Goodbye, Gutenberg: The Newspaper Revolution of the 1980s* (New York: Oxford University Press, 1980), pp. 300, 301.
2. Philip Seib, *Going Live: Getting the News Right in a Real-Time, Online World* (Lanham, MD: Rowman & Littlefield, 2001), pp. 121–122. Some of the functions of the computer—especially the home computer—were replaced at that time by cell phones with touch-screen Web access and a blended nine-inch television, CD player, and Web browser attachable under kitchen cabinets, leaving obsolete early forms of acclaimed Palms. The personal computer moved from desk to pocket.
3. Jim Cox, *Sold on Radio: Advertisers in the Golden Age of Broadcasting* (Jefferson, NC: McFarland, 2008), pp. 8–9.
4. www.journalism.org/analysis_report/understanding_participatory_news_consumer.
5. Bill Kovach and Tom Rosenstiel, *Blur: How to Know What's True in the Age of Information Overload* (New York: Bloomsbury USA, 2010), pp. 173–174.
6. Eric Alterman, "Out of Print: The Death and Life of the American Newspaper," *The New Yorker*, March 31, 2008.
7. James O'Shea, *The Deal from Hell: How Moguls and Wall Street Plundered Great American Newspapers* (New York: Public Affairs, 2011), pp. 272, 273.
8. Dan Gillmor, *We the Media: Grassroots Journalism by the People, for the People* (Sebastopol, CA: O'Reilly Media, 2004), p. 236.
9. Some of the ideas in the paragraphs that follow originated in John V. Pavlik's *Journalism and New Media* (New York: Columbia University Press, 2001), pp. xi–xii. Generalizations have been expanded more broadly than in Pavlik's discourse, however.
10. James W. Carey, "The Internet and the End of the National Communications System: Uncertain Predictions of an Uncertain Future," *Journalism Quarterly*, Spring 1998, p. 28.
11. Pavlik, pp. xii, xiii.
12. Ibid., p. 62.
13. Smith, p. 3.
14. Peter Steven, *The News* (Toronto, ON: Groundwood Books, 2010), pp. 87–88.
15. www.ebizmba.com/articles/news-websites.
16. The figures given are from the first quarter of 2009 (Ken Doctor, *Newsonomics: Twelve New Trends That Will Shape the News You Get* [New York: St. Martin's Press, 2010], p. 2).
17. Ibid., pp. 10, 2.
18. Pavlik, p. 170.
19. Doctor, p. 2. The results of the Pew study cited are reported here.
20. Stephen B. Shepard, *Deadlines and Disruption: My Turbulent Path from Print to Digital* (New York: McGraw-Hill, 2013), p. 268.
21. Ibid., p. 269.
22. Leonard Downie, Jr., and Robert G. Kaiser, *The News About the News: American Journalism in Peril* (New York: Alfred A. Knopf, 2002), p. 95.
23. Doctor, p. 2.
24. The facts pertaining to the period 1990–2000 are reported in Charles M. Madigan, ed.,—*30*—: *The Collapse of the Great American Newspaper* (Chicago: Ivan R. Dee, 2007), pp. 45–46.
25. Downie and Kaiser, p. 95.
26. Rem Rieder, "Buffet's Love for Papers 'Unnatural?' No Way: Relationship Firmly Grounded on Profit," *USA Today*, March 6, 2013, p. 2B.

27. Philip Meyer, *The Vanishing Newspaper: Saving Journalism in the Information Age* (Columbia: University of Missouri Press, 2004), p. 201.
28. Paul Gillin, "Crunching the Latest Numbers on Traditional Media," February 11, 2013, www.newspaperdeathwatch.com.
29. Joseph Epstein, "Are Newspapers Doomed?," *Commentary*, January 2006.
30. www.naa.org/Trends-and-Numnbers/Circulation/Newspaper-Circulation-Volume.aspx.
31. www.npg.org/facts/us_historical_pops.htm; www.usnews.com/opinion/blogs/robert-schlesinger/2011/12/30/us-population-2012-nearly-313=million-people.
32. Doctor, p. 2.
33. Ibid., p. 265.
34. Federal Communications Commission, *The Information Needs of Communities: The Changing Media Landscape in a Broadband Age*, "Overview," June 9, 2011, www.fcc.gov/infoneedsreport.
35. Alterman.
36. Doctor, p. 265.
37. Madigan, p. 6.
38. Ibid., pp. 6–7.
39. U.S. newspaper staffs declined by more than 25 percent in a five-year span between 2006 and 2011 (Federal Communications Commission).
40. Doctor, pp. 1–2, 3.
41. Federal Communications Commission.
42. Shepard, p. 261.
43. Paul Gillin, "Forthcoming Documentary Looks at Impact of Newspaper Declines," December 6, 2012, www.newspaperdeathwatch.com.
44. Paul Farhi, "A Bright Future for Newspapers," *American Journalism Review*, June/July 2005.
45. O'Shea, p. 343.
46. Alterman.
47. Madigan, p. 9.

Chapter 5

1. Bill Kovach and Tom Rosenstiel, *Blur: How to Know What's True in the Age of Information Overload* (New York: Bloomsbury USA, 2010), pp. 22, 23.
2. The Pew Research Center's Project for Excellence in Journalism, *The State of the News Media 2009: An Annual Report on American Journalism*, www.journalism.org.
3. The Pew Research Center's Project for Excellence in Journalism, *The State of the News Media 2010: An Annual Report on American Journalism*, "Nielsen Analysis," March 15, 2010, www.stateofthemedia.org/2010/specialreports_nielsen.php.
4. Ken Doctor, *Newsonomics: Twelve New Trends That Will Shape the News You Get* (New York: St. Martin's Press, 2010), pp. 24–33.
5. This list was released April 30, 2013, by the Alliance for Audited Media, www.auditedmedia.com/news/blog/top-25-us-newspapers-for-march-2013.aspx.
6. Doctor, pp. 28, 29.
7. John V. Pavlik, *Journalism and New Media* (New York: Columbia University Press, 2001), p. 28.
8. Ibid., p. 1.

Chapter 6

1. Paul Gillin, "Crunching the Latest Numbers on Traditional Media," *Newspaper Death Watch*, February 11, 2013, www.newspaperdeathwatch.com.
2. "Just Two in Five Americans Read a Newspaper Almost Every Day: Less than One-Quarter of 18–34 Year Olds Read a Paper Each Day," Harris Interactive, January 13, 2010, www.harrisinteractive.com/NewsRoom/HarrisPolls/tabid/447/ctl/ReadCustom%20Default/mid/1508/ArticleId/258/Default.aspx.
3. Paul Gillin, "The Graying of the Newspaper Audience," *Newspaper Death Watch*, January 17, 2013, www.newspaperdeathwatch.com.
4. Suzy Post, "Loving Newsprint," *The Courier-Journal*, Louisville, KY, November 2, 2013.
5. "Just Two in Five Americans Read a Newspaper Almost Every Day."

Notes—Chapter 7

6. Gillin, "The Graying of the Newspaper Audience."
7. Bill Hoffmann, "Age of Newspaper Readers Rising Sharply," *Newsmax*, January 24, 2013, www.newsmax.com/US/news paper-readership-age-skyrocketing/2013/01/15/id/471531.
8. Gillen, "The Graying of the Newspaper Audience."
9. Tom Rosenstiel, "Newspaper Readers Are Not Graying As Quickly As Reported," Poynter, January 17, 2013, www.poynter.org/latest-news/mediawire/201042/newspaper-readers-are-not-graying-as-quickly-as-reported/.
10. Ibid.
11. Gillin, "Crunching the Latest Numbers on Traditional Media."
12. "Just Two in Five Americans Read a Newspaper Almost Every Day."
13. Douglas A. McIntyre, "The 10 Most Endangered Newspapers in America," *Time*, May 9, 2009, www.content.time.com/time/business/article/0,8599,1883785-2,00.html.
14. Ibid.

Chapter 7

1. For a brief history of the Poynter Institute, see www.about.poynter.org/about-us/mission-history.
2. Rick Edmonds, "State of the News Media 2013 Shows How Industry Is Responding to 'Continued Erosion' of Resources," www.poynter.org/latest-news/business-news/the-biz-blog/207396/state-of-the-news-m....
3. Christine Haughney, "Newspapers Cut Days from Publishing Week," *New York Times*, June 3, 2012.
4. Michaelle Bond, "For Newspapers, a Less than Daily Future," *American Journalism Review*, June/July 2012.
5. Ibid.
6. Ibid.
7. www.stateofthemedia.org/2013/newspapers-stabilizing-but-still-threatened/.
8. Ken Doctor, *Newsonomics: Twelve New Trends That Will Shape the News You Get* (New York: St. Martin's Press, 2010), p. 49.
9. Bond.
10. www.stateofthemedia.org/2013/newspapers-stabilizing-but-still-threatened/.
11. www.nytimes.com/2012/06/04/business/media/as-newspaprs-cut-analysts-ask-if-readers-will-remain.html?_r=0.
12. Ibid.
13. Rem Rieder, "Reduced Newspaper Delivery: Smart or Death Knell?," *USA Today*, February 1, 2013.
14. Doctor, pp. 46, 49.
15. www.historylink.org/index.cfm?DisplayPage=output.cfm&file_id=8956.
16. www.rockymountainnews.com/.
17. Circulation figures as of March 31, 2013, from the Alliance for Audited Media.
18. Roger Yu, "Some Major Newspapers Struggle with Changing Times," *USA Today*, June 28, 2013, p. 7B; Ted Sherman, "Star-Ledger Threatens to Close Without Concessions; Union Officials Reject Ultimatum," *The Star-Ledger*, June 26, 2013, www.nj.com/news/index.ssf/2013/06/star-ledger_threatens_to_close_without_concessions_as_union_officials_reject_ultimatum.html.
19. Sherman.
20. *You Can't Go Home Again* is a novel published in 1940 following Thomas Wolfe's death, extracted from his vast unpublished manuscript *The October Fair*.
21. www.stateofthemedia.org/2013/newspapers-stabilizing-but-still-threatened/.
22. Many of the details of the senior Newhouse's life and of Advance Publications history are gathered from www.samuelirvingnewhousejr.crazybillionaire.org/samuelirvingnewhousejr.php.
23. Bayonne is situated south of Jersey City, New Jersey, and immediately north of the New York City borough of Staten Island.
24. In mid–2013, Samuel Irving Newhouse, Jr., 85, was chairman and CEO of

Notes—Chapter 7

Advance Publications, Inc., as members of younger generations of the Newhouse clan persisted in the firm's employ. A brief profile noted Newhouse "delights in controversies." Given the uproar in the aftermath of some of Advance's shifts in publishing from seven-day-a-week dailies to two- or three-day weeks, he could be well contented (www.samuelirvingnewhousejr.crazybillionaire.org/samuelirvingnewhousejr.php).

25. www.wweek.com/portland/article-19535-stop_the_presses.html.
26. www.nytimes.com/2012/06/04/business/media/as-newspaper-cut-analysts-ask-if-readers-will-remain.html?pagewanted=all&_r=0.
27. Haughney.
28. Ibid.
29. www.stateofthemedia.org/2013/newspapers-stabilizing-but-still-threatened/. Note: New Orleans has since been eclipsed by at least one other larger market (Cleveland) for the "honor" of largest U.S. city without a printed daily newspaper. A trend stirring within the industry hints that there could be more to follow.
30. Rieder, "Battle for New Orleans on the Journalism Front," *USA Today*, May 2, 2013.
31. Bond.
32. Rieder, "Reduced Newspaper Delivery."
33. "Stop the Presses: *The Oregonian* May Not Be a Daily Newspaper Much Longer," August 8, 2012, www.wweek.com/portland/article-19535-stop_the_presses.html.
34. Sena Jeter Naslund, "Give Gift of a Courier Journal Subscription; Preserve Rich Variety of Daily Journalism," *The Courier-Journal*, Louisville, KY, January 25, 2013, p. A8.
35. Rieder, "Reduced Newspaper Delivery."
36. Bond.
37. Kevin Allman, "The Advocate Publisher on the Paper's Plans to Move into New Orleans," *Gambit*, Gambit, September 7, 2012, www.bestofneworleans.com/blog ofneworleans/archives/2012/09/07/the-advocate-publisher-on-the-papers-plans-to-move-into-new-orleans.html.
38. Eve Troeh and Bevil Knapp, "Writing the Wrongs in the Crescent City: A Year After Times-Picayune Announced Cutbacks, New Habits Changing in New Orleans," May 24, 2013, www.thelensnola.org/2013/05/24/a-year-after-times-picayune-announced-cutbacks-news-h....
39. Rieder, "Battle for New Orleans on the Journalism Front."
40. www.stateofthemedia.org/2013/newspapers-stabilizing-but-still-threatened/.
41. Allman.
42. According to figures released by the Alliance for Audited Media in March 2013, *The Plain Dealer* ranked 17th among U.S. daily newspapers with its circulation of 311,605, up 8.8 percent over the previous year. At the same point it was 15th among Sunday newspapers with a circulation of 458,838, up 4.1 percent in a year. With 95,483 total digital subscribers among its weekday aggregate reported earlier, this paper ranked 12th in dailies with digital editions in March 2013.
43. www.cleveland.com/business/index.ssf/2013/04/plain_dealer_to_remain_daily_b.html.
44. Ibid.
45. www.wweek.com/portland/article-19535-stop_the_presses.html.
46. Ibid.
47. The data that pertains to *The Oregonian* is adapted from these sources: Mallary Jean Tenore, "Oregonian to Reduce Home Delivery, Lay Off Staff," Poynter, June 24, 2013, www.poynter.org/latest-news/mediawire/216516/oregonian-to-reduce-home-delivery...; Andrew Beaujon, "Oregonian Hopes to 'Keep Reporter Numbers Where They Are Today,'" Poynter, June 24, 2013, www.poynter.org/latest-news/mediawire/216779/oregonian-hopes-to-keep-reporter-...; Floyd McKay, "The Oregonian: Going the Way of All Newspapers?," *Media*, June 23, 2013, www.crosscut.com/2013/06/23/media/115134/oregonians-cutbacks-newspapers-layoffs-de....

48. McKay.
49. www.gigaom.com/2012/05/28/print-dies-a-little-more-as-postmedia-announces-cuts/.
50. Ibid.; www.britishpapers.co.uk/publishers/johnston-press/.
51. www.nytimes.com/2012/06/04/business/media/as-newspaper-cut-analysts-ask-if-readers-will-remain.html?pagewanted=all&_r=0.
52. Roger Yu, "Media CEOs Say the Daily Newspaper Is Here to Stay," *USA Today*, June 25, 2013, p. 5B.
53. www.gigaom.com/2012/05/28/print-dies-a-little-more-as-postmedia-announces-cuts/.
54. Ibid.

Chapter 8

1. James O'Shea, *The Deal from Hell: How Moguls and Wall Street Plundered Great American Newspapers* (New York: Public Affairs, 2011), p. 334.
2. Ibid.
3. John V. Pavlik, *Journalism and New Media* (New York: Columbia University Press, 2001), pp. 157–158.
4. Ken Doctor, *Newsonomics: Twelve New Trends That Will Shape the News You Get* (New York: St. Martin's Press, 2010), pp. 5–6.
5. Ibid., p. 7.
6. Rem Rieder, "Extra, Extra: Newspapers Aren't Dead Yet," *USA Today*, April 11, 2013, p. 6B.
7. Christopher Harper, *And That's the Way It Will Be: News and Information in a Digital World* (New York: New York University Press, 1998), p. 114.
8. Ibid.
9. Parenthetically, *The Capital Times* of Madison, Wisconsin, may be the nation's first print daily to effectively go online altogether April 30, 2008, with a couple of weekly paper supplements. See Robert W. McChesney and John Nichols, *The Death and Life of American Journalism: The Media Revolution That Will Begin the World Again* (Philadelphia: Nation Books, 2010), p. 178, also www.en.wikipedia.org/wiki/The_Capital_Times.
10. Scott Kirsner, "Profits in Site?," *American Journalism Review*, December 1997, p. 43.
11. McChesney and Nichols, p. 72.
12. Steve Buttry, "Seven Reasons Charging for Content Won't Work," *Gazette*, www.stevebuttry.wordpress.com, http://www.stevebuttry.wordpress.com, May 29, 2009.
13. Walter Isaacson, "How to Save Your Newspaper: It's Now or Never for America's Dailies," *Time*, February 5, 2009.
14. Ibid.

Chapter 9

1. Jon Radoff, "A Brief History of Paywalls," November 30, 2009, www.radoff.com/blog/2009/11/30/a-brief-history-of-paywalls/.
2. Rick Edmonds, "State of the News Media 2013 Shows How Industry Is Responding to 'Continued Erosion' of Resources," Poynter, March 18, 2013, www.poynter.org/latest-news/business-news/the-biz-blog/207396/state-of-the-news-m…
3. Richard J. Tofel, *Why American Newspapers Gave Away the Future*, a Now and Then Kindle book (Now and Then Reader, 2012); www.nowandthenreader.com/why-american-newspapers-gave-away-the-future/.
4. Rebecca Rosen, "Can a Paywall Stop Newspaper Subscribers from Canceling?," *The Atlantic*, September 12, 2011, www.theatlantic.com/technology/archive/2011/09/can-a-paywall-stop-newspaper-subscribers-from-canceling/244932/.
5. Hannah Vinter, "Poynter's Bill Mitchell on Paywalls—How to Shape the Paid Experience," *Editors Weblog*, Web Editors Forum, www.editorsweblog.org/analysis/2011/10/bill_mitchell_on_paywalls_-_how_to_shape.php.
6. www.en.wikipedia.org.wiki/Paywall.
7. Rem Rieder, "Buffett's Love for Papers 'Unnatural?' No Way: Relationship Firmly Grounded on Profit," *USA Today*, March 6, 2013, p. 2B.

8. Mark Memmott, "NYTimes.com Cuts Free Articles to 10 Per Month, from 20," NPR.org, March 20, 2012, www.npr.org/blogs/thetwo-way/2012/03/20/148998882/nytimes-com-cuts-free-articles-to-10-per-month-from-20.

9. Felix Salmon, "How the New York Times Paywall is Working," *Wired*, August 14, 2011, www.wired.com/epiccenter/2011/08/new-york-times-paywall/; Lauren Indvik, "How to Hack the New York Times Paywall … with Your Delete Key," *Wired*, March 28, 2011, www.mashable.com/2011/03/28/how-to-bypass-new-york-times-paywall.

10. Rick Edmonds, "Newspapers: Missed the 2010 Media Rally," in The Pew Research Center's Project for Excellence in Journalism, *The State of the News Media 2011: An Annual Report on American Journalism*, www.stateofthemedia.org/2011/newspapers-essay/.

11. www.en.wikipedia.org/wiki/Paywall.

12. Lucia Moses, "Newspapers' Digital Circulation Climbs: NY Times, Others Crank Out Substantial Gains," *Adweek*, October 30, 2012, www.adweek.com/news/press/newspapers-digital-circulation-climbs-144889.

13. Joe Pompeo, "New Report: Circulation Is Up at Most U.S. Newspapers, but It's Skyrocketed at the 'Times' Thanks to Paid Model," *Capital*, May 1, 2012, www.capitalnewyork.com/article/media/2012/05/5816614/new-report-circulation-most-us-newspapers-its-skyrocketed-times-thanks.

14. Rick Edmonds, "Newspaper Circulation Stays the Same in Latest ABC Report, but the Mix Is Shifting to Digital," Poynter, October 30, 2012, www.poynter.org/latest-news/business-news/the-biz-blog/193003/newspaper-circulation-stays-the-same-but-the-mix-is-shifting-to-digital/.

15. Rem Rieder, "Get Ready to Pay for Online News: Soon It'll Be the Rule, Not the Exception," *USA Today*, January 22, 2013, p. 5B.

16. Michael Wolff, "Are Print Ads Seeing an Upswing?: Hints of Countertrend as Digital Hits Glitches," *USA Today*, February 4, 2013, pp. 1B, 2B.

Chapter 10

1. Seth Godin, "When Newspapers Are Gone, What Will You Miss?," January 14, 2009, www.sethgodin.typepad.com/seths_blog/2009/01/when-newspapers.html.

2. "Who Killed the Newspaper?," *The Economist*, August 24, 2006, www.economist.com/node/7830218.

3. Tim Windsor, "Resolved: Newspapers Could Die. Now What? A Panel in Baltimore," Nieman Journalism Lab, May 28, 2009, www.niemanlab.org/2009/05/resolved-newspapers-are-dying-now-what/.

4. Clay Shirky, "Newspapers and Thinking the Unthinkable," March 13, 2009, www.shirky.com/weblog/2009/03/newspapers-and-thinking-the-unthinkable/.

5. Jack Cafferty, "Would You Notice If Your Daily Newspaper Disappeared?," *Cafferty File*, May 18, 2009, www.caffertyfile.blogs.cnn.com/2009/05/18/would-you-notice-if-your-daily-newspaper-disappeared/.

6. Richard Pérez-Peña, "As Cities Go from Two Papers to One, Talk of Zero," *New York Times*, March 11, 2009.

7. Ibid.

8. Ibid.

9. Cafferty.

10. Pérez-Peña.

11. Godin.

12. Tony Rogers, "Five Things That Are Lost When Newspapers Close: What We Lose When a Newspaper Disappears," About.com Journalism, www.journalism.about.com/od/trends/a/closedpapers.htm.

13. Pérez-Peña.

14. Ibid.

15. Rachel Smolkin, "Cities Without Newspapers," *American Journalism Review*, April/May 2009, www.ajr.org/article.asp?id=4755.

16. Belinda Luscombe, "What Happens

When a Town Loses Its Newspaper?," *Time*, March 22, 2009.
17. Ibid.
18. Smolkin.
19. A pixel edition is not referenced here because most online newspapers have not yet gained the reputations and longevity citations earned by their newsprint siblings, although it's not inconceivable that this will eventually transpire.
20. Smolkin.
21. Ibid.
22. Ibid.
23. Ibid.
24. Ibid.
25. Ibid.
26. Ibid.
27. Michael Sebastian, "The Best (and Worst) Cities for Newspapers," *Ad Age*, June 11, 2013, http://adage.com/article/media/worst-cities-newspapers/242020/.
28. Smolkin.
29. Rick Green, "When the Daily Paper Disappears, What Happens?," *CTConfidential: What's Really Happening*, November 18, 2008, www.blogs.courant.com/rick_green/2008/11/when-the-daily-paper-disappear.html.
30. "If Newspapers Disappeared, Who Would Fill the Role," *The Spokesman-Review*, March 12, 2009, reprinted in *Seattle Times*, March 13, 2009.

Chapter 11

1. Leonard Downie, Jr., and Robert G. Kaiser, *The News About the News: American Journalism in Peril* (New York: Alfred A. Knopf, 2002), p. 256.
2. www.blog.realmatch.com/trade-publishers/whats-your-old-content-good-for/.
3. Victor Thorn, "Print Newspapers: Will They Survive?," *American Free Press*, March 25, 2012, www.americanfreepress.net/?p=3379.
4. Ibid.
5. www.journalism.about.com/od/printjournalisminperil/a/Newspapers-Are-Not-Dead-Not-Yet.htm.

6. Ibid.
7. Alex Alben, "Newspapers Will Survive by Doing What They Do Best," *Seattle Times*, January 24, 2008, www.http://seattletimes.com/html/opinion/2004141265_alben24.html.
8. Unidentified blogger, "In a Hurricane of Free Online News, Print Newspapers Will Survive," *News Now*, April 5, 2013, www.journalism.epals.com/article.php?id=824.

Chapter 12

1. Leonard Downie, Jr., and Robert G. Kaiser, *The News About the News: American Journalism in Peril* (New York: Alfred A. Knopf, 2002), pp. 66–67.
2. Ibid., p. 64.
3. Paul Oberjuerge, "American Newspapers: A Long, Slow Decline," March 25, 2009, www.oberjuerge.com/http:/www.oberjuerge.com/american-newspapers-a-long-slow-decline/.
4. The figures from the 2012 Pew biennial study herewith and in succeeding paragraphs are reported by Andrew Beaujon, "Pew: Half of Americans Get News Digitally, Topping Newspapers, Radio," Poynter, September 27, 2012, www.poynter.org/latest-news/mediawire/189819/pew-tv-viewing-habit-grays-as-digital-news-consumption-tops-print-radio/.
5. Martin Langeveld, "Are Newspapers Doomed?," Nieman Journalism Lab, January 22, 2009, www.niemanlab.org/2009/01/are-newspapers-doomed-intro-part-ii/.
6. "Overview," in The Pew Research Center's Project for Excellence, *The State of the News Media 2013: An Annual Report on American Journalism*, p. 6, www.journalism.org.
7. Saul K. Padover, ed., *The Complete Madison*, quoted in a letter from Madison to W. T. Barry on August 4, 1822 (Millwood, NY: Kraus Reprint, 1953).
8. Richard C. Anderson and Others, *Becoming a Nation of Readers: The Report of the Commission on Reading* (Washington, D.C.: National Institute of Education, 1985), p. 12.

9. *Consumer Reports on Health* (Harlan, IA: Consumer Reports, 2013), p. 6.
10. Philip Meyer, *The Vanishing Newspaper: Saving Journalism in the Information Age* (Columbia: University of Missouri Press, 2004), p. 5.
11. Jodi Enda and Amy Mitchell, "Americans Show Signs of Leaving a News Outlet, Citing Less Information," in The Pew Research Center's Project for Excellence in Journalism, *The State of the News Media 2013: An Annual Report on American Journalism*, www.stateofthemedia.org/2013/special-reports-landing-page/citing-reduced-quality-many-americans-abandon-news-outlets/.
12. www.bartleby.com/100/139.39.html.

Chapter 13

1. "The American Newspaper Media Industry Revenue Profile 2012," www.naa.org/Trends-and-umbers/Newspaper-Revenue/Newspaper-Media-Industry-Revenue-Profile-2012.aspx.
2. Ibid.
3. Ibid.
4. Leonard Mogel, *The Newspaper: Everything You Need to Know to Make It in the Newspaper Business* (Pittsburgh: GATF Press, 2000), p. 150.
5. Bill Kovach and Tom Rosenstiel, *Blur: How to Know What's True in the Age of Information Overload* (New York: Bloomsbury USA, 2010), p. 23.
6. Ken Doctor, *Newsonomics: Twelve New Trends That Will Shape the News You Get* (New York: St. Martin's Press, 2010), p. 5.
7. James O'Shea, *The Deal from Hell: How Moguls and Wall Street Plundered Great American Newspapers* (New York: Public Affairs, 2011), p. 246.

Chapter 14

1. Lloyd Grove, "The Grahams Sell 'the Washington Post,' and Woodward Is Sad," *The Daily Beast*, August 6, 2013, www.thedailybeast.com/articles/2013/08/06/bob-woodward-saddened-by-washington-post-sale-to-jeff-bezos.html.
2. Ibid.
3. James O'Shea, *The Deal from Hell: How Moguls and Wall Street Plundered Great American Newspapers* (New York: Public Affairs, 2011), pp. 21–22.
4. Nick Turner and Edmund Lee, "Jeff Bezos Bets $250 Million on Reviving Washington Post," Bloomberg, August 6, 2013, www.bloomberg.com/news/2013-08-05/amazon-ceo-jeff-bezos-to-buy-washington-post-for-250-million.html.
5. Brian Lowry, "Future of Print Journalism? Jeff Bezos' Washington Post Purchase Spurs Questions," *Variety*, August 15, 2013, www.variety.com/2013/biz/news/future-of-print-journalism-jeff-bezos-washington-post-purchase-spurs-questions-1200579025/; Brian Warner, "Jeff Bezos Net Worth," *Celebrity Net Worth: What's Your Favorite Star Got in the Bank?*, www.celebritynetworth.com/richest-businessmen/ceos/jeff-bezos-net-worth/.
6. Grove.
7. Ibid.
8. Turner and Lee.
9. Ibid.
10. Grove.
11. Ibid.
12. Emily Steel and Richard Waters, "Newspapers: Return of the Press Baron; Jeff Bezos's Acquisition Has Fed Hopes That the Struggling Industry Will Be Saved," *Financial Times*, August 9, 2013, www.ft.com/cms/s/0/b7d51d60-00d8-11e3-a90a-00144feab7de.html#axzz2cv7D5GiX.
13. 2 Corinthians 5:17, English Standard Version.
14. Tim McLaughlin, "From Boston Hero to Goat, Billionaire John Henry Takes On Globe Challenge," Reuters, August 3, 2013, www.news.yahoo.com/boston-hero-goat-billionaire-john-henry-takes-globe-221830613.html.
15. Ibid.
16. Ibid.
17. Lowry.
18. Matthew Rothschild, "Bezos, Wash-

Notes—Chapter 15

ington Post, and the Future of Journalism," *The Progressive*, August 6, 2013, www.progressive.org/bezos-washington-post-journalism.

19. Susan Milligan, "For the Globe, a Bid About More than Money," *U.S. News & World Report*, August 7, 2013, www.usnews.com/opinion/blogs/susan-milligan/2013/08/07/why-red-sox-owner-john-henry-really-was-the-boston-globe-high-bidder.

20. David Von Drehle, "The Fixer: What Jeff Bezos Can Do for the Washington Post," *Time*, August 19, 2013, pp. 14, 17.

21. Steel and Waters.

22. Rem Rieder, "Rich Guys Replace Chains as Newspaper Owners," *USA Today*, August 7, 2013, www.usatoday.com/story/money/columnist/rieder/2013/08/06/a-major-shift-in-who-owns-newspapers/2623293/.

23. Ibid.

24. Steve Myers, "2011 Busiest Year for Newspaper Ownership Changes Since 2007," Poynter, June 27, 2012, www.poynter.org/latest-news/mediawire/178968/2011-busiest-year-for-newspaper-ownership-changes-since-2007/.

25. Leonard Downie, Jr., and Robert G. Kaiser, *The News About the News: American Journalism in Peril* (New York: Alfred A. Knopf, 2002), p. 68.

26. Downie and Kaiser offer a couple of examples of excellent family-run regional dailies that were swallowed up by an operator focused upon improving profitability. They report some of what transpired in achieving it. See pp. 89–92.

27. www.stateofthemedia.org/media-ownership/newspapers/.

28. Aggregate as of July 18, 2013, www.stateofthemedia.org/2013/newspapers-stabilizing-but-still-threatened/.

Chapter 15

1. Pew Research Center's Journalism Project Staff, "The Changing Newsroom," Pew Research Journalism Project, July 21, 2008, www.journalism.org/2008/07/21/the-changing-newsroom-2/.

2. Eunice Chan, Shirin Ghaffarty, Jessica Choi, Ashwin Shanker, and Andrew Hsieh, "Decline of Journalism As We Know it," *The Mosaic Newspaper*, www.bazeley.net/mosaic/news/archives/news/decline_of_journalism_as_we_know_it.html.

3. Pew Research Center's Journalism Project Staff, "The Changing Newsroom," Pew Research Journalism Project, July 21, 2008, www.journalism.org/2008/07/21/the-changing-newsroom-2/.

4. Eric Alterman, "Think Again: The End of Newspapers and the Decline of Democracy," March 22, 2012, Center for American Progress, www.americanprogress.org/issues/media/news/2012/03/22/11254/think-again-the-end-of-newspapers-and-the-decline-of-democracy/.

5. "U.S. Newsroom Employment Declines," ASNE, April 16, 2009, www.asne.org/content.asp?pl=121&sl=15&contentid=151.

6. Ken Doctor, *Newsonomics: Twelve New Trends That Will Shape the News You Get* (New York: St. Martin's Press, 2010), p. 46.

7. Emily Guskin, "Newspaper Newsrooms Suffer Large Staffing Decreases," Pew Research Center, June 25, 2013, www.pewresearch.org/fact-tank/2013/06/25/newspaper-newsrooms-suffer-large-staffing-decreases/.

8. Philip Meyer, *The Vanishing Newspaper: Saving Journalism in the Information Age* (Columbia: University of Missouri Press, 2004), pp. 103, 102, 100.

9. Ibid. See pp. 83–108.

10. Doctor, pp. 12–13.

11. Leah Gentry, "Buckbobill: Journalist," Newspaper Association of America, December 1996, www.naa.org. Ms. Gentry, incidentally, did not personally subscribe to either assumption. Her theory focused on paying attention to details the professional scribes had always been taught: "Journalists who succeed ... will do solid reporting, careful editing, compelling writing, and visual storytelling, using the latest tools available. They'll tell their stories in whatever medium people use. But the

Chapter 16

1. John V. Pavlik, *Journalism and New Media* (New York: Columbia University Press, 2001), p. 17.
2. Joseph E. Persico, *Edward R. Murrow: An American Original* (New York: Dell Publishing, 1988), p. 295.
3. Ken Doctor, *Newsonomics: Twelve New Trends That Will Shape the News You Get* (New York: St. Martin's Press, 2010), p. 34.
4. Leonard Downie, Jr., and Robert G. Kaiser, *The News About the News: American Journalism in Peril* (New York: Alfred A. Knopf, 2002), p. 203.
5. Ibid., pp. 199–200.
6. James O'Shea, *The Deal from Hell: How Moguls and Wall Street Plundered Great American Newspapers* (New York: Public Affairs, 2011), p. 59.
7. Michael Antonoff, "At 75, 'World News Roundup' Thrives in Digital Age," *USA Today*, March 12, 2013, p. 7A.
8. Andrew Beaujon, "Pew: Half of Americans Get News Digitally, Topping Newspapers, Radio," Poynter, September 27, 2012, www.poynter.org/latest-news/mediawire/189819/pew-tv-viewing-habit-grays-as-digital-news-consumption-tops-print-radio/.
9. Rana Foroohar, "The End of TV As We Know It: While Cable Companies and Networks Bicker, Consumers Are Staging a Video Revolution," *Time*, August 16, 2013, p. 24.
10. Ibid.
11. Ibid.

Chapter 17

1. These quotes and the material pertaining to them are adapted from John Paul Titlow, "Why Magazines Are Using Digital to Boost Prices, Not Bolster Innovation," *readwrite*, January 24, 2013, www.readwrite.com/2013/01/24/why-magazines-are-using-digital-to-boost-prices-not-bolster-innovation#awesm=~obZLpaA5aG9fsZ.
2. To establish some common terminology for this chapter, *pulp* typically referenced a magazine launched in the 1880s measuring 10 by 7 inches printed on thick, coarse paper derived from wood pulps. It introduced mass production of cheap magazines and the name by which it is known. Meanwhile, publishers of more upscale middle-class magazines printed on better-quality, shinier stock saw their works dubbed *slicks* or *glossies* for their improved paper. To read more, see R. D. Mullen, "From Standard Magazines to Pulps and Big Slicks: A Note on the History of US General and Fiction Magazines," www.depauw.edu/sfs/back/issues/65/mullen65.htm, and "Pulp magazine," www.en..wikipedia.org/wiki/Pulp_magazine.
3. Susanna Kim, "Magazines May Follow Newsweek's Lead in Shuttering Print Version," ABCNews, October 18, 2012, www.abcnews.go.com/Business/magazines-follow-newsweeks-lead-shuttering-print-version/story?id=17508305.
4. Craig Mod, "How Magazines Will Be Changed Forever," CNN Opinion, October 21, 2012, www.cnn.com/2012/10/21/opinion/mod-digital-magazines.
5. Susan Currie Sivek, "Getting a Tablet Is Easy; Getting Digital Magazines Is a Pain," *MediaShift*, December 19, 2011, www.pbs.org/mediashift/2011/12/getting-a-tablet-is-easy-getting-digital-magazines-is-a-pain353.
6. Stephen B. Shepard, *Deadlines and Disruption: My Turbulent Path from Print to Digital* (New York: McGraw-Hill, 2013), pp. 174, 175.
7. Jane Sasseen, Katerina-Eva Matsa, and Amy Mitchell, "News Magazines: Embracing Their Digital Future," in The Pew Research Center's Project for Excellence in Journalism, *The State of the News Media 2013: An Annual Report on American Journalism*, www.stateofthemedia.org/2013/news-magazines-embracing-their-digital-future/.
8. Roger Yu, "Time Warner Spinning Off Time Inc. Magazines," *USA Today*,

Notes—Chapter 18 and Epilogue

March 6, 2013, www.usatoday.com/story/moneybusiness/2013/03/06/time-warner-spinoff/1969205/?csp=breakingnews.

9. Leslie Kaufman, "Former Time Warner Executive Is Coming Back to Run Time Inc.," *New York Times*, July 23, 2013, p. B7.

10. Much of what is reported herewith is adapted from Rem Rieder, "Magazines Don't Deserve to Be Dumped: They're Not Losers—They Make Money," *USA Today*, March 14, 2013, p. 2B.

11. Ibid.

12. Ibid.

13. Much of what is reported herewith is adapted from Roger Yu, Tim Mullaney, and Eliza Collins, "Mass Mailers Assess Options: Publishers of Magazines, Small Newspapers Especially Affected," *USA Today*, February 7, 2013, pp. 1–2B.

14. Rick Hampson, "Rain, Sleet, Snow, but Not Saturday (Starting in August): Your Reaction to Postal Service's Plan Likely Depends on Age," *USA Today*, February 7, 2013, pp. 1–2A.

15. Yu, Mullaney, and Collins.

16. Ibid.

17. The quotes from Stengel and Learmonth appear in Susanna Kim's ABCNews piece.

18. Laura Hazard Owen, "Digital Replicas Still Just a Tiny Sliver of U.S. Magazine Industry," paidContent, August 7, 2012, www.paidcontent.org/2012/08/07/digital-replicas-are-still-just-a-tiny-sliver-of-the-u-s-magazine-industry/.

19. Unless otherwise noted the figures herewith are adapted from Sasseen, Matsa, and Mitchell.

20. Ibid.

21. Christine Haughney, "Magazine Newsstand Sales Plummet, but Digital Editions Thrive," *New York Times*, August 7, 2013, p. B4.

22. Ibid.

Chapter 18

1. Let us temporarily digress. It's noteworthy that these same anxious credit card holders readily offer their cards or numbers to other strangers. They hand their cards to waiters, retailers, and service personnel of multiple persuasions who may disappear from view with them for a few moments. Meanwhile, the cardholders hardly blink an eye. While away with the cards vendors with sticky fingers have opportunities to jot down pertinent data, snap a picture, or reproduce a card's details through other photocopy means for nefarious purposes—their own fraudulent intents or to share or sell data with/to a third party with seedy plans. Many owners seldom sense the inherent liabilities until a card's issuer notifies them with bad news. That's a warning from a victim who fell prey more than once and takes precautions to limit it now.

2. "Eighty Percent of Consumers Trust Online News as Much As Off-line," Jupiter Communications news release, November 19, 1998.

3. Philip Seib, *Going Live: Getting the News Right in a Real-Time, Online World* (Lanham, MD: Rowman & Littlefield Publishers, 2001), p. 89.

4. Ken Doctor, *Newsonomics: Twelve New Trends That Will Shape the News You Get* (New York: St. Martin's Press, 2010), pp. 16, 17.

5. This data is adapted from Brett Molina and Jon Swartz, "Tablets on Pace to be King by 2015: Shipments Set to Outpace PCs," *USA Today*, May 29, 2013, p. B-1.

6. Martin Langeveld, "The Coming Death of Seven-Day Publication," Nieman Journalism Lab, December 21, 2012, www.niemanlab.org/2012/the-coming-death-of-seven-day-publication/.

7. www.worldmediatrend.wordpress.com/2012/12/21/the-coming-death-of-seven-day-publication-by-martin-langeveld/.

8. Ibid. Note: Successive references to Langeveld are from the same source.

Epilogue

1. The McClatchy Company, headquartered in Sacramento, California, is the nation's third-largest newspaper publisher

Notes—Epilogue

based on daily circulation, after Gannett (which owns *USA Today*, and News Corporation, which owns *The Wall Street Journal*). In late 2013, McClatchy owned 30 dailies in 29 U.S. markets. In each city it runs the leading local media firm with an array of print and digital systems. It owns dozens of non-daily newspapers and digital assets and has a commanding presence in a Washington, D.C., news bureau and a global one in a group of foreign bureaus. Some of its primary U.S. dailies are *Anchorage Daily News*, *The Charlotte Observer*, the *Fort Worth Star-Telegram*, *The Fresno Bee*, *The Kansas City Star*, *Lexington* [Ky.] *Herald-Leader*, *The Miami Herald*, *The News & Observer* (Raleigh, N.C.), *The Sacramento Bee*, *The State* (Columbia, S.C.), *The News Tribune* (Tacoma, Wash.), and *The Wichita Eagle*.

2. "The Decline of the Daily Newspaper," CBS News, February 11, 2009, www.cbsnews.com/2100-501763_162-3107387.html.

3. 2 Corinthians 5:17, King James Version.

4. Originally attributed to Mark Twain.

Bibliography

Alben, Alex. "Newspapers Will Survive by Doing What They Do Best." *Seattle Times*, January 24, 2008.

Alliance for Audited Media. March 31, 2013.

———. "Top 25 US Newspapers for March 2013." April 30, 2013.

Allman, Kevin. "The Advocate Publisher on the Paper's Plans to Move into New Orleans." *Gambit*, September 7, 2012.

Alterman, Eric. "Out of Print: The Death and Life of the American Newspaper." *The New Yorker*, March 31, 2008.

———. "Think Again: The End of Newspapers and the Decline of Democracy." Center for American Progress, March 22, 2012.

"American Newspaper Media Industry Revenue Profile 2012, The." Naa.org.

Anderson, Richard C., and Others. *Becoming a Nation of Readers: The Report of the Commission on Reading*. Washington, D.C.: National Institute of Education, 1985.

Antonoff, Michael. "At 75, 'World News Roundup' Thrives in Digital Age." *USA Today*, March 12, 2013.

Beaujon, Andrew. "Oregonian Hopes to 'Keep Reporter Numbers Where They Are today." Poynter, June 24, 2013.

———. "Pew: Half of Americans Get News Digitally, Topping Newspapers, Radio." Poynter, September 27, 2012.

Bond, Michaelle. "For Newspapers, a Less than Daily Future." *American Journalism Review*, June/July 2012.

Buttry, Steve. "Seven Reasons Charging for Content won't work." *Gazette*, May 29, 2009.

Cafferty, Jack. "Would You Notice If Your Daily Newspaper Disappeared?" CNN's *Cafferty File*, May 18, 2009.

Carey, James W. "The Internet and the End of the National Communications System: Uncertain Predictions of an Uncertain Future." *Journalism Quarterly*, Spring 1998.

Chan, Eunice, Shirin Ghaffarty, Jessica Choi, Ashwin Shanker, and Andrew Hsieh. "Decline of Journalism As We Know It." *The Mosaic Newspaper*, Bazely.net.

Consumer Reports on Health. Harlan, IA: Consumer Reports, 2013.

Cox, Jim. *Radio After the Golden Age: The Evolution of American Broadcasting Since 1960*. Jefferson, NC: McFarland, 2013.

———. *Radio Journalism in America: Telling the News in the Golden Age and Beyond*. Jefferson, NC: McFarland, 2013.

———. *Rails Across Dixie: A History of Passenger Trains in the American South*. Jefferson, NC: McFarland, 2011.

———. *Sold on Radio. Advertisers in the Golden Age of Broadcasting*. Jefferson, NC: McFarland, 2008.

"The Decline of the Daily Newspaper." CBS News, February 11, 2009.

D'Innocenzio, Anne. "Change Management: Cash Registers Fade." *The Courier-Journal*, Louisville, KY, March 23, 2013.

Doctor, Ken. *Newsonomics: Twelve New*

Bibliography

Trends That Will Shape the News You Get. New York: St. Martin's Press, 2010.

Downie, Leonard, Jr., and Robert G. Kaiser. *The News About the News: American Journalism in Peril.* New York: Alfred A. Knopf, 2002.

Edmonds, Rick. "Newspaper Circulation Stays the Same in Latest ABC Report, but the Mix Is Shifting to Digital." Poynter, October 30, 2012.

———. "Newspapers: Missed the 2010 Media Rally." In The Pew Research Center's Project for Excellence in Journalism, *The State of the News Media 2011: An Annual Report on American Journalism.*

"Eighty Percent of Consumers Trust Online News As Much As Off-line." Jupiter Communications, November 19, 1998.

Emery, Michael, Edwin Emery, and Nancy L. Roberts. *The Press and America: An Interpretive History of the Mass Media.* 9th ed. Boston: Allyn and Bacon, 2000.

Enda, Jodi, and Amy Mitchell. "Americans Show Signs of Leaving a News Outlet, Citing Less Information." In The Pew Research Center's Project for Excellence in Journalism, *The State of the News Media 2013: An Annual Report on American Journalism.*

Epstein, Joseph. "Are Newspapers Doomed?" *Commentary*, January 2006.

Farhi, Paul. "A Bright Future for Newspapers." *American Journalism Review*, June/July 2005.

Federal Communications Commission. *The Information Needs of Communities: The Changing Media Landscape in a Broadband Age.* June 9, 2011.

Fitzgerald, Mark. "Get Out of the Printing Business, Moody's Tells Newspapers." *Editor & Publisher*, June 4, 2009.

Foroohar, Rana. "The End of TV As We Know It: While Cable Companies and Networks Bicker, Consumers Are Staging a Video Revolution." *Time*, August 16, 2013.

Gardner, Howard, Mihaly Csikszentmihalyi, and William Damon. *Good Work: When Excellence and Ethics Meet.* New York: Basic Books, 2001.

Gentry, Leah. "Buckbobill: Journalist." Newspaper Association of America, December 1996.

Gilbert, Clark. "Newspapers and the Internet." *Nieman Reports* 56:2 (Summer 2002).

Gillin, Paul. "Crunching the Latest Numbers on Traditional Media." *Newspaper Death Watch*, February 11, 2013.

———. "Forthcoming Documentary Looks at Impact of Newspaper Declines." *Newspaper Death Watch*, December 6, 2012.

———. "The Graying of the Newspaper Audience." *Newspaper Death Watch*, January 17, 2013.

Gilmor, Dan. *We the Media: Grassroots Journalism by the People, for the People.* Sebastopol, CA: O'Reilly Media, 2004.

Godin, Seth. "When Newspapers Are Gone, What Will You Miss?" Sethgodin.typepad.com, January 14, 2009.

Green, Rick. "When the Daily Paper Disappears, What Happens?" *CT Confidential: What's Really Happening*, November 18, 2008.

Grove, Lloyd. "The Grahams Sell 'the Washington Post,' and Woodward Is Sad." *The Daily Beast*, August 6, 2013.

Guskin, Emily. "Newspaper Newsrooms Suffer Large Staffing Decreases." Pew Research Center, June 25, 2013.

Hampson, Rick. "Rain, Sleet, Snow, but Not Saturday (Starting in August): Your Reaction to Postal Service's Plan Likely Depends on Age." *USA Today*, February 7, 2013.

Harper, Christopher. *And That's the Way It Will Be: News and Information in a Digital World.* New York: New York University Press, 1998.

Harris Interactive. January 13, 2010.

Haughney, Christine. "Magazine Newsstand Sales Plummet, but Digital Edi-

Bibliography

tions Thrive." *New York Times*, August 7, 2013.

———. "Newspapers Cut Days from Publishing Week." *New York Times*, June 3, 2012.

Hoffmann, Bill. "Age of Newspaper Readers Rising Sharply." *Newsmax*, January 24, 2013.

Holy Scriptures. Psalms 24:4, NIV; 2 Corinthians 5:17, ESV/KJV.

Hudson, Frederic. *Journalism in the United States, from 1690 to 1872*. New York: Harper & Brothers, 1873.

"If Newspapers Disappeared, Who Would Fill the Role?" *The Spokesman-Review*, Spokane, WA, March 12, 2009.

"In a Hurricane of Free Online News, Print Newspapers Will Survive." *News Now*, April 5, 2013.

Indvik, Lauren. "How to Hack the New York Times Paywall … with Your Delete Key." *Wired*, March 28, 2011.

Isaacson, Walter. "How to Save Your Newspaper: It's Now or Never for America's Dailies." *Time*, February 5, 2009.

Jarvis, Jeff. "My Testimony to Sen. Kerry." *Buzz Machine*, April 21, 2009.

Jones, Alex S. *Losing the News: The Future of the News That Feeds Democracy*. New York: Oxford University Press, 2009.

Kaufman, Leslie. "Former Time Warner Executive Is Coming Back to Run Time Inc." *New York Times*, July 23, 2013.

Kim, Susanna. "Magazines May Follow Newsweek's Lead in Shuttering Print Version." *ABCNews*, October 18, 2012.

Kirsner, Scott. "Profits in Site?" *American Journalism Review*, December 1997.

Kovach, Bill, and Tom Rosenstiel. *Blur: How to Know What's True in the Age of Information Overload*. New York: Bloomsbury USA, 2010.

Langeveld, Martin. "Are Newspapers Doomed?" Nieman Journalism Lab, January 22, 2009.

———. "The Coming Death of Seven-Day Publication." Nieman Journalism Lab, December 21, 2012.

Lee, Henry K. "Cronkite Pans TV News at Caen Lecture; He Says Internet Presents Society 'Frightful Danger.'" *San Francisco Chronicle*, November 13, 1996.

Lowry, Brian. "Future of Print Journalism? Jeff Bezos' Washington Post Purchase Spurs Questions." *Variety*, August 15, 2013.

Luscombe, Belinda. "What Happens When a Town Loses Its Newspaper?" *Time*, March 22, 2009.

Madigan, Charles M., ed. *—30—: The Collapse of the Great American Newspaper*. Chicago: Ivan R. Dee, 2007.

McChesney, Robert W., and John Nichols. *The Death and Life of American Journalism: The Media Revolution That Will Begin the World Again*. Philadelphia: Nation Books, 2010.

McIntyre, Douglas A. "The 10 Most Endangered Newspapers in America." *Time*, May 9, 2009.

McKay, Floyd. "The Oregonian: Going the Way of All Newspapers?" *Media*, June 23, 2013.

McLaughlin, Tim. "From Boston Hero to Goat, Billionaire John Henry Takes on Globe Challenge." *Reuters*, August 3, 2013.

Memmott, Mark. "NYTimes.com Cuts Free Articles to 10 Per Month, from 20." NPR.org, March 20, 2012.

Meyer, Philip. *The Vanishing Newspaper: Saving Journalism in the Information Age*. Columbia: University of Missouri Press, 2004.

Milligan, Susan. "For the Globe, a Bid About More than Money." *U.S. News & World Report*, August 7, 2013.

Mod, Craig. "How Magazines Will Be Changed Forever." CNN Opinion, October 21, 2012.

Mogel, Leonard. *The Newspaper: Everything You Need to Know to Make It in the Newspaper Business*. Pittsburgh: GATF Press, 2000.

Bibliography

Molina, Brett, and Jon Swartz. "Tablets on Pace to be King by 2015: Shipments Set to Outpace PCs." *USA Today*, May 29, 2013.

Moses, Lucia. "Newspapers' Digital Circulation Climbs: NY Times, Others Crank Out Substantial Gains." *Adweek*, October 30, 2012.

Mott, Frank Luther. *American Journalism: A History of Newspapers in the United States Through 250 Years, 1690–1940*. New York: Macmillan, 1941.

Mullen, R. D. "From Standard Magazines to Pulps and Big Slicks: A Note on the History of US General and Fiction Magazines." depauw.edu.

Myers, Steve. "2011 Busiest Year for Newspaper Ownership Changes Since 2007." Poynter, June 27, 2012.

Naslund, Sena Jeter. "Give Gift of a Courier-Journal Subscription: Preserve Rich Variety of Daily Journalism." *The Courier-Journal*, Louisville, KY, January 25, 2013.

Neuman, W. Russell. *The Future of Mass Audience*. New York: Cambridge University Press, 1995.

Nichols, John. "Newspapers and After." *The Nation*, January 12, 2007.

Oberjuerge, Paul. "American Newspapers: A Long, Slow Decline." Oberjuerge.com, March 25, 2009.

O'Shea, James. *The Deal from Hell: How Moguls and Wall Street Plundered Great American Newspapers*. New York: Public Affairs, 2011.

Oswald, John Clyde. *Printing in the Americas*. New York: Hacker Art Books, 1968.

"Overview." In The Pew Research Center's Project for Excellence in Journalism, *The State of the News Media 2013: An Annual Report on American Journalism*.

Owen, Laura Hazard. "Digital Replicas Still Just a Tiny Sliver of U.S. Magazine Industry." paidContent, August 7, 2012.

Padover, Saul K., ed. *The Complete Madison*. Millwood, NY: Kraus Reprint, 1953.

Pavlik, John V. *Journalism and New Media*. New York: Columbia University Press, 2001.

Pérez-Peña, Richard. "As Cities Go from Two Papers to One, Talk of Zero." *New York Times*, March 11, 2009.

Persico, Joseph E. *Edward R. Murrow: An American Original*. New York: Dell Publishing, 1988.

Pew Research Center's Journalism Project Staff. "The Changing Newsroom." Pew Research Journalism Project, July 21, 2008.

The Pew Research Center's Project for Excellence in Journalism. *The State of the News Media 2009: An Annual Report on American Journalism*.

_____. *The State of the News Media 2010: An Annual Report on American Journalism*.

Pompeo, Joe. "New Report: Circulation Is Up at Most U.S. Newspapers, but It's Skyrocketed at the 'Times' Thanks to Paid Model." *Capital*, May 1, 2012.

Post, Suzy. "Loving Newsprint." *The Courier-Journal*, Louisville, KY, November 2, 2013.

Potter, Deborah. "Pessimism Rules in TV Newsrooms." *Columbia Journalism Review*, November/December 2002.

"Pulp magazine." Wikipidia.org.

Radoff, Jon. "A Brief History of Paywalls." Radoff.com, November 30, 2009.

Rainie, Lee. "Tablet and E-Book Readership Nearly Double over Holiday Gift-Giving Period." Internet, January 23, 2012.

Rieder, Rem. "Battle for New Orleans on the Journalism Front." *USA Today*, May 2, 2013.

_____. "Buffet's Love for Papers 'Unnatural?' No Way: Relationship Firmly Grounded on Profit." *USA Today*, March 6, 2013.

_____. "Extra, Extra: Newspapers Aren't Dead Yet." *USA Today*, April 11, 2013.

_____. "Get Ready to Pay for Online

Bibliography

News: Soon It'll Be the Rule, Not the Exception." *USA Today*, January 22, 2013.

———. "Magazines Don't Deserve to Be Dumped: They're Not Losers—They Make Money." *USA Today*, March 14, 2013.

———. "Reduced Newspaper Delivery: Smart or Death Knell?" *USA Today*, February 1, 2013.

———. "Rich Guys Replace Chains As Newspaper Owners." *USA Today*, August 7, 2013.

Rogers, Tony. "Five Things That Are Lost When Newspapers Close: What We Lose When a Newspaper Disappears." About.com Journalism.

Rosen, Rebecca. "Can a Paywall Stop Newspaper Subscribers from Canceling?" *The Atlantic*, September 12, 2011.

Rosenstiel, Tom. "Newspaper Readers Are Not Graying As Quickly As Reported." Poynter, January 17, 2013.

Rothschild, Matthew. "Bezos, Washington Post, and the Future of Journalism." *The Progressive*, August 6, 2013.

Salmon, Felix. "How the New York Times Paywall Is Working." *Wired*, August 14, 2011.

Sasseen, Jane, Katerina-Eva Matsa, and Amy Mitchell. "News Magazines: Embracing Their Digital Future." In the Pew Research Center's Project for Excellence in Journalism, *The State of the News Media 2013: An Annual Report on American Journalism*.

Sebastian, Michael. "The Best (and Worst) Cities for Newspapers." *Ad Age*, June 11, 2013.

Scib, Philip. *Going Live. Getting the News Right in a Real-Time, Online World*. Lanham, MD: Rowman & Littlefield, 2001.

Shakespeare, William Henry. *Macbeth*. Act V, scene 1.

Shepard, Stephen B. *Deadlines and Disruption: My Turbulent Path from Print to Digital*. New York: McGraw-Hill, 2013.

Sherman, Ted. "Star-Ledger Threatens to Close Without Concessions; Union Officials Reject Ultimatum." *The Star-Ledger*, Newark, NJ, June 26, 2013.

Shirky, Clay. "Newspapers and Thinking the Unthinkable." Shirky.com, March 13, 2009.

Sivek, Susan Currie. "Getting a Tablet Is Easy; Getting Digital Magazines Is a Pain." *MediaShift*, December 19, 2011.

Smith, Anthony. *Goodbye, Gutenberg: The Newspaper Revolution of the 1980s*. New York: Oxford University Press, 1980.

Smolkin, Rachel. "Cities Without Newspapers." *American Journalism Review*, April/May 2009.

Steel, Emily, and Richard Waters. "Newspapers: Return of the Press Baron; Jeff Bezos's Acquisition Has Fed Hopes That the Struggling Industry Will Be Saved." *Financial Times*, August 9, 2013.

Stephens, Michael. *A History of News: From the Drum to the Satellite*. New York: Viking, 1998.

Stephens, Mitchell. "History of Newspapers." *Collier's Encyclopedia*, ca. 1992.

Steven, Peter. *The News*. Toronto, ON.: Groundwood Books, 2010.

"Stop the Presses: *The Oregonian* May Not Be a Daily Newspaper Much Longer." Wweek.com, August 8, 2012.

Tenore, Mallary Jean. "Oregonian to Reduce Home Delivery, Lay Off Staff." Poynter, June 24, 2013.

Thorn, Victor. "Print Newspapers: Will They Survive?" *American Free Press*, March 25, 2012.

Titlow, John Paul. "Why Magazines Are Using Digital to Boost Prices, Not Bolster Innovation." *readwrite*, January 24, 2013.

Tofel, Richard J. *Why American Newspapers Gave Away the Future*, a Now & Then Kindle book. Now and Then Reader, 2012.

Troeh, Eve, and Bevil Knapp. "Writing the Wrongs in the Crescent City: A Year

Bibliography

After Times-Picayune Announced Cutbacks, New Habits Changing in New Orleans." Thelensnola.org, May 24, 2013.

Turner, Nick, and Edmund Lee. "Jeff Bezos Bets $250 Million on Reviving Washington Post." Bloomberg, August 6, 2013.

"U.S. Newsroom Employment Declines." American Society of Newspaper Editors, April 16, 2009.

Vinter, Hannah. "Poynter's Bill Mitchell on Paywalls—How to Shape the Paid Experience." *Editors Weblog*, Web Editors Forum.

Von Drehle, David. "The Fixer: What Jeff Bezos Can Do for the Washington Post." *Time*, August 19, 2013.

Warner, Brian. "Jeff Bezos Net Worth." *Celebrity Net Worth: What's Your Favorite Star Got in the Bank?* Celebritynetworth.com.

Weaver, David, et al. *The American Journalist in the 21st Century*. Mahwah, NJ: Lawrence Erlbaum Associates, 2007.

"Who Killed the Newspaper?" *The Economist*, August 24, 2006.

Windsor, Jim. "Resolved: Newspapers Could Die. Now What? A Panel in Baltimore." Nieman Journalism Lab, May 28, 2009.

Wolfe, Thomas. *You Can't Go Home Again*. A novel published in 1940 following the author's death, extracted from an unpublished manuscript, *The October Fair*.

Wolff, Michael. "Are Print Ads Seeing an Upswing?: Hints of Countertrend as Digital Hits Glitches." *USA Today*, February 4, 2013.

Wood, James Playsted. *The Great Glut: Public Communication in the United States*. Nashville: Thomas Nelson, 1973.

Wyatt, Edward. "Most of U.S. Is Wired, but Millions Aren't Plugged In." *New York Times*, August 19, 2013.

Yu, Roger. "Media CEOs Say the Daily Newspaper Is Here to Stay." *USA Today*, June 25, 2013.

_____. "Some Major Newspapers Struggle with Changing Times." *USA Today*, June 28, 2013.

_____. "Time Warner Spinning Off Time Inc. Magazines." *USA Today*, March 6, 2013.

_____, Tim Mullaney, and Eliza Collins. "Mass Mailers Assess Options: Publishers of Magazines, Small Newspapers Especially Affected." *USA Today*, February 7, 2013.

Index

AAA Living 163
AARP Bulletin 163
AARP The Magazine 163
ABCNews 42
Ad Age 104
Advance Publications, Inc. 70–76, 77–79, 80, 140, 163, 164, 177–178
Advertising Age 168
advertising revenue 27–28, 45–46, 60, 66, 68, 81, 82, 83–84, 86, 88, 92, 96, 110, 122–123, 125, 126, 132, 136, 169, 183
The Advocate (Baton Rouge) 76–77
Adweek 94
Adweek Media 56, 57
aggregator defined 67
aging of newspaper readership 56, 57, 58, 86, 96–97
A.H. Belo Company 140
Alben, Alex 109
Alden Global Capital 141
Alliance for Audited Media 130, 163–164, 170–171
Allman, Kevin 74
Alpha Media Group 163, 168
Alterman, Eric 5–6, 49, 57
Amazon 63, 129
America Online 22
American Association of Retired Persons 163
American Automobile Association 163
American Broadcasting Company 51, 153
American Journalism Review 33, 66–67, 102, 103, 104
The American Legion Magazine 163
American Legion Society 163
American Life Project 36
American Marketing Association 60
American Press Institute 58, 177, 178
American Society of Magazine Editors 47
American Society of Newspaper Editors 28–29, 37, 146
The Ann Arbor News 72
AnnArbor.com 72, 73
Annenberg, Walter 137

Annenberg School Center for the Digital Future 109
Anschutz, Philip 137
Anschutz Company 141
Antonoff, Michael 154
AOL 162, 164
Apple 63
Aquent 60
Architectural Digest 72
The Arizona Republic 176
Arkansas Democrat-Gazette 93
Aspen Institute 88
Associated Press 1, 19, 51
Astroturf 133
The Atlanta Journal-Constitution 22, 105, 140, 176
The Atlantic 169
Audit Bureau of Circulations 45, 72, 94–95, 163
Austin American-Statesman 176
author's stance 2–3

Bacon, Sir Francis 121
The Bakersfield Californian 105
The Baltimore Sun 47, 48
Baquet, Dean 37, 38
Batten, Jim 85
Bayonne (NJ) *Times* 71
BBC News 42
Berkshire Hathaway 140
Bernstein, Carl 129
Better Homes & Gardens 163
Bettinger, Jim 69
Bezos, Jeffrey P. 129, 130–131, 132, 133
The Birmingham News 73
Black Press, Ltd. 140
Bloomberg 51, 130
Bonnier Publishing 163, 164, 168
Booth Newspapers 71
Booth School of Business 102
The Boston Globe 61, 131, 132, 135
Boston News-Letter 18
Boston Red Sox 131, 132, 135
Boston University 131

215

Index

Bradlee, Ben 129
Bride 72
Brinkley, David 153
The Bristol (Conn.) *Press* 106
British Broadcasting Corporation 23, 51
Broad, Eli 132
Brown, Chip 130
Budde, Neil 86
The Buffalo News 93
Buffett, Warren 93–94, 132
bundling subscriptions on mixed platforms 33
Bush, George W. 115
Business Week 47, 162
BusinessWeek Online 162
Buttry, Steve 87
Buzz Machine 30

Cable News Network 41, 51, 88, 100
Cablevision 141
Calgary Herald 80
Campbell, John 18, 38
Candid Camera 106
Capital (online) 95
Carey, James W. 40
Carroll, John 37
CBS News 183
CBS World News Roundup 154, 155
Center for American Progress 146
Charles I 16
The Charlotte Observer 176
Chicago Sun-Times 52, 57, 61, 95, 140
Chicago Tribune 29, 46, 52, 125, 133, 176
The Christian Science Monitor 65
The Cincinnati Post 102
circulation losses 28, 29, 45, 60, 183
City University of New York 101
"civilian reporters" 155
classified advertising 29, 132, 183
Codex Journal of Typography 159
Cohn, Steven 171
Cole, Jeffrey 109
Collins, Steve 106
Columbia Broadcasting System 51, 68, 116, 153, 154, 155, 183
Columbia Journalism Review 31
Columbia University 53
Comedy Central cable channel 45
The Commercial Appeal (Memphis) 140
Community Newspapers Holdings 140
CompuServe 22
computerized information advantages 20
Condé Nast Publications 71, 158, 168, 169
Condé Nast Traveler 72
confidence in news sources 52–53
conglomerate media ownership 29, 30, 39
Consumer Reports 120

Contents Magazine 159
"cord cutting" in TV 156
Cosmopolitan 163, 168, 171
Courage Campaign 133
Courant (Hartford) 105
Cox Media Group 140
Craigslist 33, 46, 125
Cribb, John 137
Cronkite, Walter 12, 52, 153
Crowe, E. Odell 23–24

Daily News (New York) 52, 61, 140
Daily News Corporation 140
The Daily Show 45
The Dallas Morning News 140
D.E. Shaw & Company 129
de la Rochefoucauld, Francois 49
The Denver Post 52, 183
Detroit Free Press 64, 65
The Detroit News 61, 62, 64, 65
Dickens, Charles 98
Dickey, Robert J. 81
Diffusion Group 156
"Digital Decade" 66
"Digital Dozen" 51
digital replicas of magazines 168
diversification in media revenues 33
Doctor, Ken 7, 47, 51, 52, 66, 72, 82, 85, 130, 147, 151, 170
Doherty, Carroll 103
Dow Jones 136
Downie, Leonard, Jr. 12–13, 44, 107–108, 114–115, 138, 152–153
Drudge Report 42

The Eagle-Tribune (North Andover, Mass.) 140
Eastern Michigan University 72
eBay 28
The Economist 99, 169
Editor & Publisher 87
Edmonds, Rick 63, 90–91, 104
Edmonton Journal 80
EH Publishing 169
Eisendrath, Charles R. 73
electricity, inception and influence 18
Electronic House 169
electronic newspapers' pervasiveness 7
Empirical Media 130
Entertainment Weekly 165
Epstein, Joseph 45
e-readers' pervasive impact 175–176
ESPN 163, 168
ESPN The Magazine 163, 168
Essence 165
Evening Courier (Halifax, U.K.) 81
Evening News (Scarborough, U.K.) 81

Index

E.W. Scripps 140
The Examiner (San Francisco) 140
E-Z Pass 177

Facebook 63, 103, 117, 170
Family Circle 163
Farhi, Paul 48
Fairleigh Dickinson University 155–156
Farley Post Office (New York City) 166
Federal Communications Commission 39
Fenway Park 132
Financial Times 51, 136–137, 183
First Amendment 85
Fitch Ratings 100
Foroohar, Rana 156
Forrester Research 156
Fortune 165
Fourth Estate 143, 154, 162
Fox News 42, 51
fragmented news consumption 36–37
Friedlich, Jim 130
Funt, Allen 106

Gambit 74
Game Informer 163, 168
GameStop 163, 168
Gannett Company 42, 81, 82, 95, 139
Gardner, Howard 31
Garrido, Miguel 102
GateHouse Media 140
The Gazette (Colorado Springs) 137
Geffen, David 132–133
Gentleman's Quarterly 72
Gentry, Leah 148
Gentzkow, Matthew 102
Georges, John 77
GigaOm 93
Gilbert, Clark 11–12
Gillin, Paul 48, 58, 109
Gillmor, Dan 38
Glamour 72, 163, 171
Godfrey, Paul 80
Godin, Seth 98, 101
Golf Magazine 165
Good Housekeeping 163
Google 63, 130, 170
Google News 41
Gould, Jack 151
Gourmet 72
GPS technology 14
GQ 169
Graham, Donald 129, 130
Graham, Philip L. 135
Granvill, Joseph 16–17
The Guardian 51, 92, 183
Gutenberg, Johannes 4, 16, 21, 179

Halifax Media 140
Hampson, Rick 166–167
Harden, Kari Dequine 77
Harper, Christopher 14, 22
Harris, Benjamin 18
Harris Poll 56, 57
Harvard Business School 11
Harvard College 17
Harvard University 31, 32, 176
Health 165
Hearst, William Randolph 137
Hearst Corporation 69, 140, 163, 164, 168, 171
Heath, Max 167
Henry, John W. 131, 132, 133, 134
Hoffmann, Bill 58
House & Garden 72
The Houston Chronicle 105, 140
Huber, Craig 68
Huber Research Partners 68
Huffington, Arianna 92
Huffington Post 42
Hughes, Lisa 170
Huntley, Chet 153
The Huntsville (Ala.) *Times* 73
Husni, Samir 164, 165
Hussman, Walter, Jr. 93
hybrid interval 2, 10, 171, 181

I Love Lucy 153
IDC research 174
Industrial Revolution 18
Information Age 21, 35, 39, 46
informational illiteracy 112–113
Ingram, Matthew 93
Internet: acceptance 84–85, 173–174; disenfranchised audience 13; effects on newspapers' "gravy train" 136; effects on television 13; launched 22; rise 8–9
Isaacson, Walter 27, 88

Jaclynn B. Jarrett Publishing 168
Jarvis, Jeff 30, 101
John S. Knight (journalism fellowship program) 69
Johnston Press 80–81
Jones, Alex S. 32
The Journal News (White Plains, N.Y.) 140
Jurkowitz, Mark 110

Kaiser, Robert G. 12–13, 44, 107–108, 114–115, 138, 152–153
Katz, Lewis 137
Keller, Bill 6
Kennedy, John F. 17
The Kentucky Post 102
Kindle 161, 174, 175

217

Index

King, Charles 174
Knight-Ridder (news syndicate) 85, 170, 183
Knight Wallace Journalism Fellows 73
Kotok, Steven 166
Kovach, Bill 36–37, 50, 124–125
Kramer, Joel 100
KRON-TV, San Francisco 23
Kushner, Aaron 137

Ladies' Home Journal 163
Langeveld, Martin C. 118–119, 176–178
Larcom, Geoff 72–73
Las Vegas Review-Journal 105
Learmonth, Michael 168
Lee, Edmund 130
Lee, Peggy 119
Lee Enterprises 140
legacy news providers 51–53
Linfield College 160
Lippmann, Walter 26
Little, Caroline 124
Los Angeles Times 22, 29, 37–38, 42, 52, 83, 125, 132, 133, 136, 140, 148, 164, 176, 183
Lowry, Brian 132–133
Luce, Henry 88, 164
Luthor, Lux 133

Macbeth 4
Mademoiselle 72
Madigan, Charles 46, 49
Madison, James 120
Magazine Innovation Center 164, 165
Mail Online 42
Main Street Media 46
Mainichi Shimbun 22
mainstream media 183
Major League Baseball 132
Manchester, Doug 137
Manship, David 76–77
Maraniss, David 32
Martore, Gracia 82
Massachusetts Bay Colony 17
Massachusetts Institute of Technology 103
Maxim 163, 168
McChesney, Robert W. 11, 27, 28, 30–32, 87
McClatchy Company 81–82, 95, 140, 183
McIntyre, Douglas A. 61
mechanical power's influence 18
Media General Corporation 93
Media Industry Newsletter 171
MediaNews Group 95, 139
MediaShift 160
membership model packaging 177
Men's Health 169
mercantile innovations 1
Meredith Publishing 163, 164

metering system 9–10
Meyer, Eugene 135
Meyer, Philip 5, 12, 44, 104, 120, 147
The Miami Herald 61, 140
Milligan, Susan 134–135
MinnPost.com 100
Mitchell, Bill 92
Mod, Craig 159–160
Mogel, Leonard 124
Money 165
Moody's Investors Service 23
Moritz, Michael 130
Morse, Samuel F.B. 19
Morton, John 33, 66–67, 74, 104, 137
The Mosaic Newspaper 144
MSNBC 41, 51
multimedia's interconnectedness 150–151
multiplatform distribution 51
Murdoch, Rupert 37, 133, 136
Murdock, Ian 87
Murrow, Edward R. 151, 154, 155
Mutter, Alan D. 44, 56, 58–59, 137, 146

National Broadcasting Company 51, 68, 153
National Geographic 160, 163, 168
National Geographic Society 163, 168
National Newspaper Association 167
National Post 80
National Public Radio 51, 156
nationalgeographic.com 160
"netizens" 53
Neuman, W. Russell 21
New Jersey Nets 137
The New Orleans Times-Picayune/States-Item 88
New Scientist 159
New York Post 52
The New York Times 6, 13, 22, 42, 51, 52, 72, 73, 82, 94, 95, 96, 100, 105, 109, 117–118, 128, 132, 135, 136, 140, 151, 155, 165, 176, 183
The New York Times Company 82, 128, 131, 132, 134, 140, 165
The New Yorker 57, 72, 169, 170
Newhouse, Donald 71
Newhouse, Samuel Irving, Jr. ("Si") 71, 76
Newhouse, Samuel Irving, Sr. 70, 71
News & Observer (Raleigh, N.C.) 22
News & Record (Greensboro, N.C.) 93
News Corporation (New York) 140, 165
"news grazers" 36
Newsday 141
Newsmax 58
Newsom, Gavin 99–100
Newspaper Association of America 7, 85, 122–123
Newspaper Death Watch 58, 109

218

Index

Newspaper Next 177
newspapers: costs and selling prices 83; criteria 17; family owners 128, 138, 139, 141, 142; non-readers 56, 117; potential demise 11, 27, 28, 30, 32, 33, 36, 59, 61, 62, 69, 79, 88, 91, 98–101, 109, 129, 131, 157, 175, 181, 183; revenue sources 122–123; traditional revenues 88, 123–124; trends in future 178–179, 181–183; values and assets 115
newsprint days' reduction 62, 64–70, 72, 73–76, 77–81, 82, 125, 176, 177–178
Newsweek 47, 159, 160, 168, 169, 171
niche journalism 11
Nichols, John 11, 27, 28, 30–32, 87
Nieman Journalism Lab, Harvard 176
Nixon, Richard 127, 129, 130, 135
NOLA.com 74
non-unionization of operations 72
Nook 161, 175
Norcross, George 137
Northampton Chronicle & Echo (U.K.) 81
Northamptonshire Evening Telegraph (U.K.) 81
Nylon 168
NYTimes.com 159

O, the Oprah Magazine 163, 168, 171
The Oakland Press (Pontiac, Mich.) 141
Oberjuerge, Paul 116
The Oklahoman 176
Omaha World-Herald 93, 140
The Orange County Register 137, 141
The Oregonian (Portland) 71, 78–79
OregonLive.com 79
O'Shea, James 29–30, 37–38, 48–49, 83, 125, 128, 153
Ottawa Citizen 80
Outsell, Inc. 130
Owens, Howard 93

Parade 71
Parenting 163, 168
Pathfinder 22
The Patriot-News (Harrisburg, Pa.) 78
Pavlik, John V. 40, 53, 84, 150
pay vs. free debate 86–89, 90–91
paywalls 80, 82, 85, 87, 89, 90–97, 177
Pedroia, Dustin 132
People 163, 165
Pérez-Peña, Richard 100, 101–102
periodicals for narrowly defined audiences 20
Person to Person 151
Peterborough Evening Telegraph (U.K.) 81
Pew Internet 36
Pew Research Center 42, 43, 46, 57, 58–59,
66, 88, 94, 103, 105–106, 110, 117–118, 119, 121, 144, 145, 147, 169, 170
Philadelphia Daily News 61, 137
The Philadelphia Inquirer 137, 141, 176
Philadelphia Media Group 141
pictograms 15
Pilgrims 17
pixel defined1
The Plain Dealer (Cleveland) 61, 62, 71, 78, 79, 105, 140
Poder Hispanic 168
Politico 67, 130
Popular Science 168
Portfolio 72
The Post and Courier (Charleston, S.C.) 176
Post-Gazette (Pittsburgh) 105
Post Office Square (Boston) 166
The Post-Standard (Syracuse) 78
Postmedia 80, 82
Potts, Mark 99
Poynter Institute 58, 63, 90, 92, 95, 104
press as gatekeeper 26
Press-Register (Mobile) 73
Prevention 163
Princeton Research Associates 87
Princeton University 102
The Progressive 133
Project for Excellence in Journalism 36, 50–51
ProPublica 67, 91
Publick Occurrences, Both Foreign and Domestick 18
Pulitzer Prize 32, 79, 129
Pund-IT 174

radio envisioned 16–17
Random House 71
Rather, Dan 115–116
Reader's Digest 163
Reader's Digest Association 163, 164
readwrite blog 158
Redbook 163
Reuters 42, 51
Reynolds, Frank 153
Rieder, Rem 33, 44, 95–96, 137, 164–165
Rocky Mountain News (Denver) 69
Rodale Publishing 163, 164, 169
Rogers, Tony 101
Rosen, Jay 93
Rosenstiel, Tom 36–37, 50, 58–59, 124–125
Rothschild, Matthew 133–134

St. Louis Globe-Democrat 71
St. Louis Post-Dispatch 140, 176
Salmon, Felix 94
San Antonio Express-News 87, 105

219

Index

The San Diego Union-Tribune 137
San Francisco Chronicle 61, 69, 99–100
San Jose Mercury News 139
San Jose Urban Journalism Workshop 145
Sarasota Herald-Tribune 140
Saturday Night Live 45
Scarborough Research 59, 104–105
Schulhofer-Wohl, Sam 102
Seattle Post-Intelligencer 68–69
The Seattle Times 109
See It Now 151
Self 72
Shakespeare, William L. 4, 33, 139
Shapiro, Jesse 102
Shepard, Stephen B. 6, 9–10, 47–48, 161–162
Sheridan Institute of Technology 41
Shirky, Clay 99
Siegel, Randy 75–76
Simmons, Debra Adams 78
Simonton, Mike 100
Sivek, Susan Currie 160–161
sivekmedia.com 160–161
Smith, Anthony 8, 9, 20–21
Smolkin, Rachel 104
Snyder, Jim 103
Sony Reader 174
Sorkin, Andrew Ross 132
Southern Living 163, 165
The Spokesman-Review (Spokane, Wash.) 106
Sports Illustrated 163, 165
Stanford University 42–43, 69
Star-Ledger (Newark) 69, 79
Star-Telegram (Fort Worth) 22, 61
The Star Tribune (Minneapolis) 61, 100
start-up competition 61
State of the News Media 106, 139, 169–170
Staten Island Advance 71
Staten Island Advance Company 71
Stengel, Richard 168
Steven, Peter 41
Stewart, Jon 45
Stockholm University 103
Strömberg, David 103
subscriptions, converted to e-readers 161
Sulzberger, Arthur Ochs, Jr. 128
Sun-Times Media Holdings 140
The Sunday Times (London, U.K.) 88
synergy created by re-packaging media 152–153

tablets 174, 178
Talamantes, Patrick 81–82
A Tale of Two Cities 98
Tampa Bay Times 176
Taste of Home 163
Telecommunications Act of 1996 39

The Telegraph 51
telephone answering devices 14
Televisa Publishing 168
television 17, 20
Temple University 158
Thompson, Mark 82
Time 27, 61, 88, 129, 135, 156, 164, 165, 167–168, 169
Time Inc. 22, 158, 164
Time Warner 163, 164, 165
Time Warner Cable 164
The Times (London, U.K.) 92
Times Online 51
The Times-Picayune (New Orleans) 71, 73–76, 77, 79, 82, 88
Times Union (Albany, N.Y.) 105
Titlow, John Paul 158–159
Tofel, Richard J. 91
TPStreet 77
Tribune Company (Chicago) 37, 133, 140
Tribune-Review (Pittsburgh) 105
Tulsa World 93
Turner, Nick 130
24/7 Wall Street 61
2100 Trust LLC 137, 141

U-T San Diego 137
Union-Tribune (San Diego) 100
"unique visitors" defined 41
United Press International 46
U.S. Census 59
U.S. Commission on Reading 120
U.S. Defense Department 22
U.S. News & World Report 134
U.S. Postal Service 165, 166, 167, 172, 178
University of Chicago 102
University of Miami 110
University of Michigan 73
University of Mississippi 164, 165
University of Missouri Press 104
University of North Carolina 104
University of Southern California 109
Ureneck, Lou 131, 132
USA Today 22, 33, 42, 44, 51, 52, 81, 84, 85, 95, 96, 109, 137, 139, 154, 155, 164, 174

The Vanishing Newspaper 104, 147
Vanity Fair 72
Variety 132–133
Veronis Suhler Stevenson investment firm 170
videotext 23
Vogue 72
VoiceofSanDiego.org 100
Von Drehle, David 135–136

Wales, Jimmy 92

Index

The Wall Street Journal 51, 52, 85–86, 96, 109, 136, 140, 155, 183
The Wall Street Journal Interactive Edition 22
Warner Communications 164
Warner Music 164
Washington Examiner (Washington, D.C.) 141
The Washington Post 32, 42, 43–44, 48, 51, 52, 82, 85, 93, 109, 114, 127–131, 133–134, 135–136, 138, 140, 152, 183
Washington Post Company 140
Watergate 130, 135
Wayne, Bruce 132
The Week 166, 169

Weymouth, Katharine 82
Wikipedia 92, 94
Wired 159, 169
Wolfe, Thomas 70
Wolff, Michael 96–97
Women's Health 169
Woodward, Bob 129
Woolley, Buzz 100
World Series 132
writing's inception 15

Yahoo 130, 170
Yahoo! News 41

Zaurus (portable electronic display) 22

www.ingramcontent.com/pod-product-compliance
Ingram Content Group UK Ltd.
Pitfield, Milton Keynes, MK11 3LW, UK
UKHW041951140426
5217IPUK00015B/746